James of St George and the Castles of the Welsh Wars

Caernarfon: The Eagle Tower from the east, with the water gate at its base.

James of St George and the Castles of the Welsh Wars

Malcolm Hislop

Pen & Sword
MILITARY

AN IMPRINT OF PEN & SWORD BOOKS LTD.
YORKSHIRE – PHILADELPHIA

First published in Great Britain in 2020 by
PEN & SWORD MILITARY
An imprint of
Pen & Sword Books Ltd
Yorkshire – Philadelphia

ISBN 978 1 52674 130 1

A CIP catalogue record for this book is
available from the British Library

Typeset in Ehrhardt 11/13.5
by Aura Technology and Software Services, India.

Printed and bound in India by Replika Press Pvt. Ltd.

Pen & Sword Books Ltd incorporates the imprints of Pen & Sword Archaeology,
Atlas, Aviation, Battleground, Discovery, Family History, History, Maritime,
Military, Naval, Politics, Social History, Transport, True Crime, Claymore Press,
Frontline Books, Praetorian Press, Seaforth Publishing and White Owl

For a complete list of Pen & Sword titles please contact

PEN & SWORD BOOKS LTD
47 Church Street, Barnsley, South Yorkshire, S70 2AS, England
E-mail: enquiries@pen-and-sword.co.uk
Website: www.pen-and-sword.co.uk

Or

PEN & SWORD BOOKS
1950 Lawrence Rd, Havertown, PA 19083, USA
E-mail: Uspen-and-sword@casematepublishers.com
Website: www.penandswordbooks.com

In memory of Alexander and Margaret Hislop

Contents

Preface

Researchers have expended much effort on the castles of Edward I in Wales, and there is, in consequence, a considerable body of scholarly literature about them. However, the only lengthy survey of the whole group is that of Arnold Taylor, first published in 1963, and later (1974) as a separate volume, which was itself reissued in a revised edition in 1986. Principally, however, this is an historical account in which the appraisal of the architecture is minimal. Despite the fact that a considerable amount of work has been done on the architecture, the buildings as a group have never been the subject of an extensive study. The primary aim of the current work, therefore, is to provide a general introduction to the architecture, encompassing not only the royal works, but contemporary baronial castles as well.

In addition to concentrating on the royal and baronial castles of the Edwardian era in Wales, chapters are included on castle building by the northern Welsh, by the English in Wales prior to the Edwardian invasion, and by the English and their supporters in Scotland during the Edwardian occupation there; it is intended that these will contribute to a more rounded picture of the Edwardian castle. The penultimate chapter discusses the impact of Edward's project over a wider geographical area, and the final section comprises the denouement of a pervading theme of the book: the role of the King's principal mason, James of St George, in shaping the character of the architecture. It is hoped that this work will provide a useful starting point for general readers, and serve as a companion for those conducting further research on the Edwardian castle.

In a book of this nature, with a large degree of descriptive writing, there can never be enough illustrations. Given the space restrictions, the priority has been to include as many castle plans as was reasonably possible in the circumstances; they are presented at a common scale in order to assist comparisons between them. However, there are also plenty of photographs, and this is, all in all, a well-illustrated book. Building measurements in the text are given in British imperial units with metric equivalents rounded up to one decimal point; longer distances are given in miles. British sites are located with respect to pre-1974 county boundaries.

Acknowledgements

I would also like to express my gratitude to a number of people for their assistance: Rachel Swallow for allowing me to see a draft of her article on the landscape of Caernarfon Castle; Will Davies of Cadw for advising me on recent work and thinking on the sequence of construction at Denbigh Castle, and for permitting me to see his unpublished report on the subject; Will also read and commented on a draft of Chapter 8. Many thanks too to Neil Ludlow for reading and commenting on a draft of Chapter 9, and suggesting various sites that might be pursued with profit, and particularly to John Kenyon who read through a draft of the entire book and raised various issues to be addressed. My dear wife Anne also read each chapter as it was completed and provided a general reader's critical (but encouraging) assessment, as well as picking up on issues of punctuation and syntax. Of course, none of them are responsible for the manner in which I might have responded.

All the photographs are the author's own but a few drawings are reproduced here by the kind permission of a number of individuals and organisations. Each of these is acknowledged in the respective captions, but I take the opportunity here to offer my thanks in a more heartfelt manner. I am much indebted to Cadw and the Welsh government for their generosity in allowing the reproduction of numerous castle plans, and to Verity Hadfield of Cadw for her assistance in this matter. A debt of gratitude is also owed to Mike Salter for permission to publish his plan of Ruthin Castle, and likewise to the Gwynedd Archaeological Trust in respect of the plan of Carndochan Castle and to David Hopewell for facilitating it. Thanks are also owed to Nigel Dodds for redrawing and rescaling a number of published and unpublished drawings.

I am also grateful to Kathryn Laws and Karen George of the National Trust for organising two seminars at Chirk Castle in the summer of 2018, to Neil Guy for inviting me as a delegate from the Castle Studies Group, and again to Karen George for facilitating a later visit. It came at a most opportune moment and gave the chance to explore some of the lesser known parts of the building in the company of experts. Neil Guy also organised the Castle Studies Group 2019 Spring Meeting based in Northampton, another fortuitous occasion, which included a number of buildings that filled out the picture of the influence exerted by the Edwardian castle.

Chapter One

Introduction

The Castles of the Welsh Wars

Of all the castles of the Western world, those resulting from Edward I's containment, and then conquest, of the Welsh principality of Gwynedd, are amongst the best known and admired. Long regarded as some of the most significant examples of castle building in Britain, the Edwardian castles also represent a watershed in the development of castellated architecture, at once epitomising the zenith of military developments yet also heralding a change of direction in which stateliness, ostentation, symbolism, and domestic convenience were all aspects that seemed to count for as much as, or even more than, defence, even though they might be presented in a martial wrapping.

Edward built, or entirely rebuilt, eight castles as a consequence of his Welsh campaigns (Aberystwyth, Builth, Flint, Rhuddlan, Conwy, Harlech, Caernarfon, and Beaumaris). In addition, his followers, with some help from the King, built or entirely rebuilt, another six castles in north Wales (Caergwrle, Chirk, Denbigh, Hawarden, Holt, and Ruthin). We therefore have a group of fourteen castles that are directly related to the conquest of Gwynedd, all of which were being raised within a comparatively short time span and in a compact locality. Despite that geographical constriction, there is nothing regional about the character of the buildings, which embrace the most recent developments in military and domestic architecture and which hold their own upon the international stage.

The immediate appeal of the Edwardian castle, of course, lies in its antiquity and architectural quality, but that interest is compounded by the survival of a large amount of contemporary documentation relating to construction. Thus, we not only know the dates, but also a good deal about the building process and the personnel involved. The documents, indeed, provide fleeting glimpses of hundreds of human stories, a few of which will be touched upon in this book, as responsibility for the design of the castles is explored and attributions considered. It is not possible to recover the whole story, but the main contributors are known, most of all Master James of St George, Edward's principal craftsman in north Wales, who had overall responsibility for the construction of the royal castles, and who also had a degree of involvement in at least some of the baronial castles listed above.

Whilst there is no doubt that Master James fulfilled a highly significant role, it is apparent that a number of other master builders, known and unknown, also made contributions to the character of the royal and baronial castles that were consequent upon the conquest of Gwynedd. It is an aim of this book to evaluate the extent of their involvement, whilst re-assessing that of Master James. Although Gwynedd was the target of Edward's Welsh wars, its political dominance amongst the free Welsh meant that the conflict extended to most parts of Wales, and the castle-building phenomenon that accompanied the suppression of Welsh Wales was not confined to the northern principality.

For the first three-quarters of the thirteenth century it was the marcher lordships that had been the dynamo for castle design and construction in Wales, and Edward's campaigns from 1277 onwards did not immediately obviate the need for such buildings in those territories, or displace the impetus or creativity that existed therein. Several major schemes were indeed engendered within the marcher lordships by the Welsh wars, and these also need to be seen as part of the architectural legacy of the period, and examined with regard to their role in shaping or being shaped by the character of the Edwardian castle.

Building Design and Construction

Several people were involved in bringing a castle (or, indeed, any substantial architectural work) to its final form. First amongst these was the patron who provided the initial vision and, importantly, the finance. 'Patron' is something of an 'umbrella title', including, as it might, one or more advisers. Patrons no doubt varied in the degree of their involvement, but there is evidence to show that some could be exacting in their critical evaluation of a design. The best proof we have for a high level of patronal involvement is to be found in the successive specifications for Eton College which show Henry VI bending his mind to the architectural character of his pet project, his interventions suggesting an attempt to micromanage the design to the point of obsession.[1]

This is an unusual case and unlikely to be typical, but there are other, less well-documented instances of English monarchs clearly being involved in the design of major architectural works, at, for instance, Westminster Abbey and Knaresborough Castle.[2] Documentary evidence for a patron's participation is rarely specific, and it has to be a matter of judgement, based on the character of the building, and the circumstances surrounding its construction, as to how deep this was. The patron, then, had a vision; it might be vague or it might be detailed, or it might be partial, such as an idea regarding the most significant aspect of the building, be it a keep, gatehouse, or hall, or, indeed, particulars regarding the defences.

The two main aspects of a castle were the fortifications and the accommodation, domestic and administrative. Regarding the first of these, at the outset of the

Welsh castle-building programme, Edward I was an experienced soldier. He had fought in the Barons' Wars and in Palestine, had taken part in sieges and had been involved in the construction of defences; he was familiar with castle architecture and would have been able to proffer informed opinions on its defensive aspects. There were, in addition, numerous members of his noble entourage who had their personal experiences of castles, including the military advantages and drawbacks of particular aspects; there would, therefore, have been no shortage of opinions and advice to draw upon.

An important impetus to a patron taking an active role in designing a castle was that he or she usually had to live and work in it, hence, attention to domestic convenience was greatly to his or her advantage. The formalities of medieval royal and noble life are reflected in the provision of a number of stock elements, but, nevertheless, accommodation varied according to a castle's purpose and the size of the entourage it might be expected to house. These were aspects for the patron to decree, but these strictures are likely to have been broad outlines rather than detailed specifications.

There are also instances in which psychological, political, and symbolic messages have been discerned in castle design.[3] Even now, several hundred years removed from the circumstances in which it was raised, viewing a judiciously sited castle can engender an emotional response, but, in the medieval period, when such buildings were also centres of power, the effect is likely to have been much more laden with significance. The visual impression might have been fortuitous, a side-effect of a tactically advantageous site, for example, but there are certainly instances where there seems to have been a deliberate policy to create an effect. For the most part this may have been a general statement of authority and wealth, but it is probable that in other cases there was a more pointed meaning.[4] The intended allusions are not easy to pin down, but folklore and legend, including Arthurian legend, have been cited as sources of architectural expression.[5] Such connotations were obviously dictated by the patron.

More generally, Edward himself had greater experience than most when it came to castles. As King he was the paramount castle holder in the realm and heir to a long history of castle building by his forebears. His father, Henry III, was an inveterate castle builder who made major contributions to Dover, the Tower of London, Windsor, and York, to name but a few. Henry's works, which acted as beacons of royal authority, include many innovative and appealing aspects. An interest in Arthurian legend within the royal family is evident in the construction of Tintagel Castle by Edward's uncle, Richard, Earl of Cornwall and King of Germany, the site having seemingly been chosen largely for its reputation as King Arthur's birthplace. One can't help thinking that the well-travelled Uncle Richard might also have been a conduit of ideas on castle design following his 1241 crusade, during which he completed the re-fortification of Ascalon, and during his return journey, which included a four-month sojourn at the court of

Frederick II in Sicily. Also pertinent were his subsequent travels in Italy, where he must have seen some of Frederick's recently erected castles, including, perhaps, Castel del Monte in Puglia.

Although a patron's vision might initiate the design process, his ideas were naturally matters for discussion with the master builder; normally, in the case of a stone building, this would be a mason. The master mason was responsible for devising and directing the building work, but also for design. Although the first of these functions is unambiguous, the second is more open to question. Whilst the patron would naturally be involved in determining the character of the building because he or she had a set of requirements, design was almost certainly a collaborative process; the patron may have provided the vision but the master builder had to give it substance through a drawing or a model, and to consider too the structural feasibilities. There might be some to-ing and fro-ing, but this is how the system must have worked, to a greater or lesser extent, and how it still works between patron and architect today. Whilst patrons differed, and their degree of involvement varied accordingly, these were the fundamentals of the relationship.

In debating architectural authorship it is important to point out that, theoretically, the media of drawings and models allowed a building to be designed remotely, without the designer visiting a site, thereby opening up the possibility that the senior craftsman on site was not always the originator of the design. Nevertheless, even should this have been the case, such a template could only have been an ideal, the final product having to take into account the terrain and below-ground geology of the site itself. There are numerous instances of medieval castles in which the plan seems to be based on a symmetrical figure, but which for some reason (known, unknown, or presumed) diverges from the model.[6] A geometrical basis can be noted in the plans of many of Edward's Welsh castles, and a number of contemporary baronial castles, though few maintained the precision of the underlying geometry.[7] Unless the design was made with knowledge of the site conditions, compromises would have to be made by the master builder on the spot. The castles with the most symmetrical plans were those on low-lying sites free from topographical constraints.

In the case of large-scale projects, in addition to the master builder, there was usually an undermaster, who assumed control in the master's absence. A much sought-after master may have been in charge of more than one project simultaneously, in which case there might be a resident subordinate master at each of his sites with his own deputy or undermaster. In the case of Edward's castles in Wales, there were several subordinate masters, and whilst they had a lower level of responsibility, they were clearly highly capable figures and there may have been occasions on which they were able to make contributions to the design of the building of which they had day-to-day charge.

Another factor to consider is the contractor, who undertook to produce a certain amount of work for a fixed price. Thus, the town walls of Conwy were built by contractors, although the manufacture of the arrow loops themselves, which were incorporated into the defences, were the subject of a different contract. Contracts would have been fulfilled according to the instructions of the master builder, but the degree of control may have varied, and perhaps in the case of a trusted stalwart may have amounted to little more than a verbal instruction. As far as the walls of Conwy are concerned the laying out must have been done as a single project in consultation with the King or his representative, but their construction involved at least two, and possibly more, teams of contractors. Although the Conwy defences are broadly of a piece, and the accounts show that there was a specification standard, the three gatehouses, each of which belongs to a separate phase, differ in points of detail.[8] It is unlikely that such subtle distinctions were deliberately incorporated into the design by the master builder, and far more probable that they represent the contractors' slightly different interpretations of a restricted brief.

James of St George

James of St George has a reputation as one of the most significant castle builders of the Middle Ages. His origins and early career at the heart of Europe and his subsequent masterminding of Edward I of England's extensive castle-building programme in Wales and Scotland, all bestow upon him an international status afforded to few other master builders retained by the English Crown. This view of Master James is very much the product of Dr Arnold Taylor (1911–2002), Chief Inspector of Ancient Monuments and Historic Buildings in the Ministry of Works (1961–70) and Department of the Environment (1970–2), whose research into the Savoyard mason and his colleagues was revealed and refined in a series of publications between 1950 and 1986.[9] Taylor's exposé of Master James, his Continental origins, and his role in the Edwardian castles of Wales, was a masterpiece of historical detective work that far from being simply the study of an individual craftsman, went to the heart of how medieval building design and construction worked in the later thirteenth century and also laid bare the world of the medieval master builder.

Seldom is it possible to reconstruct the career of a medieval master craftsman with any degree of completeness or certainty. Nevertheless, in Edward I's subjugation of Wales and his associated castle-building activities during the last quarter of the thirteenth century and beyond, Taylor found the ideal opportunity to attempt to elucidate the life of just such an individual. Here was a substantial group of well-documented and dated buildings, raised over a compact period for the same patron, many of which were in a comparatively good state of preservation. Throughout nearly the entire period of Edward's massive expenditure on the castles of north Wales, from 1278 until his death *c.* 1309, Master James served as the King's leading building craftsman in Wales, apart from the years 1299–1306 when he was serving with Edward in Scotland, during the greater part of which period the Welsh project was in abeyance. Clearly these were promising conditions with which to begin a study of an individual's contribution to the architecture of the Middle Ages. Furthermore, Taylor's identification of Master James with a Continental namesake, who, there is reason to believe, was involved in the design of a succession of castles for the counts of Savoy between 1261 and 1275 in what is now Switzerland, Italy, and France, revealed a master craftsman with a documented career span of forty-eight years, a situation that is rare indeed.

Taylor's documentary research was augmented by structural analysis. In the Edwardian castles of north Wales he had noted a number of distinctive architectural, or structural, features that were otherwise (to his knowledge) unknown in English or Welsh castles.[10]

One of these peculiarities was an inclined arrangement of putlog holes, which, when applied to cylindrical towers resulted in a helicoidal pattern. In north Wales the inclined pattern manifests itself at the castles of Conwy (Caernarfonshire), Harlech (Merioneth), and Beaumaris (Anglesey), and in the town walls of Caernarfon and Conwy. Although such configurations had been in use in France since the early thirteenth century, they were largely unknown in Britain prior to the later thirteenth century, when they appeared in Edward's north Walian castles. However, they were in common usage in the castles of the dukes of Savoy during the 1260s and 1270s, specifically at Chillon (Vaud, Switzerland), Saxon (Valais, Switzerland), La Bâtiaz (Valais, Switzerland), and Saillon (Valais, Switzerland).

A second feature was the semi-circular arch, which is encountered in various situations at Flint, Conwy, Caernarfon, Harlech, and Beaumaris. To Taylor it was a form that was uncommon in thirteenth-century England and Wales, but which would be featured in several thirteenth-century Savoyard structures of the 1260s–70s including the town and castle of Saillon, and the castles of Saxon and Yverdon, Saint-Georges-d'Espéranche (Isère, France), and La Bâtiaz in Martigny.

Thirdly, there are two types of latrine turret which Taylor saw as having been borrowed from Savoyard practices. One was a shallow rectangular projection extending from ground level to a little below the parapet and situated at the re-entrant angle between a corner tower and the curtain wall. In Wales it is to be found at Rhuddlan, Conwy, and Harlech, but it was also used in Savoy during the 1260s at the castles of Saint-Georges-d'Espéranche and Yverdon (Vaud, Switzerland). The other type, which in the Edwardian castles is found only at Harlech, is in the form of a round turret corbelled out from the curtain; it is a feature that has no known precedents in Britain but which is paralleled at the Savoyard castle of La Bâtiaz.

Fourthly, at Conwy, the battlements are adorned with pinnacles, a most unusual feature in an English castle, but one that occurs at the Savoyard castle of San Giorio di Susa (Piedmont, Italy), and which probably existed at other castle sites in Savoy.[11]

Fifthly, Taylor cited the shallow segmental-headed two-light windows used in the great gatehouse of Harlech, which were found to be of comparable dimensions to windows of similar basic form at Chillon dating from the 1260s. Segmental-arched windows were also used at the castles of Saint-Georges-d'Espéranche and Yverdon.

Taylor's two-fold approach was to confirm without question that Master James of Wales and Master James of Savoy were one and the same, and he conferred upon his subject a stature of European dimension, not only for his origins and transnational sphere of influence, but also as the mastermind behind one of the Continent's most lauded groups of castles. However, it was also made clear that, far from being a one-man band, James of St George imported a number of key associates from Savoy who were strategically deployed amongst the royal castles of Wales, and whose presence supports the idea that, despite his multiple responsibilities, Master James maintained a high degree of control over the building process. To Taylor, James of St George 'displayed a versatility that was characteristic of the great master builders of the medieval world', and that he was 'pre-eminent among the military architects of his generation'.[12]

Whilst a combination of documentary references and distinctive architectural or structural features are essential for determining the authenticity of attributions to a particular medieval master builder, the evidence is not always as straightforward as it may seem, and there has, inevitably, been a reaction to Taylor's conclusions. Some of the features that Taylor thought of as indicative of a Savoyard presence, and, by extension, James of St George's practices, are no longer thought to be quite so diagnostic. For instance, the early thirteenth-century employment of helicoidal scaffolding has been noted at two sites in Wales, and the use of semi-circular arches in English castles is attested in the 1260s.[13]

These evidences may weaken the impact of Taylor's argument, but on the other hand they do not disprove it even in respect of these particular instances, and the significance of other features is unchallenged.

A more contentious criticism of Taylor's thesis asserts an overemphasis on Master James as the architectural mastermind behind the Edwardian castle, and a downplaying of the contributions to design made by the King, his advisers, and other technical staff including the subordinate masters.[14] In the attempt to redress the balance, the reputation of Master James as an architect has suffered. Thus, King Edward initiated design whilst Master James 'merely obeyed his master's orders, whether they were for particular features . . . or for what those features were to look like'. Instead, his high rank is attributed to 'his organisational skills, rather than his perceived abilities as a military engineer'.[15] This particular criticism will be considered in the following chapters as the present investigation of the buildings proceeds, and conclusions are drawn regarding the respective contributions of Master James and his colleagues and the qualities needed to fulfil effectively the demands of such a far-reaching position as that of Master of the King's Works in Wales.

Master James and his Colleagues in Savoy

A number of the castles raised for the counts of Savoy were in the Valais, in the upper Rhône valley, a border area between Savoy and the territory of the bishops of Sion. At Conthey, where a *turris* was under construction in 1257–8, one of the contractors was a *Franciscus cementarius*, who Taylor identified with a *Johanni Francisco* listed in the accounts for Chillon castle and the 'Johanni Franceys', or John Francis, of the Conwy accounts.[16] Little remains of the castle at Conthey, but it had an unusual D-shaped donjon.

Three years later, in 1261, Franciscus built a great tower for the counts at Saillon (Valais, Switzerland) about 8 miles to the south west of Conthey, under the supervision of the Gascon engineer Sir John Mesoz (also Maso, Masot, Masouz, Massout, Maysoz, Mesot), formerly in the employ of King Henry III, by whom he was knighted, and now one of Savoy's senior technical officers, with whom Franciscus agreed the form and position of the keep.[17] The castle is sited on a north-east to south-west aligned rocky ridge of such precipitous character that it is now hard to imagine how it might have functioned as a castle. The principal remains are the south-west curtain, which is punctuated by a series of D-shaped open-backed towers that reminded Taylor of the town walls of Conwy, and the cylindrical keep, also situated towards the south-west end and sited on the line of, but largely inside, the north-west curtain, which crowns the ridge (Figure 1.1).

Nestling at the foot of the ridge, to the north east, is the little walled town, its fortifications, which date from the 1250s, enclosing an area of *c.* 2.75 acres (1.1ha). The semi-circular arches of the four town gates were one of the Savoyard features that Taylor compared to examples at several of the north Walian castles, and in particular with the outer gateway at Harlech (Figure 1.2). Semi-circular open-backed towers project from the walls, an arrangement not unlike the south-west curtain of the castle.[18]

At first glance, the donjon of 1261 appears to have absolutely perpendicular sides, but, in fact, a slight batter rises from the ground to first-floor level, a sensible if subtle precaution on a steeply sloping site. The tower has an external diameter of 9.96m (32ft 8in) and rises through four storeys, being entered via a first-floor doorway; otherwise the openings are all slits at second- and third-floor level. From the first floor a mural staircase wound clockwise around the tower to the second floor, separate lengths leading from second to third floor and from the third floor to the roof. Like the town gateways, the entrance has a semi-circular arch, so too does a pair of opposed doors at second-floor level.

Remnants of a first-floor fireplace include a pair of stone corbels and above them the stubs of two timber beams that supported the hood. The third-floor room had the facility of a latrine, corbelled out from the tower and discharging outside the curtain. Otherwise there is little sign of comfort and indeed the internal diameter of the upper floors at 3.12m (10ft 3in) is hardly spacious.

Figure 1.1: *Saillon. The castle from the south showing the south-west curtain and wall towers with the donjon of 1261 behind.*

It is a watch tower in the *Bergfried* tradition rather than a residence. In constructing the great tower, John Francis used a helicoidal system of scaffolding, one of Taylor's indicators of Savoyard workmanship in north Wales. This was in direct contrast to the enceinte and the town walls, where a horizontal pattern of scaffolding holes is retained in walls and towers alike (Figure 1.3).

Figure 1.2 (left): *Saillon. South gateway to the walled town.*

Figure 1.3 (below): *Saillon. Town walls from the north east.*

A third great tower of the same date as Saillon, which is considered to be by the same architect, is that of Brignon (Valais), some 7 miles to the east of Saillon in the Val de Nendaz on the south bank of the Rhône.[19] The castle is sited above and to the south west of the village, on a headland on the west side of the road between Brignon and Nendaz, a precipitous cliff giving protection on the south and west sides. There were two principal courtyards arranged concentrically, the inner one, which was slightly more regular, with a sub-triangular form, its prow pointing towards the eastern approach and capped by the keep. A narrow outer ward was enclosed by another curtain wall to the east containing the gateway from which there was a circuitous approach to the inner ward, the entrance to which was protected first by an apsidal-ended tower, which had to be circumnavigated, and, second, by a rectangular tower or bastion.

Some eighteen years later, in 1279–80, between the first and second Welsh wars, a tower of comparable design was raised 2 miles to the south west of Saillon, on the opposite side of the river, at Saxon. Similarly sited on a height above the town, the tower rises through four storeys above a basement to a height of around 21m (36ft) and has an external diameter of 9m (30ft) and walls 2m (6ft) thick. It has a more pronounced batter than Saillon's keep, but also has the helicoidal putlog pattern. The round-arched entrance is at second-floor level and, at third-floor level, there is a corbelled-out latrine like that of Saillon. Like Saillon too, the floor was carried on two parallel cross beams, on which the joists were laid.

The contractors for the Saxon tower included the brothers Giles of St George (*Giletus de sancto Georgio*) and his brother Tassin, the former being identified by Taylor as the Giles of St George (*Egidio de Sancto Georgio*) who subsequently worked at Aberystwyth in 1282 as resident master, and perhaps at Harlech in 1286.[20] Furthermore, a third contractor at Saxon was one *Beynardus*, who dug the foundations for the tower. Taylor matched *Beynardus* with Adam Boynard, who was also working at Harlech in 1286 in association with a certain *Gilet*, who Taylor believed was none other than Giles of St George.[21] The recognition that *Franciscus*, *Giletus de sancto Georgio*, and *Beynardus* of the Savoyard records and their namesakes in Wales were respectively one and the same provided additional evidence for Taylor's thesis regarding James of St George's Continental origins, and the influence that he exerted over the character of the Edwardian castles of Wales.

The comital castles of the Valais were spartan outposts in a mountainous and disputed territory occupying rugged and tactically advantageous sites. A different aspect of thirteenth-century Savoyard castle architecture was a group of regularly planned courtyard castles which were essentially residential in character. One that James of St George was associated with was Yverdon-les-Bains (Vaud, Switzerland), which is situated at the south-west end of Lac de Neuchâtel within the *Pays de Vaud*, an area controlled by the future Count Peter II. Work on the castle lasted from 1261 until *c.* 1271, the principal mason being a Master John, the father of Master James, who worked as his associate, and who took over from him *c.* 1268.[22] Yverdon is a quadrangular castle with four cylindrical corner towers, of which the south-eastern one is enlarged to form a great tower, or keep (Figure 1.4). The domestic apartments were ranged around the central courtyard, which was entered via an unobtrusive gateway in the curtain wall.

A similar arrangement is found at neighbouring Champvent (Vaud), another quadrangular castle lying some 3½ miles to the east of Yverdon. At Champvent, it is the north-east tower that forms the keep, and the courtyard contains two adjacent residential ranges, which Taylor compared with the L-shaped arrangement of the royal apartments within the inner ward of Conwy (see below, Chapter 6).[23] The castle's existence can be attributed to Peter of Champvent, who made a career at the courts of both Henry III and Edward I, and who was Lord of Champvent between *c.* 1251 and 1303, when he died.

Another related castle is Saint-Georges-d'Espéranche, from which Master James may have taken his English toponymic.[24] Built for Count Philip probably between 1268 and 1275, it too was a quadrangular castle with an L-shaped arrangement of apartments ranged along the inside of the curtain.[25] Taylor emphasised the connection between Saint-Georges and Yverdon through the comparison of the remains of thirteenth-century first-floor windows then visible in their respective curtain walls.[26] These openings had shallow segmental heads and were divided into four lights by a transom and mullion. A second common trait that survived at Saint-Georges, and had existed at Yverdon, was a slim latrine turret set within the re-entrant angle of corner tower and curtain. There is some reason, then, to believe that the two buildings were designed by the same architect.

However, Saint-Georges-d'Espéranche differed from the other Savoyard castles in that it employed corner towers of polygonal (rather than circular) plan. The use of polygonal towers was in itself quite uncommon, although, nearly thirty years earlier, the emperor Frederick II had set a precedent in Puglia, where, *c.* 1240, he had built an octagonal courtyard castle (Castel del Monte) with corner turrets of similar plan. The choice of polygonal towers in these instances was probably due to aesthetics, or rarity value, because they had no special merit from a defensive perspective. At Saint-Georges-d'Espéranche, the main protection against mining was a water-filled moat, said in 1794 to have been 30–50ft (9–15m) wide and 10–18ft (3–5.5m) deep and then a broad berm 30–40ft (9–12m) wide.[27] This berm represents both an outer ward and the principle of concentricity.

Straddling the architectural gap between these castellated stately residences and the frontier castles of the Valais is Chillon (Vaud), a multi-phase castle of tenth-century origin, situated at the east end of Lake Geneva. Chillon has an irregular plan, a result of being sited on a narrow rocky platform that extends into the lake, its encirclement by water being completed by the creation of a moat on the landward side (Figure 1.5).

Figure 1.4: *Yverdon. Great tower from the north east.*

Figure 1.5: *Chillon. The castle from the south east.*

The early core of the castle occupied the crest of the rock and comprised a curtain-walled enclosure of sub-elliptical plan on a roughly north–south alignment, containing a rectangular great tower; there was a talus in front of the landward (eastern) curtain extending down the slope of the rock (Figure 1.6). However, during the thirteenth century, this rather austere fortress was transformed into a palatial and extensive residence.

Early developments included the thickening of the curtain, the addition of a number of rectangular flanking towers and other buildings around the perimeter of the old enclosure, the provision of an outer curtain in front of the talus and the extension of the castle to the south by the enclosure of the low-lying ground at this end. The central position of the keep provided a natural focus for a bipartite division of the old enclosure, and the extension of the castle to the south created a third courtyard, resulting in (from north to south) a lower, middle, and outer ward.

Further remodelling during the mid to late thirteenth century included the construction of three D-shaped wall towers to the eastern curtain and a substantial addition to the domestic accommodation. The latter was achieved by extending the castle towards the lake (west), beyond the crest of the rock, an operation that necessitated the construction of vaulted undercrofts over which a substantial two-storey range was raised. This work resulted in two major residential blocks centred on the middle and upper wards, the latter the preserve of the counts and probably dating from *c.* 1250.

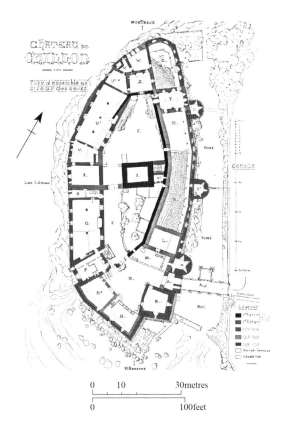

Figure 1.6: *Chillon. Castle plan. From Naef 1908.*

0   10   30metres

0   100feet

The middle ward block is slightly later and may date from the time that James of St George was engaged at Chillon, his presence having been recorded in 1266–7.[28] The ground-floor hall within this range is lit by segmental-arched fenestration of twin lancet lights with trefoil-cusped heads surmounted by a central trefoil; the central mullion was embellished by a colonette with foliate capital, and surrounds had multiple chamfered rebates. These windows, which are also found elsewhere at Chillon, notably within the *Domus Clericorum* (G) at the north-east apex of the castle, were one of the crucial elements considered by Taylor as evidence of Savoyard influence in Wales, notably at Harlech, where the gatehouse contains windows that appear to be derived from their Chillon counterparts (Figure 1.7).

Figure 1.7: *Chillon. Restored later thirteenth-century window in the curtain from the north east.*

Figure 1.8: *Chillon. The towers of the east front from the south east with the great tower in the background.*

It is probable too that the three eastern wall towers were rebuilt during this period, when they were provided with a timber hoard, no longer extant, the beam slots for which survive below two later medieval heightenings (Figure 1.8).[29] Other works include the refurbishment of the twelfth-century Allinges Tower at the northern end of the upper ward including the first-floor *Camera Domini.*

This brief summary of castle building in Savoy is a reminder that there was a Continental hinterland within the development of the Edwardian castle, one which manifested itself in various ways in Wales (although Savoy was only one of the sources of inspiration that were to mould the character of Edward's Welsh castles). Other antecedents will be discussed during the course of the book, but the first task, which is the subject of the next chapter, is to consider the main castles raised by the Welsh princes prior to the invasion of 1277. Some were retained for a time by Edward and his successors, and repairs and additions made, but they now serve as monuments to the old regime that came to an end with the English conquest.

Chapter Two

The Castles of the Northern Welsh

Problems of Chronology

S tone castle building in thirteenth-century north Wales prior to 1277 was largely carried out by the Welsh princes, notably Llywelyn ab Iorwerth (*c.* 1173–1240), also known as Llywelyn Fawr (Llywelyn the Great), and his grandson Llywelyn ap Gruffudd (d. 1282), each in his turn ruler of Gwynedd and the dominant force in Welsh politics. Castles usually attributed to Llywelyn Fawr include Carndochan (Merioneth), Castell-y-Bere (Merioneth), the first phase of Criccieth (Carnarvonshire), Deganwy (Carnarvonshire), Dolbadarn (Carnarvonshire), and Dolwyddelan (Carnarvonshire); those attributed to Llywelyn ap Gruffudd are the second phase of Criccieth, Ewloe (Flintshire), and Dolforwyn (Montgomeryshire). Another major castle, Dinas Brân (Denbighshire), at Llangollen, was probably built by Gruffudd ap Madog (d. 1269), the ruler of northern Powys, or Powys Fadog.[1] Thus far then, these details are clear enough, but, in fact, the chronology of the Welsh castle is not nearly so straightforward.

The main obstacle is a paucity of documentation. There are no building accounts from the Welsh period, and indeed only a few isolated historical references, which simply indicate the existence of a castle. Moreover, any date, if there is one, might only signify the foundation or the earliest mention of a castle, whereas a perusal of the physical evidence, as might be expected, clarifies that most of the castles under discussion here comprise more than one structural phase, and the fabric of the building may, therefore, belong to two or more historical periods.

This seems to be true of Criccieth, where three principal structural phases have been discerned, two belonging to the Welsh period and one to the English occupation, although the identification of the structural phases with the historical periods has not been without controversy, and there may, even now, be considered to be an element of doubt. On the other hand, it should be stressed that structural phasing may simply be an indication of a particular building sequence in which the dates of construction are actually very close to one another. This seems to have been the case at Dolforwyn, where the Round Tower and the Keep were built first and the linking curtain walls second, but the whole complex dating from the Welsh period is very closely dated to the four years 1273–7.

Another difficulty arises when attempting to establish a relative chronological framework for the whole group through typology, because there appears to be a lack of typological development. Diagnostic details are few and stock features seem to crop up time and again between 1221 and 1277, the earliest (Castell-y-Bere) and latest (Dolforwyn) dates we have for the Welsh stone castles of the thirteenth century. The apsed tower, the rectangular keep, the round tower straddling the curtain, and the D-shaped tower are all recurrent aspects of the Welsh castle that do not seem to change their character.[2] For these reasons the following review can only describe, point out the obstacles to interpretation, and come to tentative conclusions.

The Castles of Llywelyn ab Iorwerth

Castell-y-Bere (Merioneth)

Castell-y-Bere, situated 7 miles north east of the coastal town of Tywyn, is as good a starting point as any for a review of the castles of Llywelyn ab Iorwerth for two reasons. Firstly, it provides one of the few firm dates on which a chronology can be based, being generally accepted as the castle built by Llywelyn after taking the cantref of Meirionnydd and the commote of Afon Lliw from his son, Gruffudd, in 1221.[3] Secondly, it contains several of the elements that are thought of as being typical of native Welsh castles. It seems therefore to represent a rare datum for contributing to a sequence of architectural development. This sounds promising, but, although the fabric displays a number of modifications, the ruinous state of the complex and the lack of a detailed programme of structural analysis and excavation means that the physical development of the castle is far from clear. Bere is clearly a prime target for future work on the evolution of the Welsh castle, but, for the time being, we have to be content with a degree of assumption and supposition.

Castell-y-Bere occupies a hilltop site which narrows from south west to north east, the main enclosure being formed by straight lengths of curtain, the configuration of which is dictated by the natural topography (Figure 2.1).

The main approach, which is from the south east, is interrupted by three consecutive ditches, the second of which is immediately in front of the outer gatehouse. This gatehouse comprises a small rectangular tower set within the wall of an outwork, or barbican. Within the gate passage is a drawbridge pit, implying a turning bridge pivoted on the threshold. The outer gatehouse gave access to an entrance passage containing a staircase, the sides of the passage narrowing with the ascent. At the top, there was the innermost ditch to be traversed before reaching the inner gateway, another single tower pierced by an entrance, as was the outer gateway, and also provided with a pivoted drawbridge.

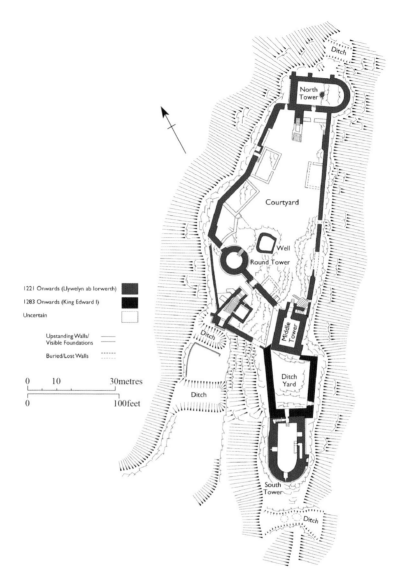

Figure 2.1: *Castell-y-Bere. Castle plan. © Crown copyright (2018) Cadw, Welsh Government*

To the north of the gatehouse, straddling the south–west curtain, is the circular Round Tower, immediately north of which the curtain contains an inserted postern. Projecting from the south angle of the main enclosure, is the rectangular Middle Tower, in effect a keep. However, the outstanding features of Bere are the North and South towers, two elongated apsidal-ended structures, respectively 65ft (19.8m) and 68ft (20.7m) in length, one at each end of the castle. The south–west wall of the North Tower forms the greater part of the north–east curtain, and, like the Middle Tower, lies entirely outside the main enclosure. The orientation of the South Tower is diametrically opposed to that of the North Tower, diverges only slightly from the axis of the south-east curtain, and was formerly isolated from the rest of the castle by a ditch. It is now linked to the Middle Tower by the Ditch Yard.

The Ditch Yard is without doubt a secondary element; its walls abut those of the Middle Tower and South Tower, and it is attributed to the work carried out by Edward after the capture of the castle in 1283 (see below, Chapter 6). The walls of the Ditch Yard, then, provide a *terminus ante quem* of 1283 for the South Tower and Middle Tower, so these can be confirmed as being of Welsh build, although it is a moot point as to whether they belong to the same construction phase. Indeed, analysis of the plan gives some reason to suppose that the entire south-west front as it is apparent today is the result of modification.

One area that is open to question is the barbican, which encloses the slopes of the summit in front of the south-west front. Although its structural relationship with the rest of the castle has not, as yet, been confirmed, it has the appearance of being an addition. Such an elaborate gate complex is unique in the castles of the Welsh princes, and is best understood as the strengthening of an earlier arrangement. Behind the barbican the rectangular Middle Tower projects almost entirely outside the south-west curtain and takes up a stolidly challenging position, apparently to dominate the gatehouse approach. The barbican gives the impression of enclosing the space formerly guarded by the Middle Tower.

The isolation of the South Tower from the rest of the castle is rather odd, but its forward position is more comprehensible if it is regarded as a successor to the Middle Tower, taking on its former role of guarding the approach. Theoretically, then, the South Tower and the barbican, with its elongated defended entrance, may be the result of a refashioning of the south-west front to strengthen the approach. If the South Tower and the barbican complex do indeed belong to the same phase then they must surely be a Welsh modification, most likely attributable to Llywelyn ap Gruffudd.

This is one possibility. On the other hand, when the castle was first built, it would have been unwise to have left such a strategic vantage point and naturally defensive position like the site of the South Tower unoccupied, because it would have seriously compromised the defence of the castle, both by weakening control over the approach and by allowing it to be occupied by a hostile force. Owing to the lack of parallels in Welsh castles it has been argued that this uncharacteristic strengthening of the entrance may have been created during the English occupation.[4] Repairs were certainly done here by Edward's men in 1283 after the castle had been captured following a siege, so such a conclusion is theoretically possible, if unproven.

During clearance and excavation at Castell-y-Bere in the 1850s, a quantity of thirteenth-century architectural sculpture was recovered, including column bases, vaulting responds, and capitals, characterised by stiff leaf, dog tooth, and waterholding bases.[5] Most of this material was found close to the south-west end of the castle, and has consequently been considered to have been concentrated near the entrance front.[6] From this point of view, potential provenances are the Middle Tower and the entrance itself. However, the North Tower is another possibility. In the centre of the ground storey is the base of a circular stone column, a feature generally interpreted as a base for a first-floor hearth, thereby indicating a hall at that level. This upper room was entered from the south west via an external stone staircase. One of the buttresses on the north-east face of the tower is strategically placed, opposite the curtain wall and at the base of the apsidal end, as though to take the thrust from a vaulting arch. Although we can't be certain about the whereabouts of the decorative work, it, together with sculpture from other sites, does provide an insight into the general character of Welsh castles, emphasising their roles as stylish residences.

Carndochan (Merioneth)

Another castle that has been associated with Llywelyn ab Iorwerth, but, on the other hand, also attributed to his son Dafydd, is Castell Carndochan, which lies some 20 miles to the north east of Castell-y-Bere on a promontory to the south west of Llyn Tegid (Lake Bala) (Figure 2.2).[7]

There are no historical records to draw on, but, the position of the castle in Meirionnydd, close to its southern border with Powys Wenwynwyn, connects it with Castell-y-Bere as a frontier castle demarcating the southern boundary of Llywelyn's territory. Although its origins remain shrouded in mystery, investigations by the Gwynedd Archaeological Trust over the period 2012–18 have revealed something of the structural character and relative chronology of this previously enigmatic fortification.[8]

A roughly semi-circular enclosure orientated from north east to south west contains the foundations of a square building with a battered base, probably a tower, or keep. Straddling the curtain at the north-east and south ends of the enclosure are the remains of a circular and D-shaped tower respectively, and, at the south-west angle, an elongated apsidal tower on the same alignment as the enclosure, its north-west wall continuing the line of the north-west curtain, projects outside the enclosure. In the south curtain, between the apsidal and D-shaped towers is the entrance, a 10ft (3m) long passage with tapered sides, widening from 5½ft (1.7m) at the outer end to 9ft (2.75m); it had an entrance arch of narrow, largely slate slab voussoirs.

Excavation has shown that the round tower is secondary; it is also possible that the D-shaped tower was secondary, though here the archaeological evidence was less conclusive. The chronology of the apsidal tower relative to the curtain is also uncertain. There is some evidence, then, that when first built, the castle

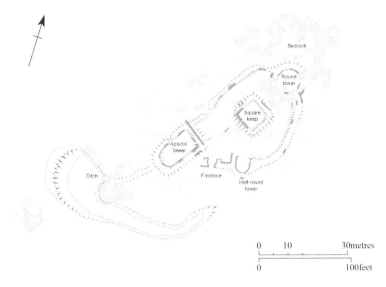

Bedrock

Round
tower

Square
keep

Apsidal
Tower

Ditch

Entrance

Half-round
tower

| 0 | 10 | 30 metres |

| 0 | | 100 feet |

Figure 2.2: *Carndochan. Castle plan. © Gwynedd Archaeological Trust (2018)*

had a simpler plan, and was perhaps no more complex than a simple enclosure containing a keep, and that the principal features of the enceinte are the result of later remodelling.

There are some obvious points of comparison with Bere. The positioning of the apsidal tower, thrusting forward of the curtain to control the approach to the gateway, parallels the rectangular Middle Tower of Bere, or, more aptly, perhaps, the apsidal South Tower. The apsidal tower of Carndochan is slightly smaller than the Bere examples (54ft/6.4m x 34ft/10.4m) but just as prominently displayed. The round tower, which was built to a comparable scale as its counterpart at Bere, has the same characteristic of being half in and half out of the curtain, although here the tower was built in two halves, which abut the curtain. Instead of forming part of the entrance front as at Bere, it is situated at the farthest remove from the gateway, occupying a comparable position to Bere's North Tower. The equivalent position of Bere's Round Tower is taken by Carndochan's D-shaped tower, an interesting and distinctive trait of which is that its projection beyond the curtain is only slight and confined to its curved prow. The layouts of the two castles, then, demonstrate similarities of concept that are too close to attribute to mere chance, and which must, therefore, represent some form of collusion.

Dolwyddelan (Carnarvonshire)

Castell-y-Bere and Carndochan were frontier fortresses. The principal features of Llywelyn's more northerly castles, in Gwynedd's heartland, are quite different. Firstly, Dolwyddelan, Llywelyn's traditional birthplace, which consists of a small irregular enclosure crowning a rocky peak with a rectangular keep forming part of the enceinte (Figure 2.3).

Ditches on the north-east and south-west sides augment the defensive character of the natural slopes on the other two flanks. The approach to the castle was from the north east, where there was a bridge and an external staircase leading to a gateway at the north-west end of the north-east front, a simple opening within the curtain wall.

At 34ft (10.4m) x 32ft (9.8m) the keep is a little smaller than the Middle Tower at Bere, but is otherwise its equivalent, here forming the principal living accommodation, essentially a first-floor hall over a basement (Figure 2.4).

The building has been much altered, firstly, by being heightened in the medieval period when it received an additional storey, and, secondly, in the nineteenth century when it was restored and reroofed. Few primary details survive, but, originally, it contained a single room open to the roof, set over a basement that was accessed through a trap in the floor. There was a fireplace in the south-east wall and a latrine at the south-west end contained within a broad projection, or turret, with a pitched stone roof that also housed the passage leading to it.

The keep cuts a striking figure from the road below although it would have been a slightly squatter building in the thirteenth century and therefore not quite so prominent. However, it would have provided a good vantage point, although the castle appears to be more of a hunting lodge or retreat

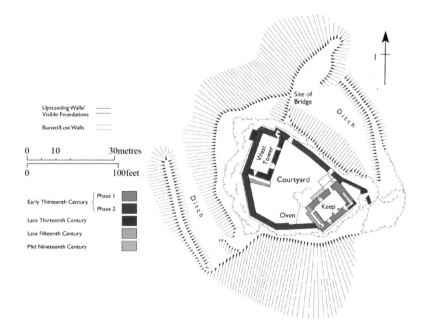

Figure 2.3: *Dolwyddelan. Castle plan. © Crown copyright (2018) Cadw, Welsh Government*

Figure 2.4: *Dolwyddelan. The great tower from the north.*

than a fortress. That Llywelyn was born in the vicinity may have been reason enough for him to build a house here, its elevated site a reminder to himself of how far he had risen from his origins, generally considered to be at the older Tomen Castell, which lies on a modest knoll rising from the floodplain beneath Dolwyddelan.

The presence of a mural latrine towards the east end of the north curtain suggests that there was another apartment in the north-east angle of the enclosure, subsequently replaced by the existing West Tower after the castle's capture by Edward's forces (see below, Chapter 6). Of this earlier building, however, we can say little; it is possible that the south and east walls were of timber.

Criccieth (Carnarvonshire)

Another rectangular keep (the South-East Tower) is to be found at Criccieth, which sits on a rocky headland at the neck of the Lleyn peninsula, a site that affords arresting views along the coast to the east and west (Figure 2.5).

The first mention of a castle here dates from 1239, shortly before Llywelyn's death. The plan of the outer ward, which probably dates from the time of Llywelyn Fawr, is in the form of an irregular triangle with its base to the south, and the gateway at the south-east angle. There are rectangular towers at the north and south-west angles and part-way along the east curtain. This latter tower (South-East Tower) and the adjoining curtain to the north form the east side of the inner ward, the other sides of which are surrounded by the outer ward (Figure 2.6).

Figure 2.5: *Criccieth. The castle from the north east.*

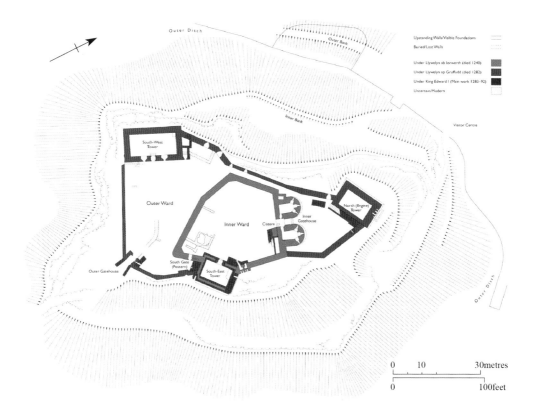

Figure 2.6: *Criccieth. Castle plan. © Crown copyright (2018) Cadw, Welsh Government*

The chronology of the castle is essentially that which was worked out in the 1930s and expounded in print by the Chief Inspector of Ancient Monuments B. H. St John O'Neil.[9] Based on a detailed analysis of the surviving fabric, it encompasses three structural phases, which are assigned to three historical periods. St John O'Neil dated the inner ward to the reign of Llywelyn Fawr, the outer ward to Llywelyn ap Gruffudd, and various alterations and additions to the English occupation under Edward I and Edward II.

Like Dolwyddelan, the inner ward encloses a small, irregularly shaped courtyard on the crown of the hill, with the keep (South-East Tower) forming part of the enceinte, although here the greater part of the tower projects outside the curtain. However, at Criccieth there is also a surprise factor: a monumental gatehouse to the north, its twin D-shaped flanking towers (the primary fabric of which survives almost to full height) forming an imposing introduction to the castle, and confirming to the observer the builder's keen eye for architectural effect (Figure 2.7).

This form of gatehouse was unprecedented in Welsh architecture, a circumstance that implies English antecedents, and which is, therefore, a reason for it having once been attributed to Edward I. The gatehouses of Beeston

Figure 2.7: *Criccieth. Inner gatehouse from the north.*

(*c*. 1220), built by Llywelyn Fawr's ally, Ranulph Earl of Chester, and the royal castle of Montgomery (1222), which Llywelyn attacked twice (1228 and 1232), have both been cited as possible sources, implying that the Criccieth gatehouse is broadly contemporary.[10] On stylistic grounds, Beeston could be considered a more likely source, its straightforward D-shaped towers having more in common with those of Criccieth. Beeston's outer gateway towers, like its Criccieth counterparts, have little or no projection into the interior (Figure 2.8).

   However, in many respects, a better visual parallel than either Beeston or Montgomery might be the outer gatehouse of Chepstow (Monmouthshire), now considered to date from *c*. 1190. Although the Chepstow entrance is flanked by

Figure 2.8: *Beeston. Inner gatehouse from the south west.*

two circular towers of different dimensions, in contrast to the twin D-shaped towers of Criccieth, the overall impression is similar, and if an architect were using a memory of Chepstow as a model then Criccieth might very well be the result. Both are rather plain structures with a highly placed blind arch above the entrance, and a line of square slots for carrying a timber hoard just below the parapet. In its day, the design of the Chepstow entrance was a radical departure from the norm, and it may well have retained a sufficient degree of celebrity to influence the builder of Criccieth (Figure 2.9).

Before taking our leave of the Criccieth gatehouse, it should be emphasised that the current chronology leaves room for doubt.[11] It is therefore worth considering the reasoning behind the now unfashionable attribution to Edward I. In 1970, C. N. Johns, the former principal investigator of the RCAHMW, proposed a radically different sequence of construction from that which had been worked out by St John O'Neil, in which the outer ward was attributed to Llywelyn Fawr, the inner ward, including the gatehouse, to Edward I, and the subsequent additions to Edward II.[12] There are several strands to the argument, which, on stylistic grounds, is both rational and plausible.

Firstly, a comparison with the Edwardian building accounts for other north Walian castles suggested that the sum of £353 spent at Criccieth between 1285 and 1292 would have been sufficient to raise the gatehouse and inner curtain in addition to paying for other minor works, even before unspecified funds for the years 1283–4 are taken into account.[13]

Figure 2.9: *Chepstow. Outer gatehouse from the east.*

Secondly, the outer ward of the castle, which covers most of the rock top, bears better comparison with other castles attributed to Llywelyn Fawr than does the curiously circumscribed inner ward (except in the case of Dolwyddelan, where the extent of the courtyard is dictated by that of the hilltop on which it was built).

Thirdly, no other native Welsh castle had a twin-towered gatehouse, although buildings similar to that at Criccieth were being raised by Edward in north Wales during the last quarter of the thirteenth century.

Fourthly, the concentric qualities of the castle, which were also to be associated with Edwardian practice in north Wales from 1277, were, conversely, otherwise unknown in other native Welsh castles.

A number of other anomalies might be added to the argument.

Fifthly, the disposition of ground–storey arrow loops in the Criccieth gatehouse are supplied in a more systematic fashion than might be expected in early thirteenth–century Wales.

Sixthly, it is also the case that the polygonal interiors of the flanking towers are not to be found in any other Welsh castle, or in possible English models of the early thirteenth century; on the other hand, they compare very well with the flanking towers of the Inner West Gate at Caerphilly, and the upper storeys of the gatehouses of Harlech and Beaumaris.

Seventhly, the narrow entrance recess between the flanking towers is not a feature of gatehouses that could have served as models in the 1230s, having more in common with some of the Edwardian castles of Harlech, Rhuddlan, and Beaumaris, although it should be noted that the width of the gateway (which is equal to that of the recess) is comparable to that of other Welsh castles.

The counter argument is that although the gateway was evidently intended as the principal ceremonial entrance to the castle, direct access to it is cut off by the presence of the northern division of the outer ward, and it can only be approached indirectly from the southern part of the outer ward via an alley between the inner and outer curtains, from which the gatehouse latrine turret was emptied. It seems highly unlikely, not to say inept, that this can have been intended when the gatehouse was built, and far more probable that it resulted from the subsequent construction of the outer ward.

Dolbadarn (Carnarvonshire)

The Criccieth gatehouse is matched, it might be said exceeded, in its architectural interest at Dolbadarn, another castle that probably dates from the 1230s (Figure 2.10).

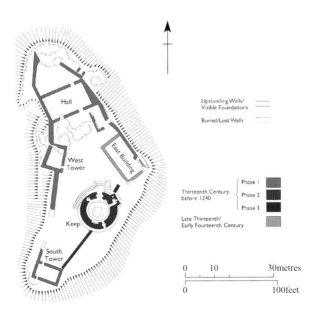

Figure 2.10: *Dolbadarn. Castle plan. © Crown copyright (2018) Cadw, Welsh Government*

Built on a rocky platform overlooking the Llanberis pass, this small and otherwise architecturally undistinguished castle is dominated by a cylindrical great tower, or keep. Built independently of the adjoining curtain wall, it may be the earliest of the castle buildings to have been raised. Its mortared masonry and fine architectural character contrasts with the dry stone walling and utilitarian nature of the other buildings (now reduced to their lower courses). These other buildings include two mural towers, both rectangular, one at the southern apex of the enclosure (South Tower) and the other on the west side (West Tower), and a hall that extends right across the courtyard towards its northern end.

The keep is perhaps the most striking building to have survived amongst the native Welsh castles and, like the gatehouse at Criccieth, is a highly unusual structure in this context, and perhaps a testament to Llywelyn's international outlook (Figure 2.11).

The inspiration comes from the round keeps that were being built in south Wales and the Marches in the early thirteenth century. This is a prestige piece, and, in this respect, together with its position on the line of the curtain, is reminiscent of Conisbrough (Yorkshire), an earlier and more ambitious building, but one that dominates that castle in the same way. Unlike other Welsh towers, none of which seems to have exceeded two storeys, the Dolbadarn keep rises through three, including a basement. It has an external diameter of 42ft (12.8m), which is larger than any of the northern Welsh round towers, and also many of the thirteenth-century round keeps elsewhere in Wales and the Marches though not one of the largest.[14] An interesting feature is the rectangular latrine turret on the north-east side with stone-corbelled roof, which provides a link with Dolwyddelan and contrasts with the semi-circular turrets common to many of the English marcher keeps. As at Dolwyddelan, access was at first-floor level by means of an external staircase, timber originally, since replaced in stone.

Although the castles attributed to Llywelyn ab Iorwerth appear to form a disparate group, there are a number of unifying factors. The first of these is the rectangular keep, which, at Bere, Dolwyddelan, and Criccieth forms part of the enceinte.[15] At Carndochan it was freestanding in the centre of the courtyard, and, unlike the others, was square (but this building may well date from an earlier period). Secondly, both Bere and Carndochan have elongated apsidal-ended towers. Thirdly, they also have large mural round towers, which are a link with Dolbadarn where the keep was similarly situated on the curtain, though it is larger and taller.[16] In at least three of these castles, the approach is dominated by a large and arresting building: at Castell-y-Bere by the South Tower and Middle Tower, at Carndochan by the south-west tower, and at Criccieth by the gatehouse. The same is possibly true of Dolbadarn, although the position of the entrance here is uncertain.

Figure 2.11: *Dolbadarn. Great tower from the north west.*

The Castles of Llywelyn ap Gruffudd

Ewloe (Flintshire)

Llywelyn Fawr's grandson, Llywelyn ap Gruffudd, is associated with three castles
in particular, the earliest of which is Ewloe, which is dated by a single reference
assigning its construction to Llywelyn following his victory over the English in
the year 1257.[17] It lies on the eastern edge of Welsh territory. There are two main
structural phases, the earlier of which is the Upper Ward to the east, containing
the freestanding D-shaped keep known as the Welsh Tower. To the west of this is
the lower ward, the curtains of which abut that of the Upper Ward and terminate
towards the west in a cylindrical tower called the West Tower (Figure 2.12).

Although the Welsh Tower has, in the past, been attributed to Llywelyn ab
Iorwerth, there is no powerful reason to suppose that it is anything other than
contemporary with the curtain or that, despite having been built in two separate
phases, the entire castle should not be attributed to Llywelyn ap Gruffudd. Even
so, there may be cause to suspect the former existence of an older fortification.[18]
The Welsh Tower is a little over 50ft in length, so it is more modest than similar
structures at Castell-y-Bere or even Carndochan. It seems to have formed the
principal residence, and its defensive function extends to domination of the
gateway. The entrance to the inner ward was a simple opening in the north-east
side of the curtain, this being approached by way of a bridge. Access to the Welsh
Tower was around the prow to a staircase on its south face, so the approach could
be tightly controlled. The Round Tower, with a diameter of *c.* 40ft (12.2m),

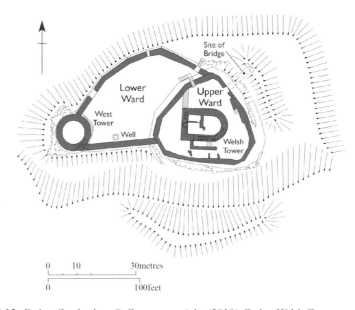

Figure 2.12: *Ewloe. Castle plan. © Crown copyright (2018) Cadw, Welsh Government*

is nearly the same size as the keep of Dolbadarn and, like Llywelyn Fawr's round towers, half in and half outside the curtain, its position at one extremity of the castle echoing its counterpart at Carndochan.

Criccieth

Stylistically, there is little to differentiate Ewloe from the castles of Llywelyn Fawr. One distinction, perhaps, is the two-courtyard plan, something that Llywelyn ap Gruffudd seems to have developed at Criccieth, where the outer ward is thought to be of his time (Figure 2.6).[19] This latter almost completely encloses the earlier inner ward; only the south wall and south-east tower of which continued to form part of the outer enceinte. The extended castle is sub-triangular in shape with rectangular towers at the north and south-west angles and a gateway at the south corner within a small square tower, wholly within the curtain; its irregular character largely results from the shape of the rocky site on which it stands. The north-west curtain with the South-West Tower at one end and the North Tower at the other came first, followed by the south and east curtains. The approach to the inner ward was now from the outer entrance across the outer ward in full view of the South-West Tower and then along a narrow passage between the inner and outer north curtains, before turning the corner to confront the inner gatehouse.

Dolforwyn (Montgomeryshire)

There is an echo of Llywelyn's Criccieth scheme at Dolforwyn, where, in 1273, on his eastern frontier, only 4 miles to the west of Montgomery, he started work on what was to be his last castle.[20] At Dolforwyn, rather than the plan being dictated by the contours of the natural terrain, as at many previous Welsh castles, the hilltop was levelled and the castle given a broadly rectangular plan. The most significant buildings were the rectangular keep that stood immediately in front of the main (south) gateway, the Round Tower at the north end, again, like its predecessors at Carndochan and Ewloe, at the farthest remove from the main entrance, and the apsidal-ended North Tower on the north-west side (Figure 2.13)

The keep measures a little over 60ft (18.3m) x 40ft (12.2m), and is therefore comparable with the South-West Tower at Criccieth, both in size (63ft/19.2m x 37ft/11.3m) and in its position in the outer ward, its long side facing the main entrance and guarding the approach to the inner ward. The Dolforwyn plan was much more compact than at Criccieth but the principle was similar – that on entering the castle by the main gateway the keep was to be seen face on, and that in order to penetrate the castle further, had to be negotiated. There are no other similarities in the planning of the two castles, but this aspect denotes a common thread in the thinking behind the entrance.

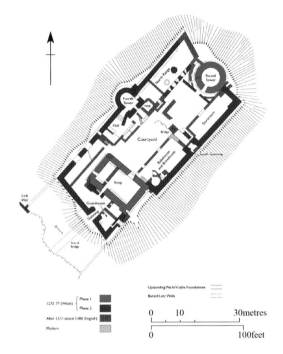

Figure 2.13: *Dolforwyn. Castle plan. © Crown copyright (2018) Cadw, Welsh Government*

The keep at Dolforwyn was one of the first parts of the castle to be raised; also dating from this initial phase was the Round Tower, which has a diameter of 35ft (10.7m) and is therefore slightly smaller than Llywelyn's earlier round tower at Ewloe, but comparable to some of the lesser keeps of thirteenth-century Wales and the Marches. As was usual with Welsh round towers, it was situated on the curtain, projecting half in and half out of the castle. The same is true of the North Tower, the apsidal north-west end projecting outside the curtain and the square south-east end extending into the enclosure, like its earlier counterpart at Carndochan.

Castell Dinas Brân (Denbighshire)

To complete this brief survey of the more significant Welsh castles in north Wales we need to look at Castell Dinas Brân at Llangollen, 30 miles to the north of Dolforwyn. This is another hilltop site, in this case built within a univallate hillfort which sits above the River Dee at a height of 1,050ft (320m). The castle was almost certainly in existence by 1270 and the builder is most likely to have been Gruffudd ap Madog, ruler of Powys Fadog.[21] There are analogies with Dolforwyn, because at Dinas Brân, too, the master builder levelled the top of the hill and created a rectangular enclosure, the building material for which came from the large rock-cut ditch that extends along the

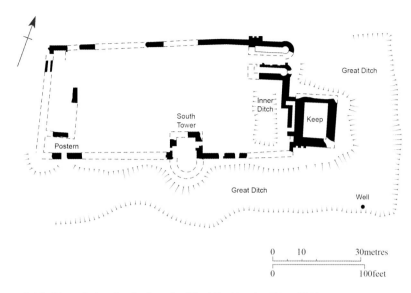

Figure 2.14: *Dinas Brân. Castle plan. By Nigel Dodds after King 1974*

south and east sides. The approach is from the east with the gatehouse at the north end of the east curtain (Figure 2.14).

In common with Dolforwyn, one of the first elements to be constructed was a rectangular keep. It was sited at the eastern end of the castle overlooking the great ditch and almost entirely outside the curtain. It shadowed the entrance, but from the outside, like the Middle Tower of Bere, rather than from within, like the keeps of Dolforwyn and Criccieth, although it is certainly arguable that it represents a similar concept. The main body of the keep was approximately 50ft (15.2m) x 45ft (13.7m), being surpassed in size, therefore, only by the South-West Tower of Criccieth, amongst the rectangular keeps discussed so far. At the west end of the south elevation, nestling in the angle with the curtain, was a shallow latrine turret housing two shafts, reminiscent in its position of the facility attached to the inner gatehouse of Criccieth built some thirty years previously. The isolation of the keep from the rest of the castle is reinforced by the presence of an inner ditch to the rear (west); this obstacle seems to have been designed to control access to the building, which was gained via a staircase on this side leading to the first-floor entrance.

The gatehouse of Dinas Brân is rather unusual, being flanked by a pair of small three-quarter-round turrets. The model for the character of these turrets might have been the inner gatehouse of Montgomery, but, if so, the builder of Brân designed miniature versions. On the other hand, the depths of the two gatehouses are similar, but Montgomery measures about 60ft (18.3m) across whilst Dinas Brân is only 40ft (12.2m). A twin-shaft latrine turret on the north side of the Dinas Brân gatehouse shows that the upper storey was residential.

The most interesting aspect of the building, however, is that the vaulted gate passage was furnished in an unusually elaborate fashion with moulded wall shafts and ribs of thirteenth-century character.[22] Quite possibly it reflects the proximity of Valle Crucis Abbey, 1½ miles to the west, and the ready access to freemasons proficient in this sort of work. Valle Crucis was founded, *c.* 1201, by Gruffudd ap Madog's father, Madog ap Gruffudd Maelor (d. 1236), but work was probably still in progress by the time Dinas Brân came to be built. If the treatment of the gate passage is any guide to the general character of the castle then it was intended to be as much palace as fortress.

Review of the Northern Welsh Castle

Given the current state of our knowledge, the castles of the northern Welsh princes might be said to represent a regional building tradition, largely, but not entirely distinct from the mainstream of English castle development. In this convention a number of stock architectural motifs, the significance of which is imperfectly understood, were used in different combinations. It is generally accepted that all or most of these aspects were in use in Llywelyn ab Iorwerth's time and continued to be employed with little typological development by Llywelyn ap Gruffudd over the course of some sixty years. Intrusions into this insular world appear to have failed to change the course of its direction. It is arguable that the reason for such conservatism is the exclusiveness of the patronal class, but such a phenomenon is nonetheless unusual.

The apsed towers that are particularly prominent at Castell-y-Bere and Carndochan are thought of as one of the most recognisably 'Welsh' elements of the native castles. If they are considered as distinct from the D-shaped wall towers (which are another common component) by virtue of their greater independence and size, then the Welsh tower of Ewloe is the only other example within the group under discussion. This is freestanding within the Upper Ward, and is easier to think of as a great tower, or keep, than those at Bere or Carndochan where there is more than one contender for the title.

Parallels for towers of this plan and magnitude amongst non–Welsh castles are scarce, but the south-west tower of Wilton Castle (Herefordshire) might be cited as evidence that it was not an exclusively Welsh phenomenon. Rectangular, with an apsidal end projecting beyond the west curtain and its south side forming part of the enceinte, the Wilton tower measured approximately 63ft (19.2m) x 31ft (9.5m). Its disposition in relation to the enclosure is echoed by the North Tower of Bere, which, incidentally, was built to similar dimensions. The latrine turret is in a similar position to that of the South Tower of Bere (at the base of the apse). The interior of the apse is semi-polygonal, a not unusual arrangement in towers with rounded prows, although the only examples to be noted in native Welsh castles are the twin towers of the inner gatehouse of Criccieth. The earliest mention of Wilton Castle dates from 1188, but, although it is generally considered to have been rebuilt in the late thirteenth or early fourteenth century by Reginald de Grey, the date of the South-West Tower is far from certain, and building work is known to have been in progress at Wilton in 1210, 1219, 1234, 1238, and 1242.[23] Architectural features include steep segmental-pointed arches with wide chamfers, a form that appears in other marcher castles, notably Goodrich, and which may be indicative of a mid to late thirteenth-century date.

The D-shaped wall towers, which straddle the curtains of the Welsh castles, seem more mainstream, but are singular in more than one sense. They are found at Carndochan, Dinas Brân, and Dolforwyn, those at the latter two being comparable in the degree of extension beyond both sides of the curtain, and therefore help to confirm the architectural relationship between the two and their proximity in date. Primarily, these were residential towers rather than military installations, although they would also have served in a defensive capacity if necessary. The larger of the two, at Brân, provided only slightly less accommodation than the keep and was only marginally smaller in scale than the Welsh Tower of Ewloe. A little more comparable in size to the Welsh Tower is the south-east tower of Caldicot Castle (Monmouthshire), which provides an English parallel for Dolforwyn and Brân. Possibly of the 1220s but remodelled in the later thirteenth century, it is a two-storey structure some 52ft (15.8m) x 33ft (10m).

The south tower of Carndochan is rather different to the other two, being more compact and built on a smaller scale. Its most notable characteristic, however, is the very slight projection outside the curtain, which is confined to the rounded end. Unique amongst the group of castles under discussion here, it too has English parallels. Perhaps the most pertinent to the discussion are the wall towers of the inner ward of Beeston Castle of *c.* 1220 which are quite distinctive, as wide as they are long (29½ft/9m x 29½ft/9m), their square backs having a pronounced projection (14¾ft/4.5m–16½ft/5m) into the courtyard, but, like Carndochan, only a slight external projection of the curved prow. This is quite an unusual configuration, not repeated at either of Earl Ranulph's other castles of Chartley or Bolingbroke, though evident in some of the wall towers erected under Henry III at Dover, notably Rokesley's Tower. The Carndochan tower does not seem to have been so regular, measuring approximately 31ft (9.5m) x 26ft (8m), and, because it is positioned at an angle to the curtain rather than at right angles to it, only one side projects in the same manner as the Beeston towers.[24] Even so, the match is good enough to suggest the direct influence of Beeston given Llywelyn's links with Ranulf.

Round towers are found at Bere, Carndochan, Dolbadarn, Ewloe, and Dolforwyn. At Bere and Dolbadarn they are in the forefront, close to the entrance, whereas at Carndochan, Ewloe, and Dolforwyn they were placed as far from the entrance as possible. They range between 30ft (9.1m) and 42ft (12.8m) in external diameter and between 18ft (5.5m) and 27ft (8.2m) internally, and would all have housed high-quality living accommodation. Dolbadarn, the largest of these five towers, is slightly unusual in its unequivocal status as the great tower of the castle, but the others are found in concert with towers of different form, including, with the exception of Ewloe, a rectangular keep. Indeed, the rectangular great tower is one of the mostly frequently encountered of buildings in northern Welsh castles of the thirteenth century. The Carndochan keep is unusual in its isolation within the courtyard; normally these structures are, like the other towers, linked to the curtain wall. It is notable that in several instances: Bere, Criccieth, Brân, and Dolforwyn, there is a close relationship with the main entrance as though the tower was intended to be seen before or as soon as a visitor entered the castle; the same role is served by the Welsh Tower at Ewloe. In some instances this overlooking of the entrance may have been conducive to a defensive role, but at Criccieth and Dolwyddelan the relationship was principally visual.

Surviving architectural details are few, but the keep of Dolbadarn, one of the better preserved buildings, retains a triangular/segmental-pointed door and window arches composed of narrow slate voussoirs. The technique is found in other Welsh castles (shale and other materials also being used) including Ewloe, Dolwyddelan, and Criccieth and may have been general, in contrast to the ashlar dressings of most arches in English castles. At Criccieth, the vaults of the loop embrasures are segmental in form, reflecting those of Beeston, the influence of which has already been discussed.

A feature that is found in a number of northern Welsh castles is the rectangular latrine turret with corbelled stone roof. At Dolwyddelan the turret occupies most of the south-west end, whereas at Dolbadarn, where one projects from the keep, it is comparatively compact. This particular example contrasts with the semi-circular turrets that are found appended to numerous early thirteenth-century keeps in south Wales and the Marches.[25] At Criccieth the inner gatehouse has a latrine turret; it sits within the re-entrant angle between the western flanking tower and the curtain, and there are two other multiple turrets serving separate wall towers. At Dinas Brân the latrine turret to the keep is similarly sited in the re-entrant angle with the curtain, and there is a second turret serving the gatehouse.

It is only at Dinas Brân that there is now any inkling of the sculptural embellishment that evidently existed in at least some of these buildings. However, the evidence of finds recovered during excavation and clearance demonstrates that carved ornamentation was not uncommon. The carved stonework from Castell-y-Bere is particularly instructive, as it includes corbelled wall shafts and capitals dating stylistically from the first half of the thirteenth century, implying that part of the castle, probably one of the towers, was vaulted.[26] Part of a capital from a shaft has also been found at Criccieth as well as a corbel carved with a human head, the latter having been found in the South-West Tower, or Llywelyn ap Gruffudd's keep.[27]

Unlike many English castles of the thirteenth century there is little evidence of a scientific approach towards defence; especially notable is the absence of the systematic deployment of wall towers or (with one or two notable exceptions) strong gatehouses. However, whilst Criccieth and Brân have the only examples of twin-towered gatehouses, tactical awareness in respect of the entrance is evident in the several castles where a tower is located close to the gateway, either projecting externally, flanking one side, as at Bere, Carndochan, and Brân, or internally as at Bere (in a later phase), Ewloe, and Dolforwyn. Two towers were so deployed at Bere (Round Tower and Middle Tower) and Carndochan (Apsidal Tower and Semi-Circular Tower). These characteristics extend from Llywelyn ap Iorwerth's earliest known castles through to the last ones to be raised by his grandsons, Llywelyn and Dafydd, at Dolforwyn and Caergwrle (see below, Chapter 5) respectively.

Llywelyn ab Iorwerth is notable for his marriage alliances amongst the English. Llywelyn himself was married to King John of England's daughter, Joan; one of their daughters married the Earl of Chester's nephew and heir, John the Scot, another daughter married Reginald de Braose, Lord of Abergavenny, and their son, Dafydd, Llywelyn's heir, married Reginald's granddaughter, Isabella, who was also a granddaughter of William Marshal, first Earl of Pembroke. These extra-Cambrian marriages typify an outward-looking attitude that is reflected in the gatehouse of Criccieth and in the three-storey keep of Dolbadarn, which, but for its height, might be classified as simply another Welsh round tower. These can be viewed as prestige pieces by a man with an international viewpoint open to new ideas. Both buildings are highly effective and recognisable types, even without the additional attraction of novelty that relocation to Gwynedd would have engendered. Earl Ranulph's Beeston, a suggested source for Criccieth and Carndochan, is usually dated to the 1220s, following his return from the Fifth Crusade, a date that would synchronise fairly well with the supposed temporal parameters of Llywelyn's castle-building activities. The cylindrical keeps of south Wales and the Marches, which appear from *c.* 1200 onwards, are the most probable models for the round towers. Indeed, Ranulph himself built a keep of marcher type at Chartley (Staffordshire).

Llywelyn ap Gruffudd's incorporation of some aspects of his grandfather's designs into his own castles suggests either a deliberate emulation of the work to draw parallels between himself and his illustrious forebear, the greatest of all the Welsh princes, or, a building tradition whose forms were symbolic of designated functions or concepts, knowledge of which has been lost. However, in contrast to the castles of Llywelyn Fawr, those of his grandson appear insular, so that apart from the more controlled plan of Dolforwyn, the latest of Llywelyn's castles, there is little evidence of a wider awareness or even a desire to incorporate new or outlandish ideas.

Chapter Three

English Castles in Wales and the Marches

A t the beginning of Henry III's reign (1216) Wales was divided between the native dynasties (*Pura Wallia*) and the marcher lords (*Marchia Wallia*). The former held sway in the north and west, whilst the marcher lordships extended in an arc from Pembrokeshire in the south west to Montgomery in the north east. The northern half of Wales was divided between Gwynedd to the north west and Powys to the south east, the border between them extending between the estuaries of the Dyfi in the south west and the Dee in the north east. Powys was split into two separate political entities: Powys Fadog (Lower Powys) in the north and the larger Powys Wenwynwyn (Upper Powys) in the south.

South Wales was less cohesive. The glory days of Deheubarth, as revived under the southern Welsh prince Rhys ap Gruffudd, or the Lord Rhys, were over. At the height of his territorial power the Lord Rhys ruled over a region stretching from the River Dyfi in the north to Carmarthen Bay in the south, an area that encompassed the later counties of Cardiganshire, Carmarthenshire, and parts of Glamorganshire and Pembrokeshire. Rhys died in 1197 and a struggle for primacy amongst his sons ensued, splitting the realm into a number of rival camps.

A formal partition was brokered in 1216 by Llywelyn ab Iorwerth, prince of Gwynedd, between Rhys's sons Maelgwn and Rhys (Rhys Gryg), and the sons of their deceased elder brother Gruffudd. Broadly, the sons of Gruffudd received Ceredigion (Cardiganshire), Rhys Gryg obtained Ystrad Tywi (Cantref Mawr and Cantref Bychan), and Maelgwn the cantrefi of Cemais, Emlyn, and Gwarthaf. Partible inheritance, the delimiter of Welsh power, brought subsequent divisions, and, thereafter, the southern Welsh princelings would never be a potent threat to English interests on their own account, only in alliance with Gwynedd.

Castles of Henry III in Wales and the Marches

In contrast to the activities of the Welsh princes, there was no established tradition of English castle building in *Pura Wallia*. The exceptions to the general dearth of thirteenth-century English strongholds prior to 1277 were the royal castles built for Henry III. The earliest of Henry's castles in Wales and the Marches was the border fortress of Montgomery (Montgomeryshire), which was built in response to the rise of Llywelyn Fawr. The castle was begun in 1222 and the first stone phase, which was confined to the Inner Ward, was constructed within a few years of the initial fortification of the site. The Middle Ward was rebuilt in the 1250s, and the domestic buildings of both wards date from the later thirteenth or fourteenth centuries.

Henry's two principal castles in Gwynedd were Dyserth (Flintshire), which was built on a new site, and Deganwy (Carnarvonshire), which was a partial reconstruction of a Welsh castle. Dyserth was fortified in 1241, and Deganwy (or Gannoc, as it was known) was rebuilt in 1244–53; both were destroyed by Llywelyn ap Gruffudd in 1263.[1] Little remains of either of these two castles; the remnants of Dyserth were mostly quarried away in the early twentieth century and the buildings of Deganwy have been largely razed.

Dyserth (Flintshire)

Built on a site about 3 miles to the east of Rhuddlan, known as the 'Rock of Rhuddlan', Dyserth Castle was sited on a promontory called Graig Bâch, to the south of the Chester road. Although no detailed study of the remains appears to have been made, the results of a survey, including a plan, were published by E. W. Cox in 1895 prior to the commencement of the quarrying that brought about the castle's almost total destruction.[2] This plan depicts some rather singular aspects that may have a bearing on the castle's Edwardian successors (Figure 3.1).

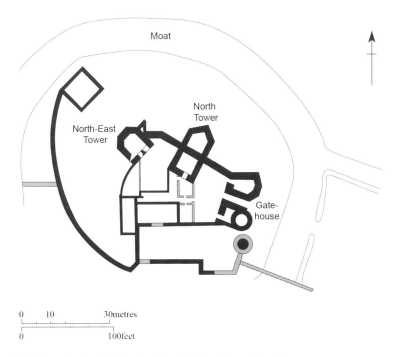

Figure 3.1: *Dyserth. Castle plan. By Nigel Dodds after Cox 1895*

A rectangular outer ward led to an oval enclosure containing a middle and inner ward arranged in concentric fashion. At the east end of the inner ward was a twin-towered gatehouse with asymmetrical flanking towers. The plan of the northern tower was that of an irregular semi-octagon, the north wall splaying outwards towards the north east. In contrast, the southern tower was bow-fronted, but seemingly constructed in a rather curious manner, as though a circular tower has been superimposed on a rectangular one or vice versa. Two other wall towers: a pentagonal north tower with a pointed prow and a semi-octagonal west tower projected both outside and inside the curtain.

Polygonal wall towers were rather unusual at this date; early examples, congregating around the turn of the twelfth and thirteenth centuries, include Dover (Kent; Avranches Tower), Framlingham (Suffolk; south-east tower), Corfe (Dorset; Butavant Tower), and Warkworth (Northumberland; Carrickfergus Tower and gatehouse); there are a couple of small towers at Barnard Castle (County Durham), probably of *c.* 1220, but, on the whole, polygonal towers are exceptions to the rule. The general outlines of the west and north towers at Dyserth are best compared with the Butavant Tower and the great tower of Mitford Castle (Northumberland) respectively. The Butavant Tower dates from the early years of the thirteenth century; Mitford keep has been dated to the mid-twelfth century, late twelfth/thirteenth century, and early thirteenth century.[3]

The asymmetrical character, though not the geometry, of the Dyserth gatehouse may be compared with that of the near contemporary inner gatehouse of Corfe, which includes one round and one D-shaped tower. These two works do not constitute a match, but they may represent a similar mindset on the part of the designer(s). The Corfe gatehouse probably dates from the 1240s, being described as 'new' in 1249.[4] A link between Dyserth and Corfe is Master Gerard, the King's engineer. There are several references to him having worked at Corfe in the 1240s and 50s.[5] In 1244 he brought siege engines to Deganwy and in 1250 was sent to view the works at Dyserth and Deganwy.[6] In 1244 Gerard was working in Northumberland and may have visited Mitford, which, at the time was in the King's hands and under the custodianship of Robert de Crepping. There is certainly no doubt that Gerard knew de Crepping, because, in 1244, the Sheriff of Northumberland was instructed to procure masons to cut stones for the King's engines 'according to the form and mould which Master Gerard and Robert de Crepping will deliver and declare'.[7]

Deganwy (Carnarvonshire)

The characteristics of Deganwy, insofar as they can be ascertained, are quite different. This hilltop site occupies a position relative to the River Conwy comparable with that of Dyserth to the Clwyd. The thirteenth-century defences encompassed two rocky peaks and the saddle, or depression, that separates them.

The larger of two heights contained the upper ward, or 'donjon', whilst the smaller was capped by a D-shaped tower known as Mansell's Tower. Between them, in the depression, was the lower ward which was entered via a gateway in the south curtain dating from 1250–2.[8]

Although the castle is thoroughly ruined, it is evident that the main outer gateway was flanked by twin D-shaped towers, a type that had been established within the royal works by the early years of the thirteenth century at Dover, where D-shaped towers flanked the outer gateway built by King John. The form did not prove popular with Henry III's engineers, so far as we know, but it may have provided inspiration for baronial castle builders, including Beeston, which has already been mentioned. Whilst the Dover gatehouse was primarily a defensive construct with open-backed towers, the south gate of Deganwy was rather different. The towers were substantially longer, being close to 45ft (13.7m), and of greater outward projection, the whole edifice forming a gatehouse proper, with two upper storeys, each containing a chamber with a fireplace, suggesting good quality residential accommodation, akin to a number of later thirteenth-century gatehouses of this type.

Cardigan and Carmarthen

At much the same time as work was being carried out at Deganwy, attention was also being given to the royal castles of Cardigan and Carmarthen, then (1248–54) under the custodianship of Robert Walerand. At Cardigan the main work was the construction of a new keep, probably to be identified with the North Tower, a building now incorporated into a nineteenth-century house, but which measured some 41ft (12.5m) x 35ft (10.7m), all of which, apart from its rear (south) wall, projected outside the curtain. Of the exterior, only the bowed northern end is visible, the rest being encased within later buildings, but, judging by the rectangular interior and the alignment of the adjacent curtain walls, it is probable that it was a built to a D-shaped plan, somewhat akin to those described in the previous chapter at a number of northern Welsh castles, but with two main differences. Firstly, the proportions of the North Tower are less elongate. Secondly, the apsidal north front was provided with a spurred base. This base is no longer visible, but, given the position of the spurs, is assumed to have been rectangular.

At Carmarthen the main work of this period was the construction of a hall and chamber for the King, a building complex that has long since disappeared but is tentatively located in the south-east corner of the Inner Ward.[9] More tangible is the South-West Tower, a building of uncertain date which has marked affinities with the North Tower of Cardigan, including the rectangular interior, the position of the staircase, the disposition of arrow loops at ground-floor level, and, most importantly, the pyramidal spur buttresses. These analogues point to a closeness in date. One suggestion is that the South-West Tower was raised in the 1230s–40s when the castle was in the custody of the Marshal family, and that it may, therefore, have served as a model for the North Tower of Cardigan.[10] Pyramidal spurred buttresses were popular in the Welsh Marches in the latter half of the thirteenth century and beyond and may well have originated in the region. These two instances at the royal castles of south Wales may be the earliest example of their type to have been noted so far.

The Baronial Castles

Chepstow (Monmouthshire) and Pembroke (Pembrokeshire)

Quite apart from the royal works, the marcher lordships of south Wales were a hot spot for castle building in the mid-thirteenth century. In 1250 two of the most important baronial castles in south Wales were Chepstow and Pembroke. Chepstow, which was an eleventh-century foundation, comprised a series of baileys arranged in linear fashion along a rocky ridge above the River Wye. The main vestige of the eleventh-century castle is the rectangular great tower that is sited at the crest of the ridge, between the Middle and Upper baileys. In 1187, Chepstow was bestowed upon William Marshal, later first Earl of Pembroke, who left his mark by making substantial additions in stone characterised by round and D-shaped wall towers, and an unusually early example of a gateway flanked by round towers.

Pembroke was also an early foundation, but, in 1199, it came, by marriage, to William Marshal, who also made his presence felt here, the inner ward being built in stone during his tenure. The outstanding feature of William Marshal's work at Chepstow was the main gateway, but the prestige of his Pembroke project was to a great extent owed to its great tower, a five-storey, stand-alone building, which formed the focus of the stone castle. A stark, but highly effective, piece of architecture, this cylindrical tower was (unusually for an English keep) covered by a semi-circular domed vault, and the dome was surmounted by an inner ring of battlements. The Pembroke keep stands at the head of a whole series of cylindrical great towers in the Welsh Marches, but although the form proliferated, none surpassed Pembroke in grandeur, and it remained for many years a paragon of keep design.

William Marshal's sons died without male issue, and, in 1247, Chepstow came to his daughter, Maud, widow of Hugh Bigod, third Earl of Norfolk, and, when Maud died, in 1248, the castle was inherited by her son, Roger, the fourth Earl. Neither the third nor fourth Earl paid much attention to the fabric of the castle, but the fifth Earl, another Roger, who succeeded in 1270, was to undertake some significant building works at Chepstow in the aftermath of Edward I's invasion of Gwynedd; these will be discussed in Chapter 8.

Pembroke passed to William de Valence, a half brother of Henry III, by virtue of his marriage to William Marshal's granddaughter, Joan. From *c.* 1258 William de Valence was rebuilding the outer ward of Pembroke Castle in stone, the new curtain wall being augmented by a series of cylindrical towers, three along the main entrance front to the south (from east to west, Barbican, Henry VII, and Westgate towers) and two larger ones (Northgate and Monkton towers) on the east and west sides respectively.[11]

The principal object of interest in respect of this investigation is the Outer Gatehouse, which is situated towards the east end of the south front. It was an unconventional building, but significant as a stage in the development of the great gatehouse as it evolved in Wales during the thirteenth century. Essentially rectangular, and located largely within the outer ward, the gatehouse has a central entrance passage, flanked by a single D-shaped tower which protrudes from the curtain to the left (west) of the entrance. A single flanking tower is unusual, but, in fact, the Barbican Tower, which lies to the right (east) of the gatehouse, and which, internally, appears to have been planned as an integral part of the gatehouse complex, was effectively being thought of as a second flanking tower. At the north end of the gate passage two semi-circular stair turrets protrude from the rear wall (Figure 3.2).

The two towers controlled the approach to the gatehouse and provided a degree of protection, but, the gate passage itself was very well defended with, from south to north, portcullis, machicolation slot, twin-leaved gate, machicolation slot, portcullis, twin-leaved gate, and machicolation slot. Next in the sequence is a pair of opposed doorways giving access to the ground-floor rooms on either side of the entry, and then the doorways to the two stair turrets, which gave access to the two upper floors and the roof.

The domestic accommodation was at first- and second-floor levels, where the same three-room plan prevailed on both floors, the central room in each case dividing and acting as a conduit between what could have been two separate residences. On the west side a single large room some 45ft (14m) x 14ft (4.3m) extended from the back (north) wall of the gatehouse to the bowed front of the flanking tower. It was equipped with a fireplace and a latrine, the latter housed in a turret sited in the internal re-entrant with the curtain. The smaller eastern room had a fireplace but no latrine, but it communicated with the Barbican Tower which had its own fireplace and latrine and its own staircase leading to the second floor of the tower. There were, then, four separate substantial chambers or suites within the gatehouse and Barbican Tower complex, which thereby formed a major residential block. This residential aspect and the strongly controlled entrance passage were to have an important influence on later gatehouse development in Wales and beyond.

Figure 3.2: *Pembroke. Outer gatehouse from the north. The first-floor gallery extending between the stair turrets is a later addition.*

Caerphilly (Glamorgan) and Related Castles

First and foremost amongst the beneficiaries of the Pembroke gatehouse development is Caerphilly (Glamorganshire), which was the most important baronial castle to be built in England and Wales in the decade before the First Welsh War, and which was to have an undoubted influence on the royal castles raised as a consequence. It was begun in 1268 by Gilbert (the Red) de Clare, Earl of Gloucester and Hertford and Lord of Glamorgan, one of the most powerful barons of the realm. The lordship of Glamorgan took its name from the old Welsh kingdom of Morgannwg, which, at the beginning of the thirteenth century, was largely under Welsh control.

Gilbert's grandfather, another Gilbert, obtained the lordship in 1217 and the de Clares gradually extended their power over the northern uplands. When Gilbert the Red's father, Richard, died in the summer of 1262 only the cantref of Senghennydd, which lay on the east side of the lordship, retained its independence. Llywelyn ap Gruffudd's invasion of Brecknock a few months later and the subsequent attack on the royal castle of Abergavenny must have highlighted Senghennydd (which bordered Brecknock) as a weak spot in the defence of Glamorgan.

In the Barons' War of 1264–7 Earl Gilbert was at first a supporter of Simon de Montfort and the reformers, but, in 1265 he changed sides, a decision that may have been influenced by Earl Simon's alliance with Llywelyn. De Clare was instrumental in the defeat and death of Earl Simon at the Battle of Evesham and was present at the siege of Kenilworth Castle (1265–6) where some of de Montfort's supporter's held out. Kenilworth was taken on 13 December 1266 and the annexation of Senghennydd began a few weeks later. The greater part of Caerphilly Castle was probably raised between 1268 and 1271, although there were to be significant additions during the next two decades.[12] Built on a gravel spur flanked by two streams, the site was carefully chosen for the tactical possibilities suggested by the water courses, which would be used to create two artificial lakes (north and south of the spur) to act as the outer line of the defences, and provide Caerphilly with one of its most defining features (Figure 3.3).

The project must have begun with a programme of ditching in which the spur was cut through to create three islands or wards. Such linear, ditch-divided sequences of courtyards were a well-established aspect of castle planning, and the site lent itself to that kind of arrangement. The initial defences were probably of timber, simply to create a defendable base for the workers and their equipment and materials, but work on the stone revetting of the islands could have begun almost immediately, and would, indeed, have been a necessary preliminary to the creation of the South Lake, which surrounds the central island. To the east, the lake is contained by the eastern island and the adjoining South Dam Platform which extends across the line of the stream; its northern extent is defined by the

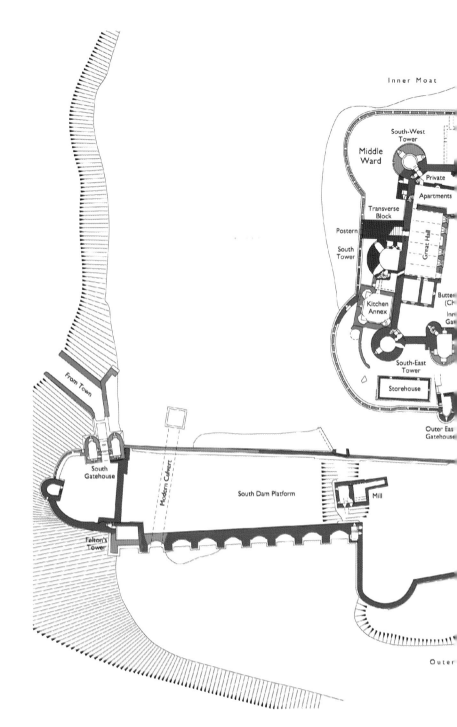

Figure 3.3: *Caerphilly. Castle plan. © Crown copyright (2018) Cadw, Welsh Government*

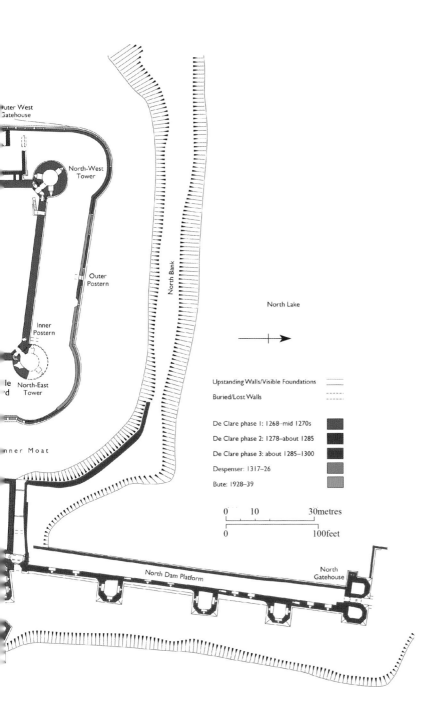

uter West
Gatehouse

North-West
Tower

Outer
Postern

North Bank

North Lake

Inner
Postern

le   North-East
d   Tower

nner Moat

Upstanding Walls/Visible Foundations

Buried/Lost Walls

De Clare phase 1: 1268–mid 1270s

De Clare phase 2: 1278–about 1285

De Clare phase 3: about 1285–1300

Despenser: 1317–26

Bute: 1928–39

0   10   30metres

0   100feet

North Dam Platform

North
Gatehouse

North Bank, an artificial earthwork now separating the North and South lakes and providing a causeway between the East and West islands. The North Lake was created at a later date and will be discussed in Chapter 8.

The construction of Caerphilly was not without its vicissitudes. At the end of the third building season, on 13 October 1270, the partly built castle was captured by Llywelyn ap Gruffudd by whom it is recorded as having been 'burnt', although it seems unlikely that the damage was substantial enough to nullify the achievements of the first three years. Work recommenced on 1 June 1271, but in the autumn Llywelyn laid siege to it again until 2 November, when a truce was negotiated, a consequence of which was that castle was temporarily taken into the hands of the King's agents. The truce also ratified Llywelyn's demand that until his territorial dispute with de Clare had been settled there should no restoration, repair, or enlargement of the castle, and this truce is generally considered to mark the end of the first main construction period, subsequent work being dated to the outbreak of the First Welsh War and its aftermath. At this stage it is probable that the three islands had been revetted in stone, that the South Dam Platform had been constructed and that the defences of the central island had been largely completed (Figure 3.4).

After the water defences, the second main attribute of Caerphilly is the concentric arrangement of the central island defences. The Inner Ward is a parallelogram with round corner towers and a large twin-towered gatehouse to the east and west, the main domestic apartments being ranged along the south curtain. Surrounding this inner enclosure is the Middle Ward which is

Figure 3.4: *Caerphilly. Central island from the south west.*

enclosed by the island's stone revetment and carried upward as a curtain wall with smaller twin-towered gatehouses to the east and west, directly in front of the inner gatehouses; rounded salients of irregular shape and size protrude from the four corners in response to the projecting corner towers of the Inner Ward. The military advantages of double lines of defence had been appreciated by the English Crown since the later twelfth century, but the compact, closely correlated, and concentric wards developed here at Caerphilly represented a new phenomenon in English castle building, something that was to be adopted by the royal works in the ensuing decades.

It is highly probable that Kenilworth Castle (Warwickshire) had acted as a model for elements of Caerphilly. The former's extensive artificial water defences, which were probably first developed in the twelfth century, came into their own during the siege of 1266. Earl Gilbert was with the besieging army, and it is quite likely that this experience coloured his inspiration when he came to build Caerphilly less than eighteen months after the conclusion of the siege.

The water defences are not the only parallel between the two buildings, because Kenilworth is another castle in which the principal of concentricity was employed. This scheme, which was created by the construction of the outer curtain, doubtless formed part of the royal works on the castle during the early thirteenth century, resulting in the construction of the outer curtain. A somewhat similar, though less complete, arrangement had been begun by Henry II at Dover and continued by his son John.

A third point of comparison is that the Brays, which forms an outer bailey outside the lake in front of the main entrance to Kenilworth, is analogous to the western island at Caerphilly, if, as has been suggested, itself was originally intended as the main approach to the castle, and that re-orientation towards the east occurred during the course of construction.[13]

Fourthly, the long narrow dam (Tiltyard) that leads from the Brays to the Mortimer Tower, or south gatehouse, is very reminiscent of the narrow North Dam Platform at Caerphilly which leads from the North Gatehouse. These analogues between Kenilworth and Caerphilly, and the separation of only two years between the siege of the former and the start of construction at the latter, gives reason to speculate that Earl Gilbert's engineer may have taken part in the siege and adapted aspects of the castle to the new foundation of Caerphilly.

An unusual and interesting aspect of Caerphilly's inner ward defences is the Braose Gallery, a vaulted passageway behind (south of) the great hall. The gallery was created from the alure that originally extended behind the parapet of the south curtain; the merlons of the parapet being pierced by arrow loops (Figure 3.5).

When the great hall was built against the north side of the curtain it rose higher than the alure, thereby enclosing it on this side; at the same time the curtain was raised and the alure vaulted over to carry that of the new, higher-level parapet.

Figure 3.5: *Caerphilly. Braose Gallery.*

In raising the curtain, the embrasures of the original battlements were filled in and the pierced merlons remained *in situ*, being incorporated into the new work, and, in the process, creating an additional tier of defence on this side of the castle. This modification to the design is generally believed to have occurred during the main construction period of 1268–71. Similar features were later to be incorporated into the design of the royal castle of Caernarfon (begun 1283) from the start.

A significant element of the Caerphilly scheme is the sequence of twin-towered gatehouses to each end of the central island, an unprecedented feature that was to be adopted and developed by the royal works. Amongst this collection of entrances, the Inner East Gatehouse may be singled out as another special characteristic of Caerphilly (Figure 3.6).

Round-fronted towers flank a narrow recessed entrance, round stair turrets project from the two inner angles, and the gatehouse contains substantial residential accommodation, a characteristic it shares with the outer gatehouse of Pembroke. A more telling comparison between the two buildings can be made in respect of the twin stair turrets (Figure 3.7); the Caerphilly examples may very well have been adapted from those of Pembroke, which, despite being semi-circular rather than three-quarters round, and projecting from the rear wall rather than the rear corners, serve the same function; it is quite possible that they represent the origin of this particular facility. A third parallel is the treatment of the gate passage: as at Pembroke, the inner East gatehouse of Caerphilly was equipped with two pairs of gates, two portcullises, and at least one but probably two sets of machicolations in the vault.

The Pembroke gatehouse is said to be the work of William de Valence, and to date from the 1260s.[14] Indeed, a construction break between the gatehouse and adjacent curtain has been seen as evidence for a hiatus in the building programme occasioned by de Valence's exile in 1264.[15] In which case, it may be significant that following Valence's banishment, his Pembrokeshire lands were briefly taken into the hands of Gilbert de Clare. The Pembroke gatehouse, then, seems to have

Figure 3.6: *Caerphilly. Outer East Gatehouse in the foreground and Inner East Gatehouse in the background.*

Figure 3.7: *Caerphilly. Inner East Gatehouse from the west.*

been a source of inspiration for the Caerphilly master, but it was too informal an arrangement to be a model for emulation. Some of the notable planning principles were indeed appropriated, and woven into his design, but a measure of the master builder's skill is that, in the process, he transformed them and created an outstanding piece of architecture far removed from the aesthetically challenged Pembroke source.

A couple of contemporary castle gatehouses from the south of England also need to be considered with regard to Caerphilly. Barnwell (Northamptonshire), a quadrangular castle dating from *c.* 1266, was built by Berenger Le Moyne. It is a building that surprises by its architectural quality when measured against the relative obscurity of its patron. As first built, the gatehouse, which has twin D-shaped flanking towers, measured some 56ft (17m) wide x 30ft (9.1m) from front to back. It had a semi-circular stair turret at the south-west corner of the north tower and the inner end of the gate passage, and is thus analogous to one of the Pembroke turrets.

Also of the 1260s is Leybourne (Kent), which was raised by Roger of Leybourne. The Leybourne gatehouse was built on a much larger scale, measuring about 70ft (21.3m) wide and at least (the building has been truncated) 45ft (13.7) from front to back. A peculiarity is the deeply recessed entrance, which is set some 24ft (7.3m) from the fronts of the flanking towers. Above the entrance is a slot, the opening for a water chute, a feature that was also incorporated into the rear elevation of Caerphilly's Inner East Gatehouse. We can't be sure about the significance of such minor details, but the links between the patrons and the movement of craftsmen between southern England and Wales are possibilities. Neither Berenger Le Moyne nor Roger of Leybourne had significant holdings in the Welsh Marches, but Roger was close to the future Edward I and strongly associated with the marcher lords in the 1260s.

The principal characteristics of the Caerphilly Inner East Gatehouse are shared with another gatehouse raised by the de Clares at Tonbridge (Kent) (Figures 3.8 and 3.9). Unlike the Inner East Gatehouse of Caerphilly, the outer front of which was almost completely rebuilt in the 1930s, the appearance of the Tonbridge gatehouse is to a great extent authentic, whereas there are serious doubts about aspects of the Caerphilly restoration. Notwithstanding the losses at Caerphilly, it is evident that the two buildings are based on the same template to create a de Clare type. The overall dimensions are similar, the general plan of round-fronted flanking towers and round stair turrets to the rear corners

Figure 3.8: *Tonbridge. Great gatehouse from the north.*

Figure 3.9: *Tonbridge. Great gatehouse from the south east.*

is identical, and the gate passages follow the same pattern of portcullis, gate, doorways to the towers, gate, and portcullis.[16] The same method of communication between floors is employed, with clockwise and anti-clockwise spiral staircases within respective turrets. Both gatehouses were also provided with rectangular latrine turrets tucked into the re-entrant angles between the flanking towers and the curtain. One of the main differences is that, at Caerphilly, the tripartite division of the ground storey (gate passage and flanking rooms) was replicated on the first floor whereas at Tonbridge there was a single chamber at this level. In both cases, however, the second floor was given over to a single room and the two gatehouses were evidently intended as major residential suites.

Planning apart, Tonbridge presents a rather different appearance from its Welsh counterpart, for it is fair to say that the Tonbridge gatehouse gives the impression of a building on which no expense was spared, combining high-class design and technical expertise with excellent quality ashlar masonry. The result was an outstanding piece of architecture of considerable aesthetic appeal, and although visual attractiveness was often an aim of the castle builder, it was seldom achieved to as high a degree as at Tonbridge. The architectural impact of the front elevation is achieved by the massing of the plain ashlar walls, pierced only by a small number of narrow loops, but accentuated by two prominent features. The first of these is the undulating spurs which rise from the polygonal bases and wrap themselves around the basements of the towers, an arrangement with no known precedents, but, one that is uniquely paralleled in the gatehouse of the royal castle of St Briavel's (Gloucestershire), which dates from 1292–3.

The second defining aspect is the entrance, which is recessed beneath a lofty outer arch of multiple chamfered orders, their feet dying into the flanking towers as they curve into the entrance. This is a device to increase the floor space at second-floor level (which contained the principal room), but it also created a stunning facade. A building with a frontage of somewhat similar appearance, though perhaps without the panache of Tonbridge, was the South Gatehouse of *c.* 1245 at York Castle, which also had a high outer arch.[17] Another royal gatehouse of similar type, though less obviously related to Tonbridge, which also dates from the middle years of the thirteenth century, is the Outer Gatehouse of Nottingham Castle (1252–5). However, there are, perhaps, closer parallels with the Edwardian castles of north Wales, from the last quarter of the thirteenth century, notably Caernarfon and Denbigh (see Chapters 7 and 8).

It is a moot point as to which of these two Clare gatehouses came first. Although the dating of Caerphilly is not controversial, estimates for Tonbridge have varied between 1220 and 1300.[18] The most promising documentary reference for pinpointing the date of the gatehouse would seem to be a licence of 1259 to enclose the town of Tonbridge with a wall and to crenellate it.[19] Although this does not constitute proof, it does indicate that building activity was being carried out on the defences of Tonbridge, which, it is not unreasonable to speculate, might have extended to the castle.

Indications of date amongst the architectural detailing include the second-floor pointed windows towards the courtyard, in which two trefoil-headed lights are surmounted by a circle. The general pattern is that of Westminster Abbey choir (begun 1245) adapted to a plainer, chunkier style, in which the thickness of the mullions and tracery is ameliorated externally by an all-over treatment of roll mouldings and broad hollow chamfers. However, the basic tracery pattern was still being used in the 1280s, when the great hall of Stokesay Castle (Shropshire) was erected, so the chronological range is too great to be of much help in refining the date of the building.

The hood moulds of these windows terminate in carved human heads, features also found internally. Externally, the sculptured heads have fared badly, only one surviving to its full extent, but they appear to have been grotesques.[20] Internally, they are better preserved, being found as termination stops to the hood moulds of the two large second-floor windows and also on the fireplace between them. It has been suggested that this group are portraits, the hood mould stops those of Richard (1222–62) and Gilbert de Clare (1243–95), the sixth and seventh earls of Gloucester, paired with their respective spouses, and the fireplace sculptures those of Edward I (reigned 1272–1307) and his queen, Eleanor (d. 1290).[21] If this is correct, then it would be reasonable to assume that the gatehouse was begun by Richard and completed by Gilbert with construction extending into the 1270s, making it a slightly earlier contemporary of Caerphilly. However, such a chronology is by no means assured and there are certainly grounds for thinking that it might be somewhat later, a possibility that will be explored in Chapter 11.

Another building that is related to the Inner East Gatehouse of Caerphilly is the main entrance to Llangynwyd Castle (Glamorganshire), nearly 20 miles to the west of Caerphilly, a building that survives in a fragmentary condition. It was probably built by Gilbert de Clare during the 1260s or slightly later, and may therefore have been under construction contemporaneously with or before, Caerphilly.[22] Slightly greater in width than its Caerphilly counterpart, but approximately equal in depth, the Llangynwyd gatehouse also had rounded flanking towers, and, within the gate passage, an identical sequence (from outside to inside) of portcullis, gate, doorways to the flanking towers, gate, and portcullis. Whether it had stair turrets at the inner angles, as at Tonbridge and Caerphilly, is as yet unknown, but the similarities are sufficient to suggest that the design had a common source. If Llangynwyd and Caerphilly are indeed contemporaries, then given the common ownership and the close proximity of one to the other, it is reasonable to suppose that the same master builder was in charge.

A third south Walian castle with a gatehouse that belongs to the same architectural grouping, but which is built on a smaller scale, is Llansteffan (Carmarthenshire) (Figure 3.10). The three-storey gatehouse was probably raised by the de Camville family during the 1260s or 1270s, and is, therefore, broadly contemporary with the Inner East Gatehouse of Caerphilly. Whereas Llangynwyd is largely destroyed, Llansteffan to a great extent survives. The general plan is slightly more regular than that of Llangynwyd, comprising a central gate passage (now blocked at both ends) and two D-shaped flanking towers. Within the barrel-vaulted gate passage the sequence of features was (from outside to inside) a line of murder holes, a portcullis, opposed doorways to the flanking towers, a line of murder holes, and a portcullis. If there was a gate at each end, then this arrangement may have matched that of Caerphilly.

At the front of the building, above the gateway, is a water chute, just as there is on the inner face of the Caerphilly gatehouse; it is a rare feature and therefore compelling evidence of the relationship between the two buildings. As at Caerphilly, there are stair turrets at the inner corners, these are solid at ground-floor level and only communicate between the first and second floors and the roof (Figure 3.11). Each of the upper floors contained a single chamber heated by a fireplace in the middle of the south wall. The second-floor fireplace

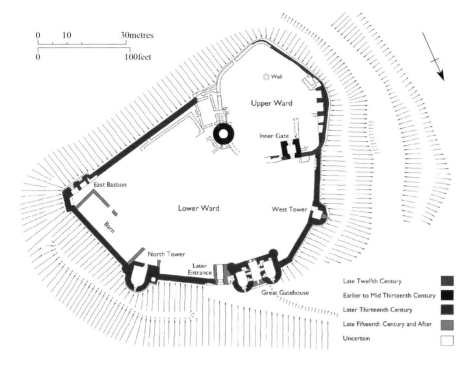

Figure 3.10: *Llansteffan. Castle plan. © Crown copyright (2018) Cadw, Welsh Government*

Figure 3.11: *Llansteffan. Great gatehouse from the south west.*

was rather elaborate, with engaged shafts and moulded capitals, the hood carried on boldly projecting corbels, of which the surviving one is carved with a human head; to each side is a quarter-round lamp bracket. The sculptured head is a reminder that similar features existed at Tonbridge, and might have done so at Caerphilly, but, if so, the evidence has been destroyed.

At much the same time as he was building Caerphilly, Gilbert de Clare was also carrying out work on a much more compact castle in southern Senghennydd, some 3 miles to the south west. Castell Coch is sited on a motte of unknown but probably Norman origin, the refortification of which included cladding the slopes of the motte in masonry and surrounding the summit with a curtain wall and three cylindrical towers, all roughly 40ft (12.2m) in diameter at the north-east (Well Tower), south-east (Keep Tower), and south-west (Kitchen Tower) angles. There was a square gatehouse adjoining the north side of the south-east tower and an integral hall range set between the two southern towers which formed the southern line of the enceinte (Figure 3.12).

Substantially ruined prior to its reconstruction by William Burges for the Marquess of Bute, the remains of the thirteenth-century castle were recorded by both G. T. Clark, who surveyed the castle in 1850, and by Burges himself, following the excavation of the remains in the early 1870s.[23] So, even though it is now largely a Victorian building, medieval elements remain and the authenticity of the plan is not in question. However, it is clear from the nineteenth-century surveys and subsequent observation that, like Caerphilly, the thirteenth-century castle was not raised in a single building programme but was rather the product of more than one phase of construction. Early features included the relatively thin curtain, the Kitchen Tower, and the attached hall range. Subsequently the curtain wall was doubled in thickness from the interior, the new work incorporating an

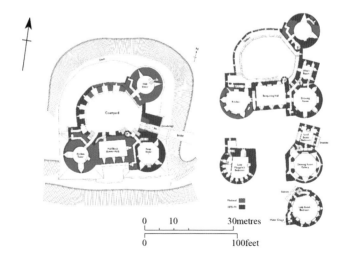

Figure 3.12: *Castell Coch. Castle plan. © Crown copyright (2018) Cadw, Welsh Government*

arcade of vaulted embrasures behind the row of loops that pierced the early wall, and the Keep Tower was added at the east end of the hall range. The position of the Well Tower in the sequence is less clear cut, having been assigned to both early and later phases.[24] However, it reasonably clear that all the medieval material dates from the later thirteenth century.

The revetting of the slopes of the motte in stone provided a steep talus around much of the castle. On the south side, where the two towers extend down to the bottom of the ditch thereby covering the slope, there is a variation of this theme which forms one of the outstanding features of the medieval castle. Each of the two southern towers is built on a square base from the exposed sides of which a talus ascends pyramid-like to envelope the tower base in a protective foot, looping down between the high points of the arrises. These 'spurred' bases were to become a particular characteristic of marcher lordship castles in the later thirteenth and fourteenth centuries, the two at Castell Coch being relatively early examples of the type. Intriguingly, this technique wasn't used for the Well Tower, which was given a more conventional, and less extravagant, battered base; this is one reason for suggesting that it belongs to a different phase and that it might be earlier than the other two.

One of the interests of these spurs lies in their chronological relationship with similar features at Caerphilly and other thirteenth–century castles. At Castell Coch they seem to be a response to the particularities of the site, extending the properties of the motte revetment to the exposed tower bases, but also spreading the load. The nature of the building site may be the reason why spurred towers are not a distinguishing feature of the early work at Caerphilly, where they are to be found almost exclusively around the North Dam Platform. One exception may be the South Gatehouse, which gave access to the primary South Dam Platform, though why they should be deployed here and not with the outer gatehouses of the central island is uncertain.

Caerphilly and related castles are testament to the existence, on the eve of war with Gwynedd, of a thriving regional 'school' of castle building. Firmly rooted in south Wales, and the English border counties, it was, on the whole, quite at odds with the architecture of the northern Welsh princes, but was a source of ideas, at least some of which would be developed in the forthcoming castle-building programme that was to follow in the wake of the English invasion of the north.

Chapter Four

The Royal Castles of the First Welsh War

Summary Narrative

The decision to move against Llywelyn ap Gruffudd was taken on 12 November 1276, and four days later the army commanders were appointed. In the initial phase of the First Welsh War, there were to be three separate lines of advance, from Chester, Montgomery, and Carmarthen, under the respective commands of Guy de Beauchamp, Earl of Warwick; Roger de Mortimer, Lord of Wigmore (Herefordshire), supported by Henry de Lacy, Earl of Lincoln; and Payn de Chaworth, Lord of Kidwelly (Carmarthenshire). Llywelyn's estranged brother, Dafydd, who was siding with Edward in pursuit of his patrimony, was with Warwick's contingent. Gruffudd ap Gwenwynwyn, deposed prince of Upper Powys, was with Mortimer. Also attached to Mortimer's army was the King's engineer, Master Bertram, his presence demanded by the impending siege of Dolforwyn, although his immediate task was to take in hand the castles of Oswestry and Montgomery and attend to their repair and strengthening.

In the north, inroads were made into the cantref of Tegeingl (the forerunner of Flintshire) as far as Mold. To the south of Tegeingl, Lower Powys, or Powys Fadog, a reluctant ally of Gwynedd, which was divided between the four sons of Gruffudd ap Madog, capitulated fairly quickly, the second son, Llywelyn, surrendering on 26 December 1276, and Madog, the eldest, early in 1277. Neither, it appears, held Dinas Brân, the main castle of the principality, which, for the time being remained in Welsh hands. On 12 May 1277 an expeditionary force led by the Earl of Lincoln arrived at the castle, to discover that it had been burnt and abandoned.

Mortimer led the main thrust against Llywelyn, and by 31 March the army had advanced to Dolforwyn and invested the castle. Siege engines were brought into play and the castle garrison surrendered on 8 April. The artillery had caused considerable damage and it was left to Master Bertram to effect repairs and make the castle tenable again, for the King wished to retain it. By early May, Builth Castle, destroyed by Llywelyn in 1260, had been recaptured and preparations for its reconstruction were in hand.

In the south, troops mustered in Carmarthen, from where Payn de Chaworth advanced up the Tywi, subduing the petty lords of the former kingdom of Deheubarth. In Ystrad Tywi, Rhys ap Maredudd, Lord of Dryslwyn, was brought to heel by 11 April, and Rhys Wyndod, Lord of Dinefwr submitted soon afterwards. By early June, the castles of Dinefwr, Carreg Cennen, and Llandovery (Carmarthenshire) were in the King's hands. At this point Edward's brother, Edmund Crouchback, Earl of Lancaster, took command, and by the end of July had advanced through Ceredigion to Aberystwyth, where work began on another royal castle.

Towards the end of this first stage of the war, during which Llywelyn's power had been broken in the south and east, and the Gwynedd heartlands besieged, Edward himself joined the campaign, reaching Chester by 16 July, and within the week had begun to advance along the Dee estuary, pausing at what was to become Flint, where a base camp was established, and reaching Rhuddlan on the River Clwyd by 19 August. Work began on constructing castles and defended towns at both Flint and Rhuddlan. By 29 August Edward had reached the River Conwy; a fleet of ships from the Cinque Ports landed troops on Anglesey, the bread basket of Gwynedd, and deprived the Welsh of the harvest. Llywelyn was forced to come to terms. The cantref of Tegeingl, in the far north east, was annexed, Dafydd ap Gruffudd being granted the lordship of Hopedale, which extended along its southern border. Adjoining Tegeingl to the west, the cantrefi of Dyffryn Clwyd and Rhufoniog were also granted to Dafydd. Llywelyn's domain was confined to the far north west, hemmed in by the four new castles of Builth, Aberystwyth, Flint, and Rhuddlan.

The Royal Castles in the South: Builth and Aberystwyth

Builth (Breconshire)

The earliest of the Edwardian castles, and the furthest south, is Builth, a fortification that had been established by Philip de Braose in the late eleventh century to a motte and bailey design. The earthworks are roughly circular with a circular motte a little to the north west of centre and a kidney-shaped bailey extending around three-quarters of its circumference. A ditch separates the motte from the bailey and the whole site is surrounded by a ditch and counter scarp bank. The bailey is divided into two unequal parts by a ditch on a roughly north–south alignment. A survey of the earthworks has been undertaken, but no archaeological excavation has taken place, and our knowledge of the superstructure is therefore limited.[1] Consequently, Builth is a prime site for further investigation towards a more comprehensive understanding of the Edwardian castle.

Destroyed by Llywelyn ap Gruffudd in 1260, work on the reconstruction of the castle started at the beginning of May 1277 and continued until mid-August 1282, when the money ran out.[2] The master builder, who may have been directing operations from the start, was the mason Henry of Leominster, about whom we know little.[3] His submaster from the beginning of the 1278 season was William of Winchcombe, a name suggesting a connection with Winchcombe Abbey in Gloucestershire, but also with Vale Royal, where there had been a mason of that name early in 1278.[4]

By 1282 William of Winchcombe had taken over as master of the works.[5] After the erection of temporary fortifications and buildings in timber, the castle was swiftly rebuilt in stone. Details are scanty, but it seems probable that in addition to walls around the two baileys there was also a twin-towered gateway with a turning bridge, possibly at the south-east edge of the motte, and, perhaps associated with it, a tower-studded wall.[6]

The architectural centrepiece of Builth, however, was a great tower, which was almost certainly built on top of the motte. A motte provided the master builder with challenges, but also presented an opportunity to create an eye-catching climax to the architectural ensemble and a striking landmark to the wider world. It has been suggested, on the basis of earthworks on the motte top, that the tower may have had a polygonal plan, and that certainly would have been one of the conventional forms for this type of building.[7] It has also been mooted that the great tower may have taken the form of a shell keep.[8] If so, it would have been quite a small one owing to the constrictions of the motte top, which has a diameter of approximately 60ft, and the supposed earthworks of the tower itself a diameter of no more than 50ft and an interior diameter of *c*. 35ft, an area that is, perhaps, more appropriate to a tower. On the other hand, Wiston Castle (Pembrokeshire), which is believed to date from the early thirteenth century, is a building of comparable size, but then Wiston was not a royal castle, and lacked the advantages that the royal coffers were able to bestow. It was built on an altogether smaller scale; its shell keep was, accordingly, a modest structure.

Aberystwyth (Cardiganshire)

Although there is little that can be confirmed about the Edwardian character of Builth until it can be revealed by excavation, we can see and conjecture a good deal more of and about Aberystwyth, which is situated some 35 miles to the north west of Builth. Known as Llanbadarn in the thirteenth century, this coastal castle is sited on a headland close to the mouth of the River Rheidol. Unlike Builth, Aberystwyth was an entirely new foundation, although it may be said to have replaced the timber castle some 1½ miles to the south, which had been raised by Gilbert Fitz Richard de Clare early in the twelfth century.

Work began on the castle at the beginning of August 1277 and continued, though not without interruption, until 1289. However, the bulk of the work must have been done during the first three seasons, which accounted for 80 per cent of the cost.[9] During these years the master builder was the mason Henry of Hereford, who may have been responsible for the initial design of the castle.[10] Following the 1279 season, little of substance appears to have been done until after the Welsh revolt of March 1282 (see below), when it was captured and slighted. In May of that year, James of St George arrived to make an inspection, and by early June his associate, Giles of St George, was in charge.[11]

Thereafter, building carried on apace, and from 1283 was being carried out under the master mason John de Ocleye (?Oakle Street, Gloucestershire) and the master carpenter John of Magull (Maghull, Lancashire).[12]

Regrettably, the castle was substantially demolished in 1649, and although clearance work at the beginning of the twentieth century elicited the main purport of the defences, the consolidation work that ensued was not carried out with sensitivity, and, consequently, aspects of the monument's historic character have been obscured or lost.[13] Excavation between 1975 and 1988 revealed further information about the early character of the castle and its construction sequence, identifying two main phases, which were attributed to the period before and after the war of 1282–3.[14]

Two concentric wards were built to a slightly irregular lozenge-shaped plan orientated from north to south, and there was a third bailey to the north west, although of this latter only a flat open space remains, and no evidence of the defences or internal components are visible. The main entrance to the castle was situated at the eastern apex facing towards the walled town that was constructed contemporaneously. There was a second entrance in the north-west curtain, which gave access to and from the north-west bailey. This was the plan as

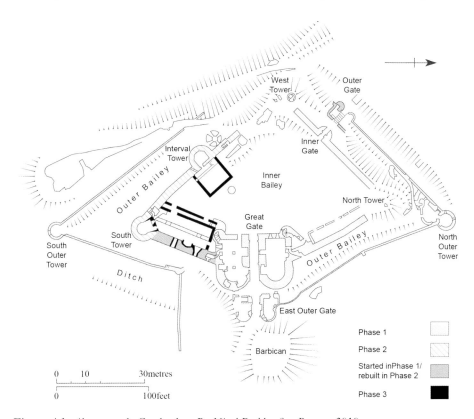

Figure 4.1: *Aberystwyth. Castle plan. By Nigel Dodds after Browne 2010*

completed by 1289, but it represents a modification to the initial layout, in that the south–west inner curtain appears to have been an afterthought, and it does not appear that the initial intention was for a fully concentric plan (Figure 4.1).[15]

The principal architectural component of the castle was the main gatehouse complex, a three-tier defence comprising a barbican, and then outer and inner gatehouses. Of the destroyed barbican, which remains unexcavated, there is little to be said, other than the earthworks suggest a rectangular structure. Round-fronted towers flanked the outer gateway, although the building seems to have been somewhat irregular in layout. An interesting feature of the adjoining north–east outer curtain is an outward bowing, which echoes the curve of the inner gatehouse tower.

Rising above the outer components of the entrance are the shattered remains of the inner gatehouse (Figure 4.2). The dimensions of the plan are impressive; at *c.* 83ft (25.3m) wide and 60ft (18.3m) from front to back, it was the largest building of its kind until the construction of the two inner gatehouses of Beaumaris, begun, though never completed, twenty years later. Despite the walls of the central gate passage having been heavily rebuilt, enough primary fabric survives to conclude that it was defended firstly by a portcullis with a groove of semi-circular section, and, beyond that, by two gates, both of which opened inwards. Between the portcullis and the first gate, on each side of the passage, there is a loop with a round termination to the basal plunge, and, situated between the two gates, the opposed entrances to the flanking towers.

Figure 4.2: *Aberystwyth. Great gate complex from the east.*

Each of the flanking towers contained a ground-floor chamber entered from both the gate passage and the inner ward, the upper storey or storeys being accessed via a pair of round stair turrets projecting from the rear angles. The stairs within these turrets have been rebuilt but fragments of newel posts survive in both. An unusual aspect of the south flanking tower is that it was divided from east to west by a three-bay stone arcade, now represented by two square pier bases and the east and west arch springers. Why this expedient should have been deemed necessary is uncertain; the southern room, which does not contain such a feature, is of similar width so it would not seem to have been a structural necessity per se for constructing the first floors.

Access from the north-west bailey was, firstly, via an outer gatehouse flanked by twin D-shaped towers with a drawbridge pit extending between them, and, secondly, and in direct alignment with it, an inner gatehouse in the form of a single semi-circular or D-shaped tower pierced by a barrel-vaulted gate passage, which was protected, firstly, by a machicolation slot in the vault, and, second, by a portcullis with a rectangular slot (Figure 4.3). There are no longer any indications of a gate, but there is a rebate for one towards the rear of the passage. The wall walk of the adjoining curtains was carried round the back of the tower; elements of this survive carried on corbelling, possibly the remnants of an east–west aligned barrel vault. Similar corbelling exists above the recessed rear entrance to the gate passage, implying that the tower extended further to the south east, and that we must think of a more elongated structure.

This inner north-west gatehouse is one of the best preserved aspects of the castle, and is of some interest, because, although single-tower gatehouses are not particularly unusual, most are rectangular, and close parallels are lacking. D-shaped gatehouse towers were also built at Caldicot, Montgomery, and Pembroke in the first half of the thirteenth century, but these were given side rather than front entrances. Nevertheless, they indicate that there was a tradition of D-shaped gatehouse towers in Wales, and that there is therefore good reason to suppose that the north-west gate of Aberystwyth derives from this regional tradition.

This notwithstanding, the most obvious model to be considered when evaluating the possible influence of

Figure 4.3: *Aberystwyth. North-west gate complex from the north west.*

earlier buildings in the design of Aberystwyth is Caerphilly, the most significant castle-building project in Wales to have been undertaken in the ten years before Aberystwyth. There are indeed a number of analogues between the Aberystwyth and the central island of Caerphilly that are worthy of consideration.

Firstly, both castles incorporate concentric defences, and although the principle of concentricity was not entirely new, Caerphilly was one of the first stone castles in Britain in which it was applied to an entire enceinte. It might be argued that Edward I's works in progress on a concentric outer circuit at the Tower of London were the source for the Aberystwyth system, but, on the whole, the western origin of Aberystwyth's master builder, and the comparative proximity of the two castles, makes Caerphilly the more likely exemplar.

Secondly, the inner wards of both Aberystwyth and Caerphilly are irregularly lozenge-shaped, and although the analogy is by no means exact, and the form in both cases was probably owed to the characteristics of the sites, it is interesting to note that in both cases the long axis of the lozenge, including the corner towers, measures approximately 300ft (91.4m).

Thirdly, in each instance, the corner towers themselves are three-quarters round and of bold projection, which, up to this point, had been a fairly unusual arrangement. Nevertheless, it was to become a standard feature in the castles of the later thirteenth century in Wales.

Fourthly, several of the openings that do survive at Aberystwyth have segmental-pointed or triangular heads, a feature that is not particularly rare, but one that was standard in the Welsh Marches, whilst not so evident amongst the Edwardian castles of north Wales.

Fifthly, it is necessary to focus on the main entrance. In this respect Aberystwyth shares the general characteristics of both the opposed gatehouse complexes of the central island of Caerphilly. However, it is its affinities with the Inner East Gatehouse of Caerphilly in particular that are striking, in that it too is served by a pair of projecting stair turrets at the inner angles, which, as we have seen, is a feature that is particularly associated with the gatehouses of the earls of Gloucester. It may therefore be stated with a reasonable degree of confidence that the main gatehouse of Aberystwyth was based on the Inner East Gatehouse of Caerphilly, in which case it is likely that the other analogues are also derived from the same source, or at least have their origins in the southern marches.

The Royal Castles in the North: Flint and Rhuddlan

English policy in the north was based on the recovery of the Four Cantrefi (Dyffryn Clwyd, Rhos, Rhufoniog, and Tegeingl). Of these, Tegeingl was in the north-east corner of Wales, contained by the River Dee and its estuary to the north east and the River Clwyd to the south west. It was here that two royal castles were established: at Flint on the Dee estuary, and at Rhuddlan next to the Clywd.

Tegeingl, which was to form the basis of the later county of Flintshire, had been periodically controlled by the English and Normans since 790 when it was seized by the Anglo-Saxon King of Mercia after defeating the Welsh at the Battle of Rhuddlan. It is uncertain how long after 790 the Anglo-Saxon occupation of Tegeingl lasted, but, in 918, Mercia was absorbed into the nascent kingdom of England, and in 921, the English King, Edward the Elder, then in alliance with the Welsh against the Vikings, established a burh, or fortified town, at a site known as Cledemutha. This name has been translated as 'Clwydmouth', implying a location next to the River Clwyd with ready access to the sea.

By the 1060s Tegeingl was once again under Welsh rule, and Gruffudd ap Llywelyn, the then ruler of Gwynedd, had established a residence for himself at Rhuddlan, where he maintained a number of ships. In 1073 the Normans seized control of the area and established a castle and borough at Rhuddlan. Rhuddlan was captured by the Welsh in 1213 but regained by Henry III in 1241, when Tegeingl was annexed. Rhuddlan was maintained, but Henry also fortified the hilltop site of Dyserth, 2½ miles to the east (described above). Llywelyn ap Gruffudd had regained Rhuddlan by 1258, and, in 1263, he captured Dyserth, which he destroyed.

A particular feature of the workforce enlisted to raise the English fortifications following the First Welsh War was the large number of diggers.[16] At both Flint and Rhuddlan these workers were the advance guard who prepared the initial defences to protect the workforce. Important in this respect were the construction of the banked and ditched circuits outside the castles, which contained the associated towns. These provided secure camps in which workers, supplies, and troops could be accommodated and marshalled.

Flint (Flintshire)

The first objective of Edward's advance along the north coast in the summer of 1277 was to secure a base camp, accessible by sea, and within marching distance of Chester. The site chosen was Flint, on the Dee estuary, some 12 miles north west of Chester, a location distinguished by a sandstone outcrop at the edge of the estuary. It is from this rocky platform, on which the castle was to be built, that the town takes its name, and it was at Flint that the workforce gathered initially and where the first fortifications were raised.[17] Here, Edward's men built a fortified town and a castle, the three elements of town, outer ward, and inner ward being separated by ditches and arranged in a lateral sequence, with the inner ward closest to the estuary. There were adjacent wharfs whereby the castle and town could be supplied by sea, but the land route to the castle was via the town. The complex is summarised in Speed's plan of 1610, at which stage the defensive complex was still largely intact.

Now, although the town defences are no longer extant, their position in relation to the plan of present-day Flint can be traced fairly accurately. Indeed, the line of the circuit was marked on the 1:2500 Ordnance Survey map of 1870, and the surviving elements appear on the 1912 map; they enclosed an area of *c.* 32 acres (13ha). The excavation of a section across the town defences in 1972 revealed a ditch 50ft (16m) wide and 10ft (3m) deep at the top with the sides sloping to a flattish bottom *c.* 15ft (4.6m) across.[18] As had been suggested by the Speed plan, the ditch was banked on each side, though only the full width of the inner bank was excavated; this was *c.* 53ft (17m) wide at its base and had survived to a height of 2ft 6in (0.75m). On each side of the ditch, at its junction with the inner and outer banks, was a shallow trench, *c.* 2ft (0.6m) wide and 1ft (0.30m) deep; these two features were interpreted by the excavator as marking-out trenches. This snapshot of the town defences is important in allowing a comparison to be made with other excavated defence systems, to be discussed below.

Although the initial labour of creating a defendable camp was carried out by the diggers, and a temporary superstructure prepared by the carpenters, masons were probably at work very shortly afterwards and to some extent contemporaneously.[19] By the spring of 1279 the masonry work of some of the towers was nearing completion or had been completed.[20] In the following two seasons, progress slowed and then ceased as Rhuddlan took priority. Preparation for a resumption of activity began in the late summer of 1280, and, in November, James of St George, who had hitherto been engaged at Rhuddlan, transferred his attention to Flint. The 1281 season saw serious advances in the construction programme, and included work on the great tower, north-west tower, and curtain wall.[21] In 1282, joists were being fitted in one of the northern towers and, at the end of the season, the great tower was fitted with a temporary roof.[22] The masons were paid off in November 1284, and were not re-engaged the following year. It is to be assumed that by this time the greater part of their work had been done. At the end of the 1286 season, the castle was largely complete and the great tower had been roofed over and covered in lead.[23]

As stated above, the castle comprised an inner and outer ward (Figure 4.4). At the north–east end of the town a bridge across the moat of the outer ward gave access to the now destroyed outer gatehouse of the castle, a building considered by its excavator to belong to the period 1279–84.[24] The gatehouse was a rectangular block (its rear wall co-terminus with the outer curtain) which projected into the moat and contained a counterbalance pit for a turning bridge pivoted on the threshold. The front wall of the building extended beyond the side walls to form a pair of buttresses. A modification was the addition of an extension that projected into the outer ward, the sides of which extended beyond those of the existing gatehouse outer section (to make a

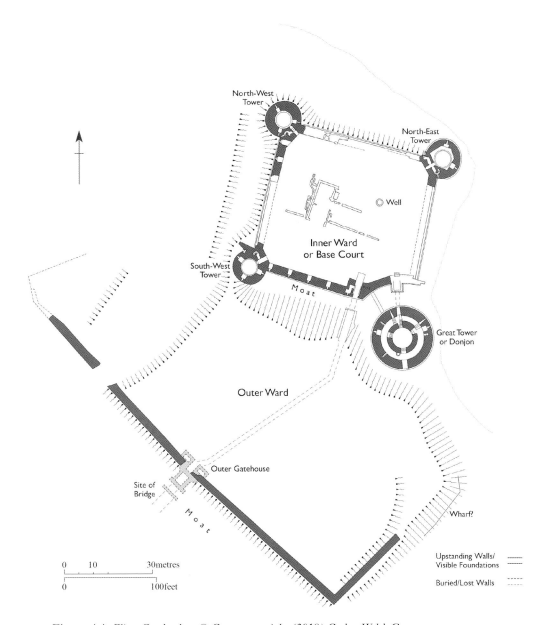

Figure 4.4: *Flint. Castle plan. © Crown copyright (2018) Cadw, Welsh Government*

T-shaped plan) and contained a small guard room on each side of the gateway. The gateway gave access to the roughly rectangular outer ward contained by a curtain wall that rose from the inclined, or battered, stone revetment of the ditch scarp.

The inner ward, which is separated from the outer ward by another ditch, comprises an almost square enclosure with three cylindrical towers projecting from the south-west and two northern angles, and, at the south-east angle, a detached great tower, also cylindrical. The curtain at this south-east corner is shaped as a concave quadrant, concentric with the great tower. At the east end of the south curtain, at its juncture with the concave south-east angle, is the gatehouse to the inner ward, which also had a simple plan. Owing to its fragmentary condition, we are limited as to what we can glean, but this one seems to have been quite different from the outer gatehouse. It too consisted of a single square tower pierced by a gate passage, but with the front of the structure flush with the curtain wall, so that it projected inwards rather than outwards (Figure 4.5).

More interesting are the drawbridge arrangements, which are also indicative of a different approach. Although the drawbridge itself does not survive, the remaining stone housings indicate that it was of a distinctive thirteenth-century type, also based on the counterbalance or turning principle. Usually, as in the case of the outer gatehouse, the turning bridge was provided with a pit immediately within the gateway to accommodate the inner end of the bridge when the outer end rose to block the gate. When lowered the outer end bridged the moat and the inner end bridged the pit. The system used at Flint was different in that only the outer end of the turning bridge was solid, the inner end comprising two counterbalance beams. Instead of a pit there were two slots designed to house the beams when the drawbridge was raised (Figure 4.6). Within the gate passage the beams and slots would have been covered by a permanent deck.

Figure 4.5: *Flint. Entrance to the inner ward from the south east with the great tower to the right.*

Figure 4.6 (above): *Flint. Inner gatehouse drawbridge counterbalance beam slots.*

Figure 4.7 (below): *Rhuddlan. Friary Gate drawbridge counterbalance beam slots (partially blocked).*

Putting the great tower to one side for the moment, the north-eastern tower, the most complete of the other three corner towers, comprises a circular basement without lighting and formerly entered from a trap in the floor above, and three irregularly hexagonal upper storeys. The entrance from the courtyard opened to a passage extending through the thickness of the wall. On the right-hand (south-east) side of the entrance passage, a corridor led to a spiral staircase leading to the upper storeys, and on the left-hand (north-west) side a corresponding corridor led to a latrine in the angle formed by the tower and curtain wall. Similar arrangements appear to have pertained at the upper floor levels. A flue on the north-west side denotes the positions of the first- and second-floor fireplaces. The few surviving details include round-arched embrasures, a form much in use by the thirteenth-century masons of Savoy. The south-west and north-west towers are badly ruined, but these too had circular basements and hexagonal upper floors. In the north-west tower, there is a fragment of a first-floor fireplace comprising a chamfered jamb with a curving head, and, adjoining it, a sconce bracket. As will be shown below, this was a standard type of hooded fireplace that was used elsewhere in the royal works of north Wales.

Now for the most interesting aspect of Flint: the great tower, or keep, which, unusually, for an English castle, lay outside the inner ward, separated from it by a moat (Figure 4.8). The relationship with the curtain wall, which has been described above, has its origins in France, where there are several examples of thirteenth-century ditched great towers isolated from the curtain (e.g. Dourdan, Lillebonne, Coucy, Aigues Mortes). The port of Aigues Mortes (Gard) on the French Mediterranean coast is the most obvious model for the general

Figure 4.8: *Flint. The castle from the south east with the stump of the great tower in the foreground.*

relationship of tower to curtain. Founded by (St) Louis IX and built between 1246 and 1302, the walled town had a detached cylindrical tower, known as the Tour de Constance, at one corner, in an arrangement that echoes that of the inner ward of Flint and its great tower. That is probably the minimum qualification for a precedent, but, the case for Aigues Mortes is stronger than most, because it was known to Edward, who embarked from there in 1270 when setting out on crusade. At that time, it would have been in the process of construction, and may therefore have had the additional attraction of modernity. A supplementary factor is that Flint measures *c*. 71 ft (21.6m) in diameter, and is therefore built at a similar scale to the Tour de Constance, which measures 72ft (21.9m). This final correlation seems to tip the scales in favour of Aigues Mortes as the principal source of inspiration, although, as we shall see, the internal planning of the Flint tower was of a rather different character.

At Flint, a bridge provided access from the inner ward to a door in the north side of the keep, opening at mezzanine level to a vestibule within the thickness of the wall. Directly ahead a straight flight of steps descended to the central area of the basement, giving unencumbered access for personnel and goods alike. The basement consists of a single circular room, but three short flights of steps to the south, north east, and north west each ascend from it to a wide segmental-pointed archway that gave access to a vaulted mural passage extending all around the tower between the inner and outer walls. Directly opposite each of these openings, in the outer wall, was a loop within a square embrasure. Inside the passage, just to the west of the southern archway, is the well, which could be drawn from first-floor level, via a trap in the vault. On the north side, the passage steps down to a lower level in order to allow for the reduced headroom occasioned by the stair from the entrance lobby.

On the left-hand side of the entrance lobby a short passage led to a newel stair which gave access to the upper storeys, rising initially to a first-floor landing. At this level there is a circular arrangement of five rooms set out above the basement-level mural passage and divided by irregularly placed wedge-shaped partitions, three of which contained single latrines equipped with ventilation shafts. There is no evidence of a fireplace in any of these rooms, but each space was lit by a window, and the latrines indicate a domestic function for the building at this level. There are few other indications of function; a barrel-vaulted room immediately to the south east of the staircase is identified with the chapel that is known to have existed in the great tower, whilst a trap above the well suggests that the southern room may have had a service function. The upper part of the tower has been destroyed, but, owing to the presence of latrine shafts, which descend from above first-floor level, we can say that the tower was probably intended to be at least three storeys high. Indeed, the other corner towers each contained four storeys including a basement, and it is unlikely that these were intended to be loftier than the great tower.

The partial survival of the great tower has presented difficulties of interpretation. Essentially, there are two alternatives regarding its intended form: the central area was either floored or it took the form of an open well.[25] Unfortunately, the structural evidence is insufficient to confirm or refute either of these possibilities. However, in considering the question, we might wish to reflect that an open area would have served no useful purpose other than as a light well. It could not, for example, have been used for storage of anything that might be spoiled by the damp, yet there is no doubt that it would have been expedient to provide a roomy storage area here in order to deposit supplies and equipment, armaments included.

It is, perhaps, pertinent that the three loops within the mural passage were situated directly opposite the openings from the central area, as though one of the objectives was to throw some light into an otherwise unlit room. It is also difficult to imagine that the circle of rooms at first-floor level functioned as 'a self-contained residential apartment'.[26] It would have been cramped, inconvenient, uncomfortable, and much less commodious than one of the corner towers. However, the presence of a central room would have provided a more flexible and capacious arrangement, and also a focus for the peripheral chambers which otherwise would be hard to envisage as a suite.

If the tower were more than two storeys high, the main challenge would have been to provide the central room with natural light. We have seen that in the basement, the central area was designed so that light from the windows in the surrounding wall passage was admitted via large open arches. Such an arrangement would have rendered the upper room useless as a conventional domestic space, so, unless it was another storage room, which, given the residential nature of this floor, seems unlikely, a modified system for the provision of light would have to have been adopted, most likely consisting of a series of windows or light shafts in the inner wall. Five years later, the designer of the Eagle Tower of Caernarfon (a building that bears an architectural relationship to Flint) would find solutions to just this sort of problem, and there is no reason to suppose that the builder of Flint was any less capable.

Rhuddlan (Flintshire)

The second of Edward's castles to be built in Tegeingl, at Rhuddlan (Figure 4.9), was begun in July 1277, and was largely complete by the autumn of 1280 after only four building seasons.[27] At this point, as we have seen, attention once more turned to Flint. Whereas Flint was built on an entirely new site, a motte and bailey castle and an associated borough had been established at Rhuddlan in 1073, the remains of which are still to be seen on the right (north-east) bank of the River Clwyd. Edward built his castle on a bluff above the river approximately 330yd (303m) to the north west of Robert of Rhuddlan's motte (Twt Hill) and bailey,

Figure 4.9: *Rhuddlan. The castle from the west, the River Clwyd in the foreground.*

the site of the Norman borough lying between the two castles. A new borough was laid out to the north west of the castle, and enclosed by a double-banked ditch, these defences extending north eastwards from the river for some 350yd (320m) turning south eastwards for another 500yd (457m) and then south westwards to meet the castle defences at the junction of Castle Street and Lôn Hylas, the lane that extends along the north-east side of the castle moat. They enclosed an area of around 22 acres (9ha).

Apart from the Norman and Edwardian defences described above there is a third earthwork at Rhuddlan, known as the Town Ditch, which lies to the south east of the Edwardian castle. The Town Ditch forms two straight sides of an enclosure, the west end of the missing northern arm being conjectured to have joined the east side of the castle defences; the fourth (west) side being represented by the River Clwyd. The extent of this enclosure is approximately 75 acres (30ha) and contains the Norman castle and borough and the Dominican friary founded by Llywelyn ap Gruffudd in 1258. Excavations undertaken in three annual seasons between 1979 and 1981 resulted in the interpretation of the earthworks as the tenth-century defences of Cledemutha (see above, p. 71).[28] Subsequently, historical and archaeological cases were made to challenge this identification and to argue that the Town Ditch does, in fact, belong to the Edwardian period; a comparison of the two sets of earthworks tend to support this later conclusion.[29]

Edward's castle was given three largely concentric lines of defence. At the core was an irregular lozenge-shaped inner ward, its long axis aligned north–south.

The outer ward is somewhat rectangular with canted northern corners, but is pulled out of shape at its southern end where it descends to the river. Here, the two arms of the curtain form a salient, at the south-western apex of which is a boldly projecting square tower (Gillot's Tower). Finally, a deep stone-revetted ditch extended around the north, east, and west sides of the outer ward, the western arm extending to the steep scarp above the river, and the eastern arm sloping right down to the river, which formed a natural barrier on this side (Figure 4.10).

At courtyard level the sloping revetment of the scarp, or inner side, of the ditch was carried up vertically as the curtain of the outer ward. The wall was pierced by some fifty arrow loops with very deep plunges, which extended down the revetment to obviate blind spots. Projecting from the curtain is a series of rectangular or sub-rectangular turrets and buttresses, four of which contained

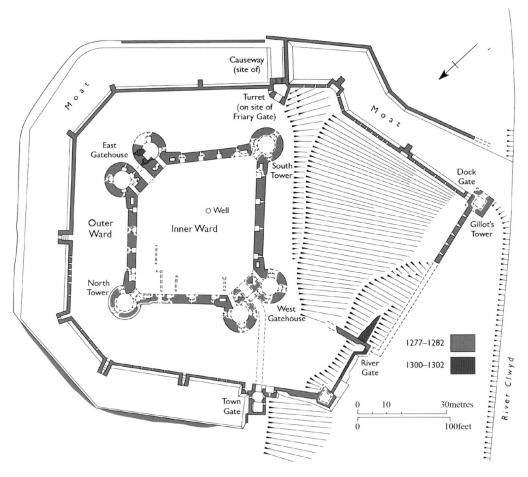

Figure 4.10: *Rhuddlan. Castle plan.* © *Crown copyright (2018) Cadw, Welsh Government*

flights of steps descending to barred postern gates giving access to the northern and eastern sections of the moat. Remnants of masonry projections to either side of some of the turrets suggest that they were flanked by wallhead bartizans, and although the remains are insufficient to reconstruct their full nature, there are indications that they had rounded faces. There is reason to believe that the buttresses also supported bartizans. The whole scheme represents an unusually lavish treatment, the revetment of the ditch in stone extending to both the scarp and counter scarp of the ditch.

There were two landward entrances to the outer ward: the Town Gate towards the north west and the Friary Gate towards the south east. The Town Gate had something in common with the outer gate of Flint, being rectangular and in projecting in front of the curtain, but the drawbridge system, in common with that of the Friary Gate, worked on the same principle as that of Flint's inner gate drawbridge. These three drawbridges, which must have been built in the very early stages of construction, are the only ones of their kind in Edward's Welsh castles. The outer gatehouses led into the broad berm that forms the greater part of the Outer Ward; it contained various ancillary buildings including stores and workshops, of which there are now no trace.

The Outer Ward is dominated by the high walls and towers of the Inner Ward, which it surrounds. At the east and west angles of the inner enclosure are twin gateways, each flanked by a pair of four-storey round towers and protected by a portcullis and a pair of gates. There is also a four-storey round tower at each of the other two angles. One element of the inner ward that is absent from Flint, but which recurs at Conwy and Harlech, is the latrine turret rising from ground level and tucked into the angles between the inner towers and curtain, one of the features that Taylor associated with Savoyard practices (Figure 4.11).

Here at Rhuddlan, where there are eight turrets altogether, one to each gate tower and two to each corner tower, these domestic conveniences also have an aesthetic purpose in effecting a graduated transition between towers and curtain, a point that is emphasised by their finely bevelled edges and a decorative quality to the masonry (see below, this chapter, for elaboration). This is a detail which contributes to the general impression that no expense was

Figure 4.11: *Rhuddlan. South tower latrine turret from the east.*

spared in the construction of what, at the time, was intended to be Edward's principal castle in north Wales. The only openings in the Inner Ward comprise a series of ground-storey loops, now very heavily eroded, some of which appear domestic in character, but which, in fact, are all arrow loops with large splayed basal plunges.

The six corner towers contained a series of self-contained chambers each equipped with a fireplace and latrine, much like those in the corner towers of Flint Castle. The gateways lack the residential accommodation block that has been noted at Aberystwyth, and contained only a single room over the gate passage, from where the portcullis was operated. The corners of the courtyard are canted, the backs of the towers being flattened in order to accommodate the continuous alure, which extended behind the towers. Like the Outer Ward, the Inner Ward is now devoid of buildings, but, traces of exposed foundations on the north-west and north-east sides, lead flashing lines in the walls, and first-floor doorways in the backs of the gate towers, all suggest that there were two-storey lean-to ranges, probably of timber-framed construction, set against the walls. The only external lighting is at ground-floor level, where the arrow loops have segmental-arched, square-sided embrasures.

A curiosity of the inner ward towers is the inconsistent configuration of the interior walls. The lowest storeys are all circular, but the interior of the North Tower is alone in being circular throughout. Also unique is the South Tower, whose upper storeys are hexagonal. In contrast, all four gate towers have heptagonal interiors; it is difficult to know how to interpret such variables. All six towers, in common with the battered plinth that extends all around the inner ward, together with the corresponding section towards the courtyard, contain some excellent quality, very finely jointed sandstone ashlar, both inside and out. The circular interiors, the spiral staircase wells and the gate passages, are all faced in ashlar, and a surviving springer on the south side of the east tower implies that the gate passages were covered with a high vault carried on ashlar ribs.

This material is just one of a number of contrasting types of masonry at Rhuddlan, which constitute a particular characteristic of the castle, and which is especially noticeable in the walls and towers of the inner ward. To some extent, the patchwork appearance of these diverse colours and textures simply reflects changes in the sources of supply and the matching of particular materials to particular jobs, but, on the whole, there does seem to have been a deliberate attempt to use the polychromatic distinction to produce an ornamental effect. Thus, the tower bases were built in grey sandstone ashlar with yellowish sandstone rubble above; pink sandstone ashlar was used for the plinth of the curtain wall, the bases and quoins of the latrine turrets, and the window frames and embrasures. The curtain walls were built in limestone rubble, which was also the principal material used in the outer curtain and ditch revetment. However, describing thus is to generalise, for the treatment is far from consistent, and the materials seldom used exclusively. There are some hints of patterns being picked out by contrasting stones in areas in which one type of material predominates, but such instances are difficult to evaluate by eye. Detailed archaeological recording of the elevations, with particular emphasis on mapping the different materials, would doubtless throw some light on the rationale (or lack of it) behind the masonry configurations and give insights into the building sequence.

Review of Flint and Rhuddlan

In several respects, the architectural character of the two northern castles is quite different from one another. Partly this can be explained by the respective possibilities of the two sites, but perhaps the dissimilarity is also owed to their different functions. However, despite their many differences, there are also several unifying factors that allow us to group Flint and Rhuddlan together and view them as representative of a common approach.

The first of these common elements is the configuration of the borough defences, which in each case consist of a roughly flat-bottomed ditch flanked by inner and outer banks, which is an arrangement peculiar to these two sites, and indicative of a single directing hand at work. Also interesting is a comparison of the dimensions. At Flint the ditch was 50ft (16m) wide and 10ft (3m) deep, and the inner bank *c.* 53ft (17m) wide. At Rhuddlan, where two archaeological sections have been dug through the defences, the corresponding dimensions are 44ft (13.40m)/46ft (14m), 9ft (2.75m)/9ft (2.75m) and 59ft (18m)/44ft (13.40m). The outer bank at Rhuddlan was 40ft (12.20m)/45ft (13.7m) wide.[30] It shouldn't be expected that the dimensions would correspond exactly, but they do show that the two works were built on a similar scale and to a similar design.

Having compared the borough defences, let us consider the Town Ditch to the south east of the castle, which was identified as the defences of Cledemutha. The ditch itself was *c.* 49ft (15m) wide with a maximum depth of *c.* 3m (10ft); inner and outer banks measured *c.* 36ft (11m) and *c.* 41ft (12.5m) in width respectively. Again, they don't correspond exactly, but they are built at a similar scale and to a similar design as the borough defences of both Flint and Rhuddlan. On these grounds alone it is difficult to see them as anything other than contemporary.[31]

If this is so, then the enclosure requires some explanation. As we have seen, it contained the old castle and borough and the thirteenth-century friary. The castle had been refurbished by Henry III in 1242, but was in Llywelyn's hands by 1258, when he founded the friary nearby, and might thereafter have served as a princely residence, and the old Norman borough as a centre of population. Two houses excavated within the Norman borough defences have been dated to the thirteenth century, although it is uncertain whether they relate to the Welsh or English periods.[32]

In the light of what was to occur in the second wave of Edwardian castle building a few years later, in which the annexation of sites with a political or symbolic significance to the royal house of Gwynedd formed a strand, the recapture of Rhuddlan, for so many years a possession of the Normans and English, presented the King with an opportunity to make his mark in a forceful fashion by establishing not only a new castle but also a major new town. The area enclosed by the Town Ditch was twice the size of Flint, but then Rhuddlan was intended to be the shire town and the new seat of the episcopal see of St Asaph. In the event, neither scheme was realised, because after 1282 the focus of Edward's Welsh interests moved west, and Rhuddlan lost much of its significance.[33]

A second point of comparison between the two castles is that the gatehouses of Flint were rather unusual in their simplicity and rectangularity. The same is true of the outer gatehouses of Rhuddlan, in contrast to those of the inner ward. The turrets and towers of the outer curtain are also notable for their rectangular plans, an unusual design in the 1270s, and could be thought of either as old fashioned, or, in another way, avant-garde in that they anticipated the widespread re-adoption of the rectangular tower, especially in northern England during the fourteenth century.

Thirdly, there is the matter of the drawbridges. A castle moat would have been traversed by a timber or stone bridge. Usually, this would fall short of the gateway, leaving the final section to be spanned by a drawbridge. In the thirteenth century this was often a turning bridge, a device akin to a see-saw, being pivoted near the centre; when it was in the down position the outer half bridged the moat and the inner half covered a pit, which was often within the gate passage itself. When the bridge was raised, the inner half swung down into the pit and the outer half blocked the gateway. It is to be assumed that the pit was then either left open or covered with a temporary deck. The arrangement at the inner gatehouse of Flint exemplifies a particular variation of the turning bridge, in which the inner half of the structure was not covered with boarding, but consisted simply of the main beams (Flint had two), which, when the bridge was down, were hidden under a permanent deck; when the bridge was raised, instead of descending into a pit, the beams dropped down into two slots, or chases, beneath the deck (Figure 4.6). The advantage of this arrangement lay in the fact that it would not be necessary to deal with the exposed pit when the bridge was raised.

The only other examples of this design in the Welsh castles of Edward I were at Rhuddlan, where the two outer gatehouses (the Town Gate to the north west and the Friary Gate to the south east) were provided with the same type of drawbridge (Figure 4.7). This particular mechanism provides a link between the two northern castles of the First Welsh War, and suggests that this part of the design was carried out by the same engineer. The fact that the outer gatehouse of Flint was given a different kind of turning bridge and that none of Edward's subsequent Welsh castles made use of the method, show that it was superseded within the first few years of the building campaign. As far as we can tell, this invention had its origins in the royal works, the earliest examples to be identified so far being at the royal castle of Newcastle-upon-Tyne (1247–50), but there was also one at the Tower of London in the Lion Tower (the barbican of the new western entrance built for Edward I over the years 1275–85) and at Goodrich Castle (Herefordshire), which betrays the influence of the Tower in this respect.

It seems conclusive, then, that the concealed counterbalance beam systems used at Flint and Rhuddlan stem from the royal works. Why, then, are they only to be found at Flint and Rhuddlan, and why was the method not used in the outer gatehouse of Flint? This does not seem to be a detail that would have been expressly stipulated by the King. The main concern was that whatever the mechanism adopted it should work efficiently, so the decision more probably falls within the province of the engineer, and a change in design, as happened at Flint, is likely to be the result of a change in engineer. The engineers Bertram and Richard were both involved in the construction of Flint, but Taylor considered that Bertram had senior authority.[34]

The link with the Tower of London is particularly pertinent, because there are further comparisons to be made between Rhuddlan and Edward's work at the Tower. Firstly, there are some general resemblances, in that both castles are situated on a river bank and both comprise two concentric wards, the other three sides of which are provided with a moat. On the Thames waterfront, at the south-east angle of the outer ward, the Well Tower and the Develin Tower, both of which belong to the Edwardian phase, are rectangular. Similar to this is Gillot's Tower, the principal structure on the corresponding frontage at Rhuddlan. It is also possible that the two inner gateways at Rhuddlan are largely based on Edward's cylindrical-towered gateways, the Middle and Byward towers, at the Tower, although these in turn owe much to the Outer Gateway of Nottingham Castle, built in 1252–5 for Henry III. The Rhuddlan towers are more closely spaced but the effect is otherwise analogous (Figure 4.12).

Other correlations between Flint and Rhuddlan include the cylindrical angle towers and their polygonal interiors, the hooded fireplaces with straight brackets, and the revetting of the castle ditch in stone. Regarding this latter element, at both Rhuddlan and the outer ditch of Flint the revetment was given a pronounced batter, or talus, rising to courtyard level, at which point it changed to the vertical and continued upwards as the outer curtain. It is an attribute that wasn't repeated at any of the other Edwardian castles in Wales, and the Rhuddlan ditch, in which this treatment was taken to its fullest extent, is something of a rarity generally in this country. However several thirteenth-century fortifications in other countries display a similar treatment that might have acted as a precedent, for example, Phillipe Auguste's Dourdan, built by 1222, Frederick II's Castel Ursino in Catania (Sicily) of 1239, or the town defences of Caesarea (Israel) in the former Kingdom of Jerusalem as rebuilt by St Louis in the 1250s.

Figure 4.12: *Rhuddlan. Inner West Gatehouse from the west.*

We now have to ponder the roles of the royal craftsmen in all of this. Master James took over responsibility for the royal works in Wales in April 1278.[35] It is not known whether he had had any involvement in the Welsh project before this date, but Taylor has argued persuasively that Master Bertram was in charge before his arrival.[36] In the nine months preceding the initial reference to James of St George's involvement in the royal works in north Wales, work had begun on five new royal castles (the fifth was Ruthin, which will be discussed in Chapter 5). The first season at Flint was dominated by the construction of earthworks, including the double-banked ditch that enclosed the town, and, presumably, the ditches associated with the castle. Additionally, carpenters would have been at work in making a defensive superstructure to protect the workforce and supplies. It is also evident from the presence of masons, and subsequent indications of the rate of progress, that some work on the stone defences was afoot from the start; it is most likely that this included, at the very least, the laying of the castle's stone foundations.

At Rhuddlan, also, it was the diggers who made up the overwhelming bulk of the workforce.[37] Their principal task was the canalising of the River Clwyd, but, as has been described above, there were also substantial earthworks connected with the castle and adjacent borough. It seems probable that here too, after the arrival of Edward on 29 August 1277, the plan of the castle was laid out, and work was begun on the foundations ready for a rapid resumption of building work at the opening of the first full building season in the spring of 1278. When Master James assumed control, then, the likelihood is that the general form of both castles had already been determined.

To some extent this must have been decided by Edward himself in consultation with his technical officers in Wales, notably, Master Bertram, Master Richard, the master ditchers, William of Boston and William of March, and, perhaps, remotely with Master James. It has been suggested that the idea for the unusual double-bank and ditch arrangement that was used for the defences of both boroughs came from Edward, inspired by reading Vegetius.[38] Aigues Mortes has already been mentioned above as a plausible model for Flint. If this is correct, then it is probable that Edward himself, who had first-hand experience of the site, suggested the general form and disposition of the keep. Moreover, given its idiosyncratic internal plan, Edward must have given instructions regarding how it was to function and what accommodation was required. The province of his craftsmen would have been the technical aspects of adapting the interior to fulfil those wishes. The lost keep of Sandal Castle has been suggested as a possible influence on Flint.[39] This proposal that is given credence by the fact that its owner, John de Warenne, was a close friend of Edward. It may well be, then, that Flint incorporates aspects of the Sandal design.

All these sources may have contributed to the design of the royal castles of Wales, but the influence of the existing royal craftsmen has also been mentioned, so too that of the Tower of London. This being so, it is pertinent to note, as has been done elsewhere, the possible involvement of Robert of Beverley, the King's master builder at the Tower, in drawing up a blueprint. Nevertheless, it is also worth remembering that Master Bertram had a connection with the Tower, for in 1276 he was busily constructing engines there, in anticipation of military action against Llywelyn. What the underlying regularities of both Flint and Rhuddlan suggest is that the initial plans were created on a drawing board to a geometrical design, something of which either of the two masters could have been capable. However, the form of the drawbridges common to both was probably determined on site, so Master Bertram seems most likely to have been responsible. Once Master James had taken charge, drawbridge design changed, both for the outer gatehouse of Flint and for the later royal castles; bridges of less complicated design would now be the norm. It is perhaps reasonable to assign this change to a new regime and a break from the traditions of the royal works represented by the Tower.

Chapter Five

Baronial Castles of the First Welsh War

Castles in the North

Ruthin (Denbighshire)

In addition to the four royal castles, the genesis of three baronial castles in north Wales can be considered consequences of the First Welsh War. The first of these is Ruthin, the administrative centre of Duffryn Clwyd, which lies approximately 15 miles to the south east of Rhuddlan and 17 miles south west of Flint. In the summer of 1277, in concert with Flint and Rhuddlan, Edward's workmen began work on a new castle here, possibly under the direction of the Lincolnshire master mason Thomas of Grantham.[1] Given the speed with which the initial work at Flint and Rhuddlan was carried out, it is feasible that before the end of 1277 the plan of the castle had, in the main, been fixed, the ditches excavated, and a start made on the stonework.

In October, as a reward for his support in the war against Llywelyn, the two cantrefi of Duffryn Clwyd and Rhufoniog were bestowed upon Dafydd ap Gruffudd.[2] At that point it was presumably Dafydd who took over responsibility for the continuation of the building work, though whether any progress was made is unknown. After Dafydd's rebellion in 1282, operations were resumed at Ruthin by the King, through the agency of James of St George, but, given that it was granted to Reginald de Grey in October, it is possible that much of the castle is to be attributed to him.[3] Therefore, although the castle was initiated by the King, and the layout determined by Edward and his craftsmen, the greater part of the construction work was probably undertaken under the auspices of de Grey.

Sited on a sandstone ridge, Ruthin Castle encloses an overall area of some 2 acres (0.8ha) and comprises a large irregularly pentagonal Upper Ward (somewhat like the outer ward of Château Gaillard) to the north east and a small rectangular lower ward to the south west, arranged, like Flint, in a lateral sequence, and separated by a rock–cut ditch, closed at each end by the curtain wall. In 1826 a castellated house was built inside the castle, straddling the ditch between the wards, the two parts of the house being linked by a bridge; this house was enlarged in 1848–53. Also, during the nineteenth century, the ruins of the castle itself were adapted, subordinated to the development of a garden and romanticised; consequently, it is not always easy to distinguish the primary fabric from later alterations. Little archaeological work has been conducted, and any interpretation of the remains must be regarded as tentative (Figure 5.1).

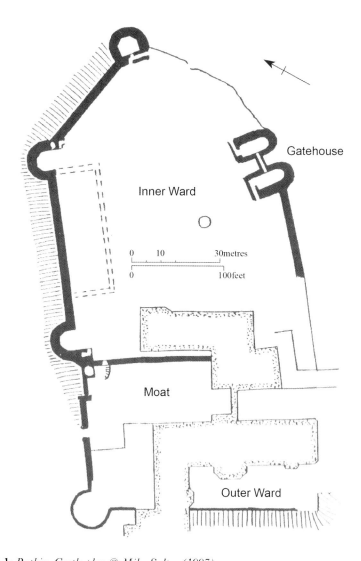

Inner Ward

Gatehouse

Moat

Outer Ward

0   10   30metres

0   100feet

Figure 5.1: *Ruthin. Castle plan © Mike Salter (1997)*

Four of the angles of the Upper Ward were marked by a D-shaped tower, the main gatehouse being at the fifth (eastern). The Lower Ward had round towers at its two southern corners. At the west end of the ditch separating the two wards was a gateway (the West Gate) set within a rectangular projection of the curtain, and, further to the north, at the north-west angle of the moat, a sally port in the curtain. The castle was surrounded by a moat, most probably fed by the River Clwyd, which lies to the west. On the north-west side, between the north angle tower and the postern, the moat opened out into a broad salient, and, beyond the postern, an arm extended towards the west and the former mill pond associated with the still extant thirteenth-century mill, suggesting quite a wide expanse of water on the north-west flank, although there must be a degree of uncertainty as to whether this was all part of the thirteenth-century scheme.

Despite an obfuscating veil of nineteenth-century fantasy, unruly undergrowth, and attrition, it is possible to discern amidst the ruins medieval masonry of two contrasting types and qualities. The Upper Ward is built from red sandstone blocks of near ashlar character (Figure 5.2), much superior to the coursed limestone rubble of the Lower Ward and the curtain at the west end of the ditch (Figure 5.3). The sandstone must be a primary fabric given that it was probably obtained from the excavation of the ditches, and was therefore being used from the start.[4] However, a supply of limestone would also have been necessary from an early date for the manufacture of lime mortar. There are carboniferous limestone deposits lying half a mile to the south west of the castle, so, although the different materials could represent separate construction phases, equally, they could be broadly contemporary.

Few of the buildings are understood well enough to provide material for a fruitful discussion. The great gatehouse was flanked by a pair of D-shaped towers, but only their basements and the (much altered) first floor of the south tower are extant, whilst the gate passage has been buried beneath a nineteenth-century ramp that leads up to an ornamental garden gate. Nevertheless, some details survive, notably a few doorways with segmental-pointed arches, quite sharply angled (possibly owing to the narrowness of the openings) and having marked affinities with a number of late thirteenth-century marcher castles, notably, Goodrich, Chepstow, and Reginald de Grey's own castle of Wilton.

Straight staircases in the rear (west) wall of the gatehouse lead individually to the basements of the two towers, a passage between the two basements has primary openings, though the passage itself is suspect, and there is a blocked staircase in the north wall of the south tower, which presumably led to the first floor. The base of a turret in the re-entrant between the north tower and the curtain may have housed a latrine servicing the upper floor of the gatehouse; similar features are associated with the Inner East Gatehouse of Caerphilly and the great gatehouse of Tonbridge, though not with the royal works in Wales. However, parallels for the general plan of the great gatehouse have reasonably been drawn with the now vanished inner and outer gatehouses of Chester Castle, which also had elongated D-shaped flanking towers, suggesting that Reginald de Grey might have been the personal link between the two buildings.[5] However, as described above (Chapter 3), a precedent had been set some years earlier in Henry III's improvements to Deganwy.

The other main area of interest is the West Gate, a rather strange structure, breaking forward from the curtain in a thickening of the wall (Figure 5.3). The emphasis placed on the gate by this projection is heightened by the

Figure 5.2: *Ruthin. West curtain showing the sandstone ashlar revetment and the sally port at the foot of the wall.*

Figure 5.3: *Ruthin. West Gate of limestone rubble with sandstone dressings around the arch.*

lighter-coloured stonework of which it is built, and which stands out against the deeper shade of the curtain on either side. This theme of contrast is carried through in the red sandstone dressings of the pointed gate arch and the darker limestone of the overhanging turret (see below). Evidently, some care has been taken to produce a pattern, suggesting, perhaps, that the broader distinction between the two wards in the use of materials is deliberate, and was intended to convey some now obscure significance.

The archway is rebated for outward opening gates; behind the rebate are square grooves for a portcullis. Above the gate is a semi-circular projection or turret comprising seven tiers of corbelling and which must have carried a semi-circular superstructure, a most unusual feature, but one which seems to have been designed to accommodate a portcullis chamber. The best parallel for the character of the West Gate is the Friary Gate in Rhuddlan Castle, which was also accommodated within a localised thickening of the curtain, only being converted to a tower in the early years of the fourteenth century, when the gateway itself was blocked.[6]

Rhuddlan might also be the source of two other aspects of the West Gate, both of which have been discussed in the previous chapter. Polychrome masonry is a particular feature of Rhuddlan, where contrasts between pink sandstone ashlar and grey limestone rubble were employed. It has also been mentioned that the rectangular staircase turrets and buttresses of the inner ward seem to have been capped by rounded bartizans. Their exact nature can no longer be determined, but they evidently had something in common with the corbelled crown of the West Gate. It is worth pointing out, too, that corbelled bartizans of more refined appearance would be used to effect at the royal castle of Beaumaris in the 1290s.[7]

Two other thirteenth-century features are to be found to the left (north) of the gate. Firstly, within the limestone walling is a broad segmental relieving arch, and, beneath it a former arched opening, probably a drain or culvert. Secondly, within the sandstone walling, is another large relieving arch, and, beneath it, tucked to one side, is a sally port or postern with a segmental-arched doorway like those in the great gatehouse (Figure 5.2). This opening was reached from the Upper Ward via a spiral staircase within the thickness of the curtain next to the west tower.

Nothing is known about the purpose of the Lower Ward, but the Upper Ward contained a number of significant buildings. The great hall, which was situated directly opposite the great gatehouse, lined the north-west curtain between the north and west towers. This was a substantial building some 100ft (30.5m) long by 40ft (12.2m) wide, dimensions comparable to those of the great hall of Caernarfon Castle (begun *c.* 1283). The kitchens were at the south-west end of the hall, and there was also a chapel on the south side of the courtyard, with the unusual feature of a polygonal east end.

Caergwrle (Flintshire)

In 1277, in addition to the cantrefi of Dyffryn Clwyd and Rhufoniog, Dafydd ap Gruffudd was granted the lordship of Hopedale, a narrow strip of land within the cantref of Tegeingl, bordering Powys Fadog to the south and south west and Cheshire to the east. Roughly in the centre of the lordship, at Caergwrle, close to the River Alyn, Dafydd began to build a castle, Edward making a donation of 100 marks towards its construction, on 12 November 1278.[8] This castle (which in the Middle Ages was known as Hope, the name of the neighbouring village some ¾ mile distant) is now much ruined, but, excavation of the entire inner enclosure in 1988–90, went some way to elucidating what had been one of the most enigmatic of the baronial castles raised in the aftermath of the Welsh wars.[9]

Dafydd's castle occupies the 450ft (137m) high summit of a hill situated at the south-east end of the village of Caergwrle, where it serves as a visual termination to High Street, the continuation of which skirts around the base of the hill on its way to Wrexham. The remains of the buildings are represented by a small, stone-built enclosure on the western edge of the hill (Figure 5.4); attached to its eastern side, sloping down from the castle, is a much larger banked enclosure which has its origins in the late Roman or post-Roman period.[10] It is probable that this earlier enclosure was utilised by the builders and/or inhabitants of the later castle.

The inner ward, of which the entire western side has been lost through quarrying, is separated from the outer enclosure by a rock-cut ditch and counter scarp bank, which cut off the south-west corner of the hill containing the summit. Within this, the curtain wall was built on a plinth with a pitched coping, now mostly robbed, although a fragment survives at the west end of the north curtain. Projecting from the east curtain are the remains of two wall towers, the North Tower at the north-east angle, and the East Tower at the south-east angle, pointing towards the north east and south east respectively. At the south-west angle of the enclosure was a great tower of circular plan, now almost entirely quarried away, although a short length of its coped plinth, similar in character to that of the north curtain, survives at its junction with the south curtain. Finally, an irregularly polygonal (four-sided) buttress turret projects roughly from the centre of the east curtain, marking a change in direction.

The position of the gateway is unknown. It cannot have been to the precipitous western side, nor was it in the south curtain, nor is there any trace of it in the extant sections of the north and east curtains. It has been conjectured that an oval 'island' of unexcavated rock left standing in the middle of the ditch on the north side of the castle indicates a barbican. If that were the case, then the main entrance would have been at the north-west angle of the enceinte, its position

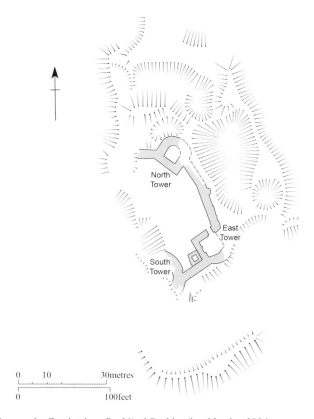

North
Tower

East
Tower

South
Tower

0   10   30metres

0   100feet

Figure 5.4: *Caergwrle. Castle plan. By Nigel Dodds after Manley 1994*

now quarried away.[11] However, excavation of a section across the ditch and
'island' has proved inconclusive. The only other possible site for a gateway is on
the east side, between the upstanding section of wall and the North Tower, which
has indeed been conjectured as a possibility.[12] The excavations showed that the
west face of the curtain extended all the way to the North Tower with which it
was bonded. This doesn't preclude a gateway in this section, because it might
have had a raised threshold, but, since there is no sign of a substantial gatehouse
structure, we should expect there to have been no more than an opening in the
curtain at this point.

Both the North and East towers were D-shaped but of uncommon form, the
prows being short segmental arcs instead of the more usual semi-circles, so that
they meet the side walls at an angle rather than segue into them in the smooth
curve that was conventional in both English and Welsh castles. The east side of
the East Tower continued the line of the east curtain, and the prow formed a
bulge in the south curtain, but was otherwise wholly within the enclosure. This
tower rose at least as high as, and probably higher than, the attached curtains. It
was entered at basement level from the north via a high arched doorway, which

seems unnecessarily large for its purpose, having more of the character of a gateway than a doorway. Inside, the basement was pentagonal, and, against the west wall, are the remains of a substantial and ornate fireplace with moulded bases carrying triple-shafted jambs, a type unparalleled in any other Welsh castle, nor one that was in use in contemporary English castles in north Wales. Access to the now destroyed upper floor was via a spiral staircase in the north-east angle of the tower.

There is no visible access to the North Tower at courtyard level, so the basement would have been entered from above, and the tower most likely had a first-floor entrance in the south-west wall, from which a wall passage led to a two-seater latrine within the adjacent north wall, and a spiral staircase at the junction of tower and curtain that must have risen to the roof of the tower and perhaps the alure of the curtain. Unlike the East Tower, neither storey had a polygonal interior, and the curve of the exterior was replicated inside. The basement was no more than a storage space, the upper room providing the main residential accommodation. It had a large fireplace against the north-west wall and, to either side of the flue at the height of the mantelbeam, a massive square opening extending through the wall. These have been interpreted as beam slots to carry the fireplace hood, though why such substantial beams should have been required is inexplicable; it's a unique but seemingly unnecessary arrangement.[13]

At the south-west angle are indications of a great tower, or keep. Round towers straddling the curtain are in the Welsh tradition, but the corner position of the Caergwrle tower and its apparent size is distinctive. The diameter has been estimated at *c.* 17–18m (56–59ft).[14] Even at the lower estimate this was a tower of substantial proportions, surpassing all other native Welsh round towers, as well as the major English constructions of an earlier period such as Conisbrough (Yorkshire) and Pembroke. It would have been only slightly smaller than the broadly contemporary keep of Hawarden (see below, this chapter). As in the case of Hawarden, the 11½ft (3.5m) thick walls were substantial enough to have accommodated staircases, passages, and chambers, and the tower is likely to have housed the principal residential accommodation in the castle. Unfortunately, owing to the building's almost total destruction, no further details of its design are ever likely to be forthcoming, but, sited as it was on the high point of the hill, it was evidently intended to be conspicuous. It would have been particularly so from the south as it was approached from Wrexham, thrust forward as it was at the left-hand (west) end of the south front. It was a clear territorial marker at the centre of the lordship of Hopedale.

King saw Caergwrle Castle as an architectural hybrid, reflecting Dafydd's ambiguous political loyalties, neither entirely Welsh nor entirely English.[15] The spiral staircases and the polygonal interior of the East Tower were considered

English traits, although they can be paralleled in the keep of Dolbadarn and the inner gatehouse of Criccieth respectively, both works of Dafydd's grandfather, Llywelyn Fawr, both of which are said to have been influenced by English models. The flanking properties of the North Tower were also considered English rather than Welsh, although towers that would have provided flanking fire are known at a number of Welsh castles. Other elements were considered to be of Welsh origin, including the two-seater latrine and the lack of flanking provided by the East Tower.

Whilst round towers are not uncommon in the castles of the princes of Gwynedd, only in the case of Dolbadarn could such a structure be described as a great tower or keep. At Caergwrle Dafydd eschewed the rectangular keep that is found in numerous native castles in Gwynedd, most recently at Dolforwyn (1273–7) and instead emulated the cylindrical great towers of the English. It was no coincidence, perhaps, that at roughly the same time, keeps of this general form were also adopted at Hawarden and Flint some 6 and 13 miles from Caergwrle respectively.

Most of the architectural features have been lost, but dressed stone recovered during the excavation represent a number of conventional thirteenth-century details, including elements of a doorway with a two-centred chamfered arch, narrow rectangular windows with chamfered surrounds, and fragments of dog-tooth ornament, roll moulding, and newel stair steps. The portion of dog tooth is interesting in that it is absent from any of the other Edwardian castles and might be said to have been rather old fashioned by 1278.

Hawarden (Flintshire)

The third castle that emerged in the aftermath of the first Welsh War was at Hawarden, to the north of Caergwrle. At the time of the 1277 invasion Hawarden was in the custody of the Crown, its lord, Robert de Montalt (also Monthaut, Mohaut, Monte Alto) having died by 16 September 1275 when his heir, Roger (1262–*c.* 1304), was a minor. The reconstruction of the castle may have been begun with Edward's encouragement either by Maurice de Craon, who relinquished custody of the Montalt estate in June 1280, or, more probably, by Roger de Clifford (d. 1286), who was granted custody of the lordships of Mold and Hawarden on 15 January 1281.[16] It is probable that construction work had started by the spring of 1282 when the castle was attacked and burnt by Dafydd ap Gruffudd in the opening act of the Second Welsh War, Caergwrle no doubt acting as the springboard of the assault. However, the details (see below) suggest a date later than 1282 for much of the superstructure giving reason to suppose that work may have carried on into the 1290s.

Built on the site of a castle destroyed by Llywelyn ap Gruffudd in 1265, substantial earthworks comprising a motte and bailey surrounded by a ditch already existed, and were to determine the form of the new stone castle. Two major stone phases are evident, the first of which is characterised by rubble masonry in common with most of the Edwardian castles of north Wales, and which includes the curtain wall, the great hall, and the keep. The second phase is denoted by the use of high-quality ashlar with many well-preserved masons' marks, and includes the addition of a substantial outwork or barbican, which extended across the ditch from the bailey curtain to the counters carp bank, a block of domestic buildings in the bailey at the foot of the motte, and a large rectangular extrusion from the east curtain. These additions to the fabric, though extensive, are heavily ruined, which hinders interpretation, but they suggest an ambitious upgrading of the castle, and probably date from the fourteenth century and the tenure of the earls of Salisbury, who held the castle from 1338.

Our concern, then, is principally with the first stone phase, comprising keep, curtain, and hall. The two-storey keep, which caps the motte, is cylindrical, a natural enough choice for a motte, for which there were several precedents. Wing walls extended down the motte slope to join a curtain, made up of several straight lengths, enclosing an irregularly shaped bailey. The only evidence for the existence of wall towers is the stump of a small round tower with a solid ground storey at the south-east angle. The main entrance was at the north-east corner, and the hall was built against the east curtain.

The hall was immediately north of the wall tower, two tall windows and the jamb of a third in the east curtain attesting to its position at first-floor level (Figure 5.5). The windows are single lancet lights with trefoil cusped heads and segmental-pointed rear embrasures, with beaded surrounds, containing stone benches. A row of corbels supported the sleeper beam that carried the first-floor timbers. Between the windows, just above the springing of the rear arches, are two blocked vertical chases, apparently to accommodate wall posts associated with the roof structure. Above the windows another row of corbels, which does not correspond with the window bays, is probably an alteration. At the south end of the hall is the scar of a transverse wall, and, below it, the richly moulded but heavily eroded jamb of a doorway. Its high quality suggests an entrance to a chamber block, of which there is no longer any other trace.

The keep, which is the principal element, is amongst the largest of its type in Britain with a diameter of 59ft (18m) above the battered base (Figure 5.6). The entrance, at motte level, is set within a (much restored) shallow two-storey projection with a pitched stone roof, or cap, flanked on either side by narrower and lower 'wings' with two-tier pitched stone caps. It is a more elaborate version of the surround to the Watergate at Caernarfon of *c*. 1283, which gives access to the basement of the Eagle Tower. The Hawarden entrance, which is the only access to the keep, has chamfered jambs and a heavily restored double-chamfered

Figure 5.5: *Hawarden. Great hall from the west.*

segmental-pointed arch; above it, at first-floor level, a moderately wide rectangular window lights the room that formerly housed the portcullis mechanism. The portcullis had square grooves terminating 3ft above the floor, behind which there was a barred door. Beyond this, still within the entrance passage, shouldered-lintel doorways to the left (south) and right (north) led to a spiral staircase and a barrel-vaulted porter's lodge respectively.

The entrance passage continues to the ground-floor room, a bare circular space lit by three light shafts with high sills and shouldered-lintel embrasures. Something of the nature of the first floor is denoted by a series of closely-set corbels for supporting a ring beam. On the north-west side about 3ft (1m) above current floor level is a two-tier corbel, and, directly opposite, the scar of another. They do not correspond with the corbels above, but rather with gaps between them. They either supported a pair of timber posts and braces associated with a beam or they represent the remains of a stone arch or arcade spanning the basement. The internal diameter of 31ft could have been bridged by a single timber, but, given that this is quite a lengthy span, it is perhaps more probable that there were two lengths with the inner ends supported on a pier or post.

The staircase led first to the portcullis chamber, which communicated with the main first-floor room via a door which could be barred from the inside, but the main access was through a doorway at the top of the staircase into a

Figure 5.6: *Hawarden. Great tower from the east.*

mural passage that extended around the western half of the tower, following the lines of the octagonal central chamber. This passage had a slab roof carried on two tiers of convex quarter-round corbels, a form that is paralleled in the royal castle of Caernarfon in work undertaken from 1295 onwards, though the general principle of slab-supporting corbelling was employed at Caernarfon from the start. The main entrance to the central room was through the south window embrasure, a wide rectangular space with segmental pointed vault; there is a third entrance at the end of the mural passage on the north side of the keep. The entrances to and from the passage on each side of the south embrasure are rather unusual. Only the eastern doorway retains its head, but it is to be assumed that the two were of uniform design. They appear to have been innovative interpretations of the shouldered lintel, with short verticals and the arc of the shoulder shallower and more elongated. Also unusual are the convex quarter-round moulded surrounds, a moulding that is shared with a cinquefoil-headed doorway in the south-east face of the room, the entrance to a mural chapel, or oratory (Figures 5.7 and 5.8).

The keep shares a number of characteristics with the great tower of Flint, suggesting that the same influence was at work in the design of the two buildings. Firstly, the entrance passage gives direct access to the lower storey, at Flint via a flight of steps, at Hawarden directly. Secondly, in both cases the entrance passage

Figure 5.7 (above left): *Hawarden. Doorways to the south window embrasure of the keep.*

Figure 5.8 (above right): *Hawarden. Great tower chapel doorway from the south.*

Figure 5.9: *Hawarden. Postern at the junction of great tower and curtain from the south east.*

gave access to a staircase leading to the upper floor. It has already been suggested that, like Hawarden, the great tower of Flint probably had a central room ringed by a mural passage at basement level and by a succession of rooms at first-floor level. Although the Hawarden keep doesn't have this outer ring of rooms it does instead have a mural passage extending around half the upper storey. It's an arrangement that seems to represent a concept similar to that evident at Flint, but, as will be described later, something of this nature is also to be observed at Caernarfon, where mural communication passages are to be found in the curtains as well as several of the towers. The connection with Caernarfon, where the shouldered lintel was employed most extensively, is interesting in that this form was also the most common type of doorway to be encountered at Hawarden (Figure 5.9).

Baronial Castles in the South

Caerphilly

Llywelyn's rebellion freed the Earl of Gloucester from any constraints on the completion of his castle of Caerphilly. The chronology of this later work cannot be dated any more closely than the last quarter of the thirteenth century, but the resumption of work affected three main areas: improvements to the principal domestic accommodation; the conversion of the two gateways to the Middle Ward into gatehouses proper; and additions to the north front, including the construction of the main outer gatehouse, the north dam, and the consequent creation of the north lake.

The work on the main domestic suite included the construction of a new chamber block at the west end of the hall, a large D-shaped kitchen tower backing onto the external face of the inner curtain within the Middle Ward, and, at its north end, the Transverse Block, which contained a covered staircase leading from the great hall to a postern in the Middle Ward south curtain and giving access to the lake. The first floor of the chamber block was lit by tall, pointed windows of two trefoil-headed lights surmounted with a central quatrefoil; affinities with the north nave aisle windows of Tintern Abbey, built under the patronage of Roger Bigod, suggest a date in the last quarter of the thirteenth century.[17]

Probably at a slightly later date came the construction of the North Dam Platform and the creation of the north lake. The character of the north dam differed markedly from that of the earlier south dam, the main feature of which was the east front where an eight-bay sequence of vertical barrel vaults alternates with square buttresses, the whole structure having the appearance of an upturned bridge. In contrast, the main distinguishing feature of the north dam's east front is a series of semi-polygonal buttress towers built on square bases from which triangular spurs rise to clasp their canted corners (Figure 5.10).

The towers of the North Gate, South Gate, and Outer Main Gate, which give access to the South Dam Platform, North Dam Platform, and eastern island respectively, are also provided with spurs. The flanking towers of the North Gate and Main Outer Gate have semi-polygonal fronts, whilst those of the South Gate are D–Shaped, but all three, like the North Dam Platform turrets, were built on rectangular bases (Figure 5.11). This coupling of spurs with polygonal towers, which was to gain a degree of currency in the late thirteenth and fourteenth centuries, may have had its genesis here at Caerphilly. It is interesting to compare these features with the spurs of the Tonbridge gatehouse which ascend from irregularly polygonal bases; the Caerphilly spurs are more regular but lack the artistic elan of Tonbridge.

Figure 5.10: *Caerphilly. North Dam from the south east.*

Figure 5.11: *Caerphilly. Outer Main Gatehouse from the east.*

Figure 5.12: *Caerphilly. South Gatehouse, drawbridge axle groove.*

An unusual and therefore significant feature of all three gateways is the arrangement for fitting the drawbridge axle. The ends of the axle slid into horizontal grooves on either side of the gateway; the grooves then turned downwards at a 45-degree angle to reach the socket (Figure 5.12). The adoption of this scheme may have been intended to provide the axle with a more secure housing in order to prevent dislocation when raising or lowering. Its curious design implies that it is an invention stemming from personal experience, and its restricted distribution suggests that it is likely to be associated with a single master craftsman. The only comparable system to have been noted is in the Upper Gatehouse of Chepstow Castle, an addition datable to the tenure of Roger Bigod, fifth Earl of Norfolk (1270–1306), who made a number of improvements at the castle.[18] The Chepstow gatehouse itself may have been built in 1272–82, but the drawbridge was replaced in 1298–1300, so the axle housing could date to either of those periods.[19] However, there is a strong possibility that it represents the hand of the second master of the Caerphilly works.

The switch to polygonal towers at Caerphilly is intriguing, but, coupled with other changes of detail, may well represent a change of personnel, as might be expected after a hiatus in construction. Precedents for the north dam towers are hard to find, although there are analogues with a number of near contemporary structures in south Wales, notably Carreg Cennen Castle (Carmarthenshire), the chapel tower of Kidwelly Castle (Carmarthenshire), and the gatehouses of Ewenny Priory (Glamorgan), and although these buildings are likely to be broadly contemporary, their relative chronology is uncertain.

Chapter Six

Royal Castles of the Second Welsh War:
Conwy and Harlech

Summary Narrative

On the night of 21 March 1282 Dafydd ap Gruffudd launched a surprise attack on Hawarden, taking the castle and seizing its constable, Roger de Clifford, an episode that marks the beginning of the Second Welsh War.[1] The capture of Hawarden was accompanied by assaults on Flint, where 'certain houses' were burnt and a number of the King's men slain, and Rhuddlan, which was unsuccessfully besieged. In what seems to have been a co-ordinated action by the southern Welsh princes, Aberystwyth was captured on 24 March, and the town and castle subsequently burnt. Two days later, on 26 March, the castles of Llandovery and Carreg Cennen (Carmarthenshire) were recaptured by the sons of Rhys Gryg. Llywelyn ap Gruffud was drawn into the conflict and Edward was faced with a full-blown rebellion.

In the north, the counter-attack was launched some three months later, once troops had been assembled at Chester. A contingent under the command of Reginald de Grey, justice of Chester, advanced on the lordship of Hope, arriving at Dafydd's castle of Caergwrle on 16 June, only to find it slighted, and the well blocked with debris.[2] A task force of building workers under the command of Richard the Engineer was brought in swiftly to make the castle tenable. Whilst work was progressing on Caergwrle, Reginald de Grey continued the advance and by the end of the month had taken Ewloe Castle.

A few days later the King set out from Chester with the main expeditionary force, reaching Flint by 6 July and Rhuddlan by the 10th. At Rhuddlan, Edward established his forward base, which, for the next nine months, served as his principal residence and the administrative centre of the realm. The effects of the siege and the King's presence provided the impetus for additional works in and around the castle. By the end of August, de Grey had taken Ruthin and the castle that had been begun in 1277; the King himself was there from 31 August until 8 September, no doubt inspecting the castle site and giving directions for its completion. From Ruthin the English moved on to besiege Denbigh, which was captured on 16 October after a month's siege.

In the south, progress had been less satisfactory. Here, the English forces were under the command of Gilbert de Clare, Earl of Gloucester, his initial objective being to regain the lost castles and reassert control over Ystrad Tywi. On 16 June 1282 the English were ambushed by the Welsh at Llandeilo Fawr (Carmarthenshire) and heavily defeated. An emboldened Llywelyn took advantage of the situation and arrived in south Wales to stiffen resistance in the region. On 6 July Gloucester was replaced by William de Valence, Earl of Pembroke, and the English counter-attack was henceforth conducted with greater vigour. Even so, the rebellion raged throughout the summer and into October, only losing its impetus when Llywelyn withdrew to the north to deal with the growing danger to Gwynedd. By the end of the month the south west had been largely pacified.

Shortly after this Edward's campaign in the north suffered a setback. An army under the command of Luke de Tany had been landed on Anglesey with the objective of securing the island and building a bridge across the Menai Strait to facilitate an invasion of Gwynedd on two fronts. On 6 November part of the army crossed to the mainland where they were attacked by the Welsh and suffered a humiliating defeat, Tany himself being killed. This debacle must have boosted Welsh morale; attempts to negotiate a peaceful end to the conflict broke down, and Llywelyn once again took the fight to the enemy, appearing unexpectedly in south-east Wales, where the insurgents were still active. It proved to be Llywelyn's last military initiative, for on 11 December he was killed in a skirmish near Builth. Dafydd attempted to carry on alone, but the northern advance resumed, and a month after Llywelyn's death, on 18 January 1283, the castle of Dolwyddelan was captured. This was a both a symbolic victory, owing to the castle's association with the birthplace of Llywelyn Fawr, but also a strategic triumph, in that it secured communications into Snowdonia and Meirionnydd.

On 15 March Criccieth was taken, and in April attention focused on Castell-y-Bere, in Meirionnydd, where Dafydd was now centring his resistance. English forces advanced towards Bere from Montgomery and Aberystwyth under the commands of Roger Lestrange and William de Valence respectively, converging there on 15 April, when the castle was laid to siege. Ten days later the garrison surrendered, though Dafydd remained at liberty, retreating northward to Dolbadarn. Towards the end of the month Otto de Grandson, coming from Anglesey, occupied Harlech, thereby completing the encirclement of the north coast.

On 2 May 1283 Dafydd was at his last stronghold of Dolbadarn; it cannot have been much later than this that the castle was captured and Dafydd became a rootless fugitive. He was captured on 21 June and executed in Shrewsbury on 2 October. Defeat was followed by the complete annexation of Gwynedd and the construction of three new royal castles at Conwy, Caernarfon, and Harlech. Royal works were carried out at a number of captured Welsh castles including Dolwyddelan, Criccieth, Dolforwyn, and Castell-y-Bere. New lordships were created centred on Chirk, Holt, and Denbigh, at each of which the construction of a castle was begun.

The Native Welsh Castles

Several of the captured Welsh castles were retained by the King, including Caergwrle, Dolwyddelan, Castell-y-Bere, Criccieth, and Dolbadarn. Dolwyddelan had a symbolic value in its association with Llywelyn Fawr, but was also strategically placed, and able to keep a watchful eye over the road from Meirionnydd to the south; Dolbadarn guarded the Llanberis Pass; Criccieth would take its place as a link in the chain of royal castles that were to extend around the coast from Flint to Aberystwyth. In several cases building works ensued very soon after they had been taken. In some instances this may have been to repair damage sustained during a siege, in others to bring the domestic accommodation up to an acceptable standard. Only in a few instances, however, is there much tangible evidence regarding the character of such works.

One thing that we can have a degree of confidence about is the new 'camera' that was built at Dolwyddelan in 1283–4 to augment the limited accommodation in the great tower.[3] This can probably be identified with what is now known as the 'West Tower', a two-storey building of rectangular plan which occupied the north–west angle of the enclosure immediately adjacent to the gateway, its north and west walls being formed by the curtain, against which the south and west walls abut. Although the building is largely ruined, the east elevation, which survives almost to full height, retains a large segmental-arched entrance to the left (south) formerly secured by a barred gate, and a window to the right (east) at ground-floor level, and another window to the left-hand (south) end of the first floor.

Otherwise, the rubble walling is devoid of openings and it is to be assumed that the upper floor received most of its light from the west. A single rectangular loop survives in the west wall of the ground-floor room. A latrine turret was added to the outside face of the west wall (curtain) to serve the upper storey, the lower floor having the benefit of an existing latrine within the north wall. Inside the building, large joist sockets in the east wall denote the position of the first floor. Above them are the remains of a large hooded fireplace with a rounded back. This seems to be a simpler version of the standard types used in the Edwardian castles, and its presence goes some way to explaining the limited fenestration on this side.

The West Tower may have been intended as the residence of the newly appointed constable, Gruffudd ap Tudur. The keep, however, would have been reserved for the King and other important guests, and there is some reason to believe that it was Edward who raised it in height, thereby making the castle more visible and reinforcing the message that it had a new master.

English work at other Welsh castles is less easy to identify. At Caergwrle (Hope), where around £300 was spent by the King in 1282, one of the first to arrive at the castle was Master Richard of Chester, who, as Richard the Engineer, had played a key role at Rhuddlan and Flint. He took charge from 16 June, and was therefore probably attached to the army that took the castle on the same day.[4]

A contingent of 340 carpenters arrived on 21 June and a further large body 4 days later. Between 25 and 30 June there was an average of 479 carpenters at Caergwrle and between 1 and 4 July an average of 359.5. The greater number then moved on leaving little more than a skeleton crew of less than ten for the rest of the season. There was a similar influx of diggers at around the same time. They were on the payroll from 18 June to 4 July, when there was a daily average of about 337, the numbers peaking at 423 for the three days 20–3 June and never falling below 300 until 4 July, after which they disappear from the records entirely, their departure coinciding with that of Richard the engineer.[5]

In contrast to these large but brief concentrations of carpenters and diggers, a more compact group of masons, averaging 35 in number, was on site from 18 June, maintaining a constant presence until the beginning of November. During the first week in July the King, and, seemingly, James of St George, were at Caergwrle, Master James directing the mason Henry of Turvey to bring down the 'tower of Hope'.[6] This was presumably the great round tower, and what is probably meant is a lowering of the building rather than total demolition, given that it formed part of the defensive circuit. The implication is that the keep had been slighted and was in a dangerous enough condition to render necessary a degree of controlled demolition; it seems likely that some rebuilding followed. From 4 July the masons were under the supervision of Master James's appointee, Master Ralph of Nottingham, but little else is known about their activities at Caergwrle.

Clues as to how the other workers were occupied are also thin on the ground. A handful of the diggers was detailed to assist the masons between 18 and 23 June, but there is no indication as to how the vast bulk of them was employed. It has been argued that their main effort may have been directed at strengthening the putative north entrance by creating a barbican within a widening of the ditch.[7] This is a possibility, but, given the lack of evidence regarding the construction sequence, can be no more than conjecture.

The extent of the carpentry work is only slightly less of a mystery. Presuming that Dafydd had destroyed the castle's timber buildings, there would have been an immediate need for domestic accommodation, workshops, and outbuildings, and it is possible that the large workforce that was concentrated here in June and early July was so engaged. The few instances relating to carpentry work to be gleaned from the accounts dates from the period after 4 July when the bulk of the workforce had departed. There are references to timber and boards for covering and constructing a chamber over the great gate, and to the new upper gate of the castle, but little else that can be unambiguously attributed to the carpenters.

The covering of the walls at the end of the season implies that the masonry work was not yet complete and that it was intended to continue the following spring. By then the castle had been granted to the Queen and any further building operations ceased to be the direct responsibility of the Crown.

Following the capture of Castell-y-Bere in April 1283, Master Bertram, together with a small number of masons and carpenters, was charged with carrying out certain works there. What these consisted of is unknown, but, it is generally accepted that the walls of the Ditch Yard belong to this period.

The works carried out at Criccieth in 1283–4 were reasonably substantial, but no individual items are recorded, there is nothing that can be ascribed to Edward on architectural grounds alone, and it is probable that there was no major change to the character of the castle. Repairs and alterations probably included the reconstruction of the South-East Tower, the construction of flights of stone steps to the North and South-West towers and the raising of the Inner Gatehouse.

The New Castles: Conwy and Harlech

Conwy (Carnarvonshire)

Immediately west of the Four Cantrefi (Dyffryn Clwyd, Rhos, Rhufoniog, and Tegeingl) the Henrician border castle of Deganwy, which was sited on the east side of the River Conwy, was replaced by a new castle on the west bank, with more immediate access to the estuary, and where a settlement was already in existence. Amongst the buildings of Welsh Aberconwy were the Abbey of St Mary and a princely residence. Some 500ft to the north east of the abbey church (now the parish Church of St Mary), on the edge of the River Conwy, and flanked on

Figure 6.1: *Conwy. The castle from the south west.*

its south side by the River Gyffin, was a rocky elevated site of considerable natural strength, which, in the circumstances, appeared to be an ideal situation for a fortress, and it was duly requisitioned for that purpose. Llywelyn's house was appropriated, no doubt serving as a temporary domicile for the King, and incorporated into the new town that accompanied the castle, where for some years it remained known as 'Llywelyn's Hall', perhaps in patronising commemoration of a doughty but vanquished foe (Figure 6.1).

Although strategic and tactical considerations were no doubt foremost in the choice of location, there was, in addition, a symbolic benefit to Aberconwy, firstly in its association with Welsh princely power, and, secondly, because the abbey was the foundation and burial place of Llywelyn ab Iorwerth. Edward's seizure of the abbey and the removal of the monks, together with Llywelyn's remains, to a replacement site at Maenan, some 20 miles further up the estuary, clearly demonstrated the eclipse of the house of Gwynedd and the power of the new regime over its most illustrious member even in death.

The castle went up with astonishing rapidity. Workmen were being recruited by March 1283, Richard the Engineer playing a major part in the preparation, and, by November 1285, after only two building seasons, the enceinte had been carried up to at least wall walk level.[8] The following year the main domestic buildings were finished, and, by the end of 1287, after which expenditure dropped dramatically, the castle must have been substantially complete, although some work continued until 1290.[9] Meanwhile, in tandem with the raising of the castle, the town defences had been under construction, but, in contrast to Flint and Rhuddlan, where new towns had also accompanied the castles, here at Conwy the defences were built in stone. The initial phase of the walls was under construction during the accounting period November 1284 to November 1285, and the circuit was probably completed within three years.

The plan of the castle is dictated by the site, a rocky ridge, located at the confluence of the two watercourses, the summit of which is some 120m (400ft) in length from east to west with an average width of about 30m (100ft) (Figure 6.2). Consequently, it is a comparatively narrow complex, slightly more spacious towards the west where the south curtain bulges outwards in following the irregular edge of the rock. The castle comprises an inner (east) and an outer (west) ward surrounded by eight round wall towers, with a courtyard barbican at each end, both furnished with open-backed turrets. The main entrance was into the east barbican, whilst a postern gave pedestrian access to the west barbican from the river. From the exterior, Conwy exudes an intimidating aura of military power, a sense that is enhanced by its domineering position on the hard, uncompromising rock.

Within the town walls, where they joined the north and west sides of the castle, was a rock-cut moat, which had to be negotiated in order to attain the main entrance. This was achieved in a spectacular and forbidding fashion via a flying

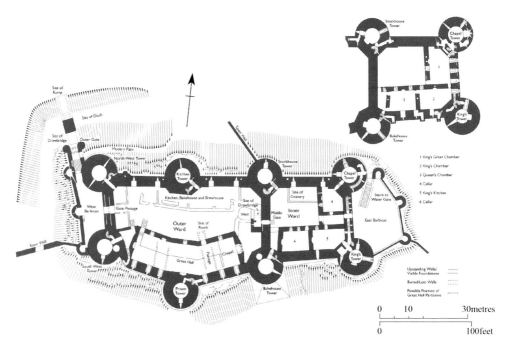

Figure 6.2: *Conwy. Castle plan. © Crown copyright (2018) Cadw, Welsh Government*

ramp or staircase (which acted as the main route into the castle until the early twentieth century, although now only the southern end survives), and then across a drawbridge to the twin-towered outer gatehouse (Figure 6.3). In addition to the drawbridge, the outer gatehouse was protected by a portcullis. Beyond this a staircase rose to a two-leaved gate into the west barbican. The line of approach to the outer ward then took a right-angled turn through a gateway in the west curtain, a principle that was adopted at Caernarfon and Denbigh as well.

Although the gateway itself is a simple pointed opening it was strongly defended, firstly, by the two western corner towers, which flank and overlook the gateway, and, secondly, by a machicolated parapet carried on six tiers of corbels, an early and extravagant form of this type, which extended all the way along the west curtain (Figure 6.4); and, thirdly, by a portcullis and barred gate within the entrance passage. This elongated entrance complex was a tightly controlled sequence of defendable barriers, displaying an intensity of purpose that is absent from the royal castles of the First Welsh War, a consequence, perhaps, of the changed circumstances in which a policy of containment had been replaced by the conquest and colonisation of the Gwynedd heartlands.

Superficially, the security precautions governing access to the inner ward from the outer ward now seem perfunctory in comparison but, in reality, they were stringent. The two wards are separated, firstly, by a rock-cut ditch, and, secondly, by a 3m (10ft) thick wall. Access to the inner ward was across an L-shaped

Figure 6.3: *Conwy. Outer gatehouse from the north east with the truncated ramp in the foreground.*

Figure 6.4: *Conwy. West barbican showing the arched entrance to the outer ward with the remains of the machicolated parapet above (1283–90).*

bridge to a square barbican, the entrance to which was in its northern side. The eastern end of the bridge could be raised from the barbican, fitting into a recess in front of the entrance. Therefore, after crossing the ditch on the fixed bridge there was a 90-degree turn to the right (south) over the drawbridge and into the barbican. Once inside, there was another 90-degree turn to the left (east) to a simple pedestrian entrance piercing the cross-wall, which was closed by a double-barred gate.

At the eastern end of the castle there was a more private entrance from the River Conwy to a postern gate in the north wall of the east barbican. Access was via a water gate situated beneath the middle tower of the barbican, which opened to a flight of steps winding around the rock to the postern being protected by a screen wall and 'a small covered hanging tower'.[10] Inside the barbican the eastern gateway leading to the inner ward was protected by a machicolated parapet similar in character to its western counterpart, and a barred gate, but the opening, which has a corbelled lintel rather than an arch, is lower and narrower, very much a back door, and the large first-floor windows of the royal apartments (widened beneath the machicolations) give the elevation more of a domestic character. There was a garden here, and the space was evidently a recreational area for the royal party.

The principal feature of the outer ward is the great hall range which occupies the entire south side, its long curving frontage bending in sympathy with the line of the curtain. Towards the courtyard (north) it was lit by three widely spaced pointed windows, each of two cusped lights surmounted by a quatrefoil (Figure 6.5, a); they may denote three internal divisions. The main entrance lies to the left (east) of centre, which, if the conventions of later medieval planning were followed, would have led into an entrance passage screened off from the lower end of the hall. The extent of the great hall is probably to be gauged by the position of two fireplaces, a large elaborate one in the south wall and a smaller one in the north wall; the purpose of the latter was to heat the dais and the high table. A third fireplace, in the west wall of the range, lit a smaller, more private room separated from the hall by a wooden partition. All the rooms in the hall range were lit to the south by plain, rectangular windows; these, together with the northern windows have segmental-rounded rear arches and stone benches within the embrasures.

The eastern end of the range has been identified as a chapel on the basis of its orientation and large east window. This opening, which has a semi-circular arch, is of three lancet lights each containing a cusped head surmounted by a trefoil (Figure 6.5, b). Taylor has drawn attention to the similarity between its tracery and that of the west window of Lausanne Cathedral of *c.* 1275, and has also linked the character of its arch with Savoyard practices, implying that the design is to be assigned to Master James.[11] Apart from this large window, there is little sign that the east end served as a chapel. It seems to have had similar window seats to the great hall and there is no trace of an integral piscina. However, neither does it contain a fireplace to indicate a domestic function.

The inner ward was given over to the royal apartments which are built against the east and south walls. In both ranges the windows have square heads set beneath segmental relieving arches, but the character of the tracery varies. Those of the south range each contain two trefoil-headed lights surmounted by three encircled trefoils beneath a pointed arch with trefoils in the spandrels (Figure 6.5, c). The design of this tracery is broadly in line with the style of the hall-range tracery, using a different combination of the same figures, except that the trefoils are encircled whilst those of the hall are unencumbered.

At the time that the Conwy apartments were being raised, designers of window tracery were moving from encircled to free geometric figures.[12] The tracery of the south range, then, is typologically earlier than that of the hall range. What this means in practical terms is uncertain, because we know that these buildings were raised simultaneously. There may have been a symbolic reason for the difference in treatment; perhaps the more elaborate (and therefore more costly) windows were considered more appropriate for the higher status of the Queen's Chamber, whilst the more modern but sparer (and therefore less costly) tracery was thought to be good enough for the hall.

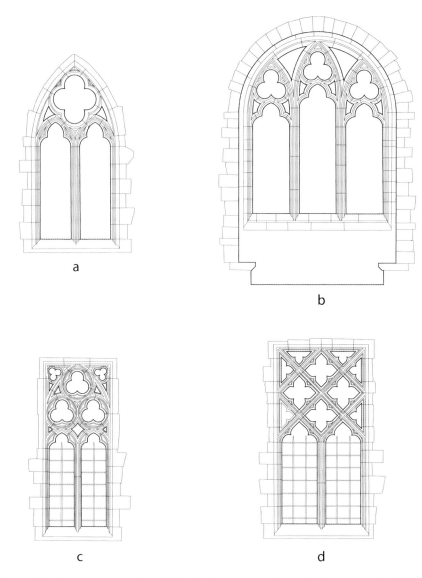

Figure 6.5: *Conwy reconstructions of the window tracery: a) great hall range south windows; b) great hall range east window; c) Queen's chamber; d) King's great chamber (1284–5).*

Such a theory would encompass the tracery of the window in the King's Great Chamber in the east range, which was different again, having a pattern of particular originality and modernity. The tracery above the two trefoil-headed lights is based on a rotated square quartered by the superimposition of a St Andrew's cross, the cusped bars creating a centrepiece of four pointed quatrefoils, and a border of smaller demi-quatrefoils (Figure 6.5, d). Repetitive geometrical designs of the late thirteenth century are often forerunners of the reticulated tracery of the Decorated period, but the

Conwy window is rather unusual in its angularity and in the emphasis placed on the centrepiece. Parallels are difficult to bring to mind, but its originality suggests that it may represent a design peculiar to Master James. In this regard it is worth considering the early thirteenth-century rose window in the south transept of Lausanne Cathedral as a possible model (Figure 6.6). The tracery pattern of this purely Geometric window is based on a series of superimposed circles and, unusually, squares. A large square forms the base figure within the circular frame, and a smaller square, rotated to an angle of forty-five degrees, forms the centrepiece of the composition, just as it does at Conwy. It only takes a short flight of the imagination to see the Lausanne rose as the progenitor of the Conwy window. That there should be two references to Lausanne at Conwy seems to confirm that the window tracery was determined by Master James. The rose is one of the outstanding aspects of Lausanne Cathedral, considered by Villard de Honnecourt to be worthy of recording in a somewhat free interpretation when he visited the building in the 1230s. So too might Master James have noted it down in own sketchbook, for future consultation.[13]

Figure 6.6: *Lausanne Cathedral. Rose window in the south transept (c. 1220).*

Another interesting aspect of the royal apartments is that although they had been planned from the outset (to judge by the provision of the first-floor windows, which, on the south side, gave access to mural latrines), they weren't built as originally anticipated. A change of plan occurred that resulted in the west wall of the east range being built across a ground-floor window, and the partition wall of the south range across a first-floor window. Why this should have been deemed expedient is unclear, but the anomaly lays bare the fluidity of planning in the Middle Ages, and also the structural compromises that are to be found in many large-scale building projects of the period. These irregularities apart, the design of the inner ward is an interesting example of integrated castle planning, even though the overall result didn't quite live up to the intention. The network of passages, staircases, lobbies, and antechambers that communicated between the main spaces to serve particular purposes are testament to the technical skill required of a master builder working at this social level.

The east and south ranges of the royal apartments rose through two storeys with the principal residential accommodation at first-floor level: the King's Great Chamber occupying the full extent of the east range and the King's Chamber and Queen's Chamber arranged east and west respectively in the south range. There were lesser rooms beneath them, including a kitchen under the King's Chamber, each with its own external entrance. The public entrances to the royal apartments, both of which survive, were at first-floor level, at the south and west ends of the east and south ranges respectively, being reached via external staircases, no longer extant. Behind the scenes, however, these rooms could be reached by a number of different routes allowing for privacy, convenience, and service.

Straight staircases within the east curtain extend from both sides of the eastern gate passage. To the south, a short flight and passage communicated with the King's (south-east) Tower, where a spiral staircase ascended to the upper storeys of the tower and south range, and with the kitchen. To the north a more lengthy flight rose to the first-floor of the Chapel (north-east) Tower. This north-eastern junction is of particular note for the complications involved in its internal design. At first-floor level a door in the north-east corner of the King's Great Chamber opened to a passage leading across the east curtain stairhead to a landing with access to a stair in the wall of the tower communicating with its basement, a spiral stair leading to the upper levels of the tower, and the chapel itself which occupies the first floor of the tower. Doorways at the ends of the passage both led north west to an irregularly polygonal vestibule, or lobby, and thence to a latrine in the north curtain. The spiral staircase ascended first to a small barrel-vaulted chamber within the thickness of the tower wall. This was the King's private pew, overlooking the chapel; it also had access to a latrine. Proficiency in the intricacies of planning was the hallmark of the competent master builder. Such practicalities are unglamorous, and often overlooked, but are nevertheless essential requisites in the process of turning the broadly expressed instructions of the patron into tangible form.

The chapel itself, which was completed during the 1285–6 season, had a circular nave, and whilst this reflected the form of the tower, the location is unusual enough to suggest that it may have been chosen deliberately for this reason. The circular form was favoured by the Templars and Hospitallers, probably for its associations with the Church of the Holy Sepulchre in Jerusalem. In view of Edward's interest in, and practical experience of, the Holy Land, where he had worked with the military orders, the round chapel of Conwy may perhaps be owed a place on the short list of medieval churches of this form, whose general character can be traced back to Palestine.[14]

The chancel, which has a polygonal apse, is set within the thickness of the wall and lit to the east by three lancet windows, each with its own embrasure; it is the most elaborately decorated space within the castle, although the ashlar details are now much eroded and the details difficult to discern. The walls are articulated vertically by eight moulded and banded shafts, and horizontally by a trefoil-headed arcade of niched sedilia (Figure 6.7); the shafts carry the ribs of a two-bay vault, the wall ribs forming an upper arcade of lancets. To the south a mural vestry was provided with a squint towards the chancel.

Apart from the ornamentation of the chapel the other principal architectural details in the castle are the fireplaces. In the towers they followed a standard design, having chamfered jambs curving forward at the head to form flat-faced corbels. Between them were keyless segmental arches surmounted by a chamfered mantle-string, above which rose the hood (Figure 6.8). In the great hall they were rather more elaborate; the corbels supporting the hoods were two-tiered, and there were triangular

Figure 6.7: *Conwy. Detail of the chapel sedilia arcade (1285–6).*

sconce brackets to either side of the arch supported on faceted inverted bell-shaped corbels. The arrangement seems somewhat over-engineered, but appears to be part of the original design, the sconce corbel, upper hood corbel, and lower part of the sconce bracket being carved from a single stone (Figure 6.9).

In considering the architectural details, it is notable that amongst the door and window heads, the pointed arch is only evident in the great hall, where the door and windows in the north side of the courtyard are so treated, and in the eastern lancets of the chapel. In the royal lodgings nearly all the windows appear to have been square headed, the smaller ones in the south range having a cusped inner order and sunken spandrels (Figure 6.10). Generally, masonry details are plain, sometimes to the extent of looking slapdash, and perhaps a testament to budgetary considerations. In several instances doorway lintels are nothing more than roughly hewn monoliths, distinguishable from the surrounding rubble walling only by their great size. There has been no attempt to emphasise or embellish the East and Middle gates, the flat heads of which are carried on plain corbels.

The main circuit of the town defences encloses a sub-triangular area of around 21 acres (8.5ha), making it the largest in extent of all the Edwardian towns that accompanied the castles. The presence of the River Conwy, which flows from south to north, and its tributary the Gyffin, which flowed from west to east, provided two natural barriers and strategic resources, which were taken into account and put to use in positioning the town walls.

Figure 6.8: *Conwy. Fireplace in the Kitchen Tower.*

Figure 6.9 (above): *Conwy. Fireplace in the great hall.*

Figure 6.10 (right): *Conwy. Window in the Queen's Chamber.*

The defensive circuit incorporates three twin-towered gateways (east, west, and south) and twenty-one wall towers, and a postern on the south side gives pedestrian access to the quay. A salient containing a postern extends the northern line of the circuit towards the east as far as the River Conwy, thereby protecting the north end of the quay; the southern end was protected by the castle from which a second salient extended southwards to the river. Most of the towers are D-shaped and open backed; those at the angles three-quarters round (Figure 6.11).[15]

All three of the gatehouses to the town are similar in having central gateways recessed between a pair of bow-fronted flanking towers. These latter are mostly D-shaped, but the south tower of the Mill Gate is three-quarters round, a result of being awkwardly positioned between two staggered sections of the south wall. The gatehouse facades are reminiscent of the inner gateways of Rhuddlan

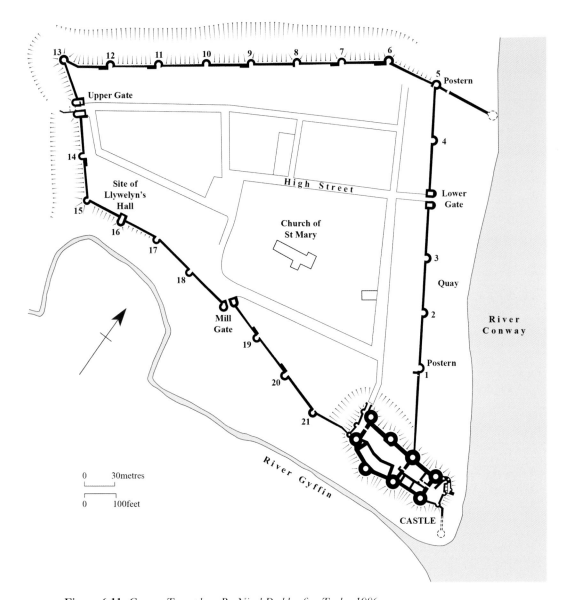

Figure 6.11: *Conwy. Town plan. By Nigel Dodds after Taylor 1986*

(Figure 4.12). The largest of the three was the Upper Gate, the approach to which was protected by a passage barbican of which a large fragment survives on the south side. In front of the gate was a drawbridge pit, and, within the gate passage, a portcullis and then barred gates. Beyond the gates the sides of the passage are splayed, widening towards the rear of the gatehouse, the only one of the three entrances to be so treated (Figure 6.12).

Figure 6.12: *Conwy. Upper Gate, town defences (1284–5).*

The defences were erected in three phases, the first of which is assigned to the accounting period 1284–5 and probably comprised the greater part of the north-western and south-western sections between the rivers Conwy (north-east) and Gyffin (south) from towers 6 to 15, and including the Upper (east) Gate (Porth Uchaf) and a short return of walling beyond Tower 15 ready to continue the defences along the south front. This first phase was followed, in 1285–6, by the construction of the southern section of the defences, including towers 16–21 and the Mill Gate (Porth-y-Felin), and, the following year, by the north-eastern section and a short northern section including towers 1–5 and the Lower Gate (Porth Isaf).

Only the builders of the southern stretch of the town defences are known by name. The greater part was raised by the mason John Francis and a number of associates. This is presumed to be the same John Francis who had worked at Chillon, Saillon, and at other sites for the Count of Savoy since the 1250s; if this is true, he was by this time a seasoned veteran and evidently a man to be relied upon. During the same season the John Francis consortium also built the now destroyed tower that terminated the wall extending from the south-east corner of the east barbican of the castle towards the Gyffin, and was subsequently employed on the Hospital of St John within the town.

The work carried out by John Francis and his colleagues on the south side of the defences included five wall towers (17–21), seven associated lengths of walling, and the Mill Gate, placed halfway along the length of this stretch (Figure 6.13). Their remit included the construction of a dozen box latrines corbelled out from the wall head between the Mill Gate and Tower 18. This section fell short of the Phase 1 work, the gap between them being filled in during the 1285–6 season by a different contractor, Philip of Darley. The reason for this division of responsibility lies in the rather anomalous character of the shorter western portion compared with the general uniformity of the defences further to the east.

The vertical joint between the work of 1284–5 and that of 1285–6 is clearly visible a little to the right (east) of Tower 15 at the south-west angle of the circuit. To the east of this line the wall is pierced by three windows, which indicate the probable position of Llywelyn's Hall. Tower 16 at its right-hand (east) end, which is known as Llywelyn's Tower by association, differs from the other wall towers in being a proper tower with a back. On the east side the tower projects beyond the face of the wall by about 14ft (4.3m), a measure commensurate with that of the other wall towers, but on the west side the distance is about 25ft (7.6m). The tower therefore masks an 11ft misalignment of the walling between towers 15 and 17. It has been suggested that the Phase 1 stub wall to the east of Tower 15 was originally built against an older building associated with Llywelyn's residential complex, possibly to be identified with a building taken down by James of St George in 1285–6, therefore immediately prior to the construction of the defences at this end.[16]

It is interesting to note that there were seven named participants in the John Francis partnership, and that their brief included seven stretches of walling

Figure 6.13: *Conwy. Mill Gate, town defences (1285–6).*

and seven towers including those of the Mill Gate.[17] That being so, it is not unreasonable to presume that each man was responsible for a separate section of the defences and headed his own gang of workers. A degree of flexibility may have been required, but, broadly speaking, that would seem to have been how the partnership would have worked. Philip of Darley's contract was broadly equivalent to one of these sections.

Whether the same personnel were involved in the construction of the other sections of the town walls is unknown, but one particular aspect of the masonry work needs to be taken into account in debating the matter. The southern defences attributed to John Francis and his men are characterised by inclined and spiral patterns of putlog holes, features noted by Taylor as Savoyard practices. This is fair enough in a project headed by a Savoyard, but, such features are also prominently displayed in the section made by Philip of Darley, who was, presumably, an Englishman from one of several English settlements of that name. It seems, then, that Savoyard techniques were transferring themselves to non-Savoyard craftsmen. In this case a reasonable deduction is that Philip of Darley had previously worked under Savoyard direction.

The Continental putlog patterns appear to be absent from the north-western section of the town defences, but, they are prominent in the south-western section which includes towers 13 to 15 and the Upper Gate. Indeed, a near vertical break may be discerned in the curtain eight paces south west of Tower 12, suggesting that the south-west section between Tower 12 and Llywelyn's Hall and the main north-western length were, like the southern stretch, erected under two separate contracts. Again, inclined putlog-hole patterns are not generally discernible in the Phase 3 work, but they are very noticeable in Tower 2 and there are slight indications elsewhere to show that the system was in use.

Another anomaly is evident in the upper part of Tower 6, near the north-eastern end of the north-west section, which is largely composed of a yellow rhyolite, a stone that stands out in startling contrast to the dark grey Silurian grit that characterises the lower part of the tower, the greater part of the town defences and the castle.[18] This is also the predominant material to the east of Tower 6, including the wing wall that extended to the River Conwy where it terminated in a round tower (no longer extant), and along the entire length of the defences that stretches along the north-eastern waterfront; in the Lower Gatehouse it is prominently displayed in bands. The compact geographical location of this material (within the town walls) supports a view that these parts of the defences are contemporary.

It is also interesting to note that the architectural details for the town walls were accounted for separately and undertaken by different contractors, who supplied the builders of the walls. The stone cutter, John Flauner, for instance, who had dressed stone for use at Flint and Caergwrle, worked the dressings for the arrow loops that are found in the towers and in the merlons of the battlements, as well as the voussoirs for the Upper Gate and Mill Gate.[19] This separation of specialisms is an arrangement that confirms the central direction of the design.

Conwy is one of the north Walian castles with which James of St George seems most intimately connected, and at which we can best appreciate the characteristics of his work. It was here that he established his headquarters from which he directed the King's works in Wales, and the survival of the records is such that his close involvement in the building operations can be attested both as a director of personnel and as a major contractor.[20] In this latter role he undertook the construction of the stonework of the great hall in the outer ward and the royal apartments in the inner ward in 1284–5, and, in 1285–6, the rebuilding of an estimated 6 perches of thick walling next to the castle well, apparently the wall between the outer and inner wards.[21]

Also, a number of structural traits found at Conwy have been associated with Savoyard building practices, including the semi-circular arch of the great hall east window, the latrine turret in the angle of the curtain with the North-West Tower, putlog holes in inclined patterns, and merlon copings capped by pinnacles, a feature that, in this country, is rare and does not seem to have occurred before the Welsh castles of Edward I (Figure 6.14). None of these features is evident at Flint, and the only one to appear at Rhuddlan is the latrine turret, which is systematically applied to the corner towers of the inner ward. It might be argued, then, that it was only in the castles of the Second Welsh War that the influence of Savoy came to the fore. This is particularly so in the case of Conwy, and to a similar extent at Harlech as is described below.

Figure 6.14: *Conwy. Chapel Tower merlon pinnacles.*

Harlech (Merioneth)

Harlech Castle is sited on the west coast approximately midway, as the crow flies (*c.* 35 miles), between Caernarfon in the north and Aberystwyth to the south.[22] Built on a rocky headland it has been cut off from the land to the east and south by the excavation of a rock-cut ditch. The castle comprises a quadrilateral inner ward with round corner towers centred on the angles, and a large eastern gatehouse with twin drum towers flanking the central entrance passage and stair turrets at the inner angles. A concentric outer ward is contained by a low curtain with eastern and northern gatehouses, the former being the main entrance and the latter giving access to the rock. At the angles the curtain bows out around the inner ward corner towers, in the manner of the middle ward of Caerphilly, but at Harlech the outer curtain hugs the inner ward more closely. From the north-east and south-west angles of the outer ward another curtain extends around the rock to create an additional enclosure and secure the access to the sea (Figure 6.15).

Harlech is dominated by its great gatehouse, a massive twin-towered entrance, which, despite its stark character, delivers a sharp visual impact and impresses itself upon the consciousness as the defining aspect of the castle. In the simple massing of this eastern frontage, and its gradations of height and depth: the low outer curtain and gatehouse, and the inner curtain and corner towers rising behind them, the architect has achieved a palpable success in which the great inner gatehouse is the potent climax (Figure 6.16). The prime purposes

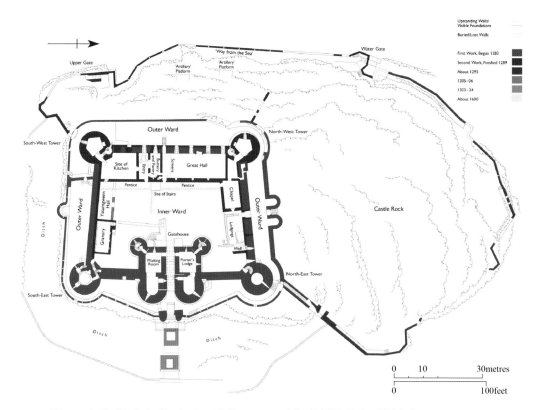

Figure 6.15: *Harlech. Castle plan. © Crown copyright (2018) Cadw, Welsh Government*

of the gatehouse were to maintain effective control over access to the castle by means of a well-defended entrance, and, at the same time to provide a major accommodation block, but in view of the effectiveness of its looming presence, it does not seems fanciful to suggest that it was also intended to create a powerful psychological impression.

It is highly probable that Aberystwyth acted as an exemplar, both buildings containing spacious residential accommodation, being equipped with twin staircase turrets to the rear corners, and sharing the composition of inner and outer gateways. These characteristics are derived from Caerphilly, but at Aberystwyth and Harlech the alignment of inner and outer gatehouses is direct, whilst at Caerphilly it is slightly skewed. Harlech also differs from the two earlier buildings in that rather than being D-shaped in plan, each of the flanking towers forms the greater part of a circle like those of Rhuddlan. The facade also has strong similarities with Rhuddlan, notably the narrow recessed entrance between two large round drum towers, which is a reason for thinking that Rhuddlan may have been the source of this aspect of the design. Other divergences from the Aberystwyth and Caerphilly models incorporated at Harlech are a more deeply recessed entrance and staircase turrets of bolder projection that form

Figure 6.16: *Harlech. Great gatehouse from the east.*

more emphatic components of the western facade. Generally, the design of Harlech is more confident and regular and implies a designer who knew how to maximise an effect.

In considering the process by which the form of the Harlech gatehouse took shape, we should remember that James had taken charge of Rhuddlan in the spring of 1278 and saw it through to completion. Whether he was the designer of the castle's inner gateways or not, he was certainly familiar with them. He had also visited Aberystwyth, in May 1282, nearly a year before work began on Harlech, surely before its design had been settled. On that occasion he must have seen the great gatehouse and no doubt taken note of its attributes, using the information he had gleaned when he came to produce his own version at Harlech. As we have seen, however, Harlech was no mere slavish copy of an existing model, but an original interpretation of a type. It is unfortunate that its predecessors at Caerphilly and Aberystwyth have both suffered too badly to allow a full comparative assessment to be made. Nevertheless, the other great example of this category survives at Tonbridge, and the rear elevation of Caerphilly is sufficiently well understood to allow a useful comparison. One innovation at Harlech was the first-floor entrance reached by an external staircase. Another is the horizontal articulation provided by a series of string courses, which define the window sills and parapet, loop over the entrance, and wrap themselves round the enlarged stair turrets that frame the elevation. A third is the regularity and form of the fenestration which suggests accommodation of equal character on the two upper floors (Figure 6.17).

The appearance of a handful of building craftsmen at Harlech in June 1283 is usually considered to mark the beginning of building operations, and it is probable that the general layout of the castle had been established by 1285, when the excavation of the ditch 'in front of the castle' was recorded.[23] This feature, which is to be identified with the rock–cut ditch that protects the castle on the east and south sides, is the first item to receive a specific mention in the accounts. How much progress had been made by this date is uncertain, but, it has long been recognised that the inner ward was built in at least two phases, the evidence for which is as follows.[24] There is a horizontal building break in the outer faces of the north and south curtains and the inner face of the east wall at about 15ft (4.6m) above the ground level of the outer ward. Below this line the masonry consists of coursed small-stone rubble interspersed with some larger blocks. Above this the character of the masonry changes to larger blocks more regularly coursed. This dividing line can be traced around the eastern towers, although the corresponding lower stages are built in large blocks. It is also possible to discern a change in the east curtain at the same level, but here there is a greater proportion of larger stones amongst the early masonry and a lesser proportion of larger stones amongst the later stonework. No similar division has been noted in the

Figure 6.17: *Harlech. Great gatehouse from the west.*

great gatehouse where the character of the masonry seems fairly homogenous. It appears, then, that by the end of the first structural phase, the curtain of the inner ward and the eastern towers stood some 15ft (4.6m) high above current ground level at the east end of the middle ward. Work on the west towers and the flanking towers of the gatehouse had probably not progressed much above foundation level. However, provided there was a gate the castle would have been defensible.

At a later date the two western towers were added, the north, south, and west curtains were thickened before being carried up to their full height, and the eastern towers were also raised to their full heights. Although we can't be absolutely sure of the dates of the two phases, what we can infer from the accounts is that from 1286–90, by which time the castle was largely complete, the work was being carried on apace, the considerable drop in expenditure in the final year indicating that the operation was nearing its end. Unfortunately, the only opportunity for discerning the specifics of the building campaign are provided by the surviving details for task work accounted for in 1289, the last major building season. Nevertheless, they do contain some interesting information, and throw some light upon the construction sequence and the personnel involved.[25]

The operations recorded in 1289 included the raising of the two western towers to their full heights, together with their roof-top turrets; the thickening of the west curtain; the raising of this thickened wall to its full height, including the battlements and a wall head turret; the construction of buildings ranged along the south and west curtains, including the hall, kitchen, and chapel; the completion of the gatehouse south stair turret; the near completion of the north-east tower; the completion of the curtain between the great gatehouse and the north-east tower including its battlements; and the raising and roofing of the south-east tower. The heights of 49½ft (15.1m) and 52ft (15.9m) given in the 1289 accounts for the north-west and south-west towers respectively imply that they were raised from ground level, probably on foundations laid during the initial laying out of the castle. A measurement of 23ft (7m) was given for the north-east tower, which amounts to approximately half its height, an indication, perhaps, of the level to which the castle had been raised in its initial phase.

As at Conwy, various structural details at Harlech are said to betray the influence of Savoy, perhaps in greater evidence here than at any other Edwardian castle.[26] Even so, the inclined patterns of putlogs were used intermittently and do not appear in any of the work that can be verified as part of the initial phase. However, they appear on the inner face of the north curtain; on the north-west tower, between ground- and first-floor level and first- and second-floor level; on the south-west tower between the ground and first floors; on the southern stair turret of the great gatehouse between ground- and first-floor level; and on the south flanking tower of the same building between first- and second-floor level.

Of these areas the two western corner towers appear in the particulars of 1289. Interestingly, the contractor for both towers was a Master William Drygda (Drogheda).[27] He was presumably Irish or Anglo-Irish rather than Savoyard, which compounds the evidence from Conwy that the technique had been adopted by other craftsmen in north Wales. Another interesting aspect to the appearance of William Drygda in the accounts is the prefix 'Master' which hints that, as well as being a contractor, he may also have been superintending the work in general and was, perhaps, the resident master mason at Harlech for much of the main building period. William Drygda was also the contractor responsible for the upper parts of the eastern towers, which contain semi-circular-arched window embrasures, although as a contractor, he may simply have been fitting voussoirs already prepared to a specification over which he had had no control (Figure 6.18).

Semi-circular arches were also used for the outer gateway and the first-floor entrance to the great gatehouse. Other 'Savoyard' features include re-entrant latrine turrets (Figure 6.19) and a semi-circular latrine turret carried on continuous corbelling, projecting from the south side of the middle ward curtain (Figure 6.20).

Figure 6.18 (right): *Harlech. A rear arch in the North-West Tower.*

Figure 6.19 (below left): *Harlech. Latrine turret adjacent to the North-west Tower.*

Figure 6.20 (below right): *Harlech. Latrine turret on the outer curtain.*

Examples of the former were noted by Taylor at the castles of Yverdon (*c.* 1261) and Saint-Georges-d'Espéranche (*c.* 1268–75), and the latter at the Savoyard castle of La Bâtiaz, Martigny (Valais); similar corbelling was used to support the flanking turrets of the outer gateway. Finally, there are the segmental-arched windows, which, owing to a close correspondence of the dimensions, seem to have been based on examples at Chillon, and although the pattern is simpler, its derivation from the Chillon examples is readily apparent (Figure 6.21).

Like several of the other Edwardian castles, the fireplaces at Harlech were hooded, some with sconce brackets, including that on the upper storey of the great gatehouse, which had hollow-chamfered jambs, the moulding being continued along the surmounting angled arms. These arms are similar to the one noted at Rhuddlan and contribute to a sense of continuity in the direction of the design work (Figure 6.22).

Figure 6.21 (above left): *Harlech. Great gatehouse, second-floor window from the north.*

Figure 6.22 (above right): *Harlech. Great gatehouse, second-floor fireplace from the south.*

Chapter Seven

Royal Castles of the Second Welsh War:
Caernarfon and Beaumaris

Caernarfon (Carnarvonshire)

The third castle emanating from the Second Welsh War was Caernarfon, which is situated at the mouth of the River Seiont and towards the south-west end of the Menai Strait. Here, a short peninsula was expropriated for the site of a castle and its accompanying borough. The castle itself was built on the south side of the headland, on a modest bluff overlooking the Seiont, which was already occupied by the eleventh-century motte and bailey castle established by Hugh d'Avranches, the motte of which was incorporated within the Upper Ward. The walled borough was laid out on sloping ground to the north (Figure 7.1).

Architecturally, Caernarfon is the masterpiece of the Edwardian castles in Wales, and appears to have been intended as such from the outset. There are some superficial similarities with Conwy in that both are aligned from east to west and are divided into two wards with the great hall ranged against the south wall and the kitchens against the north wall. The differences, however, are far greater than the parallels, and there is no doubt that Caernarfon was intended to project a quite distinct character that set it apart from Edward's other Welsh fortresses both in scale and appearance. Amongst its distinguishing characteristics is the use of polygonal wall towers, the horizontal articulation of the elevations in which sandstone banding was interspersed amongst the lighter coloured limestone, two very imposing and powerfully defended twin-towered gatehouses, and the extensive use of mural passages pierced by arrow loops on the south side, which, together with the alure behind the parapet, form three tiers of fighting galleries and circulatory walk ways (Figure 7.2).

The main thrust of the first phase of works at Caernarfon was carried out between 1283 and 1287, the first season being given over to preparatory work including the levelling of the site, the excavation of the ditch (the greater width now infilled) that separated the castle from the town, and the preparation of the rock or the laying of the foundations ready for the masons to begin work on the walls. Thereafter work could carry on apace, but it is evident that the priority was to create a continuous defendable circuit comprising the south and east fronts of the castle (inclusive of the Eagle Tower to the west and the North-East Tower to the east) and the adjoining town walls. By the end of the third season it is probable that the south and east fronts of the

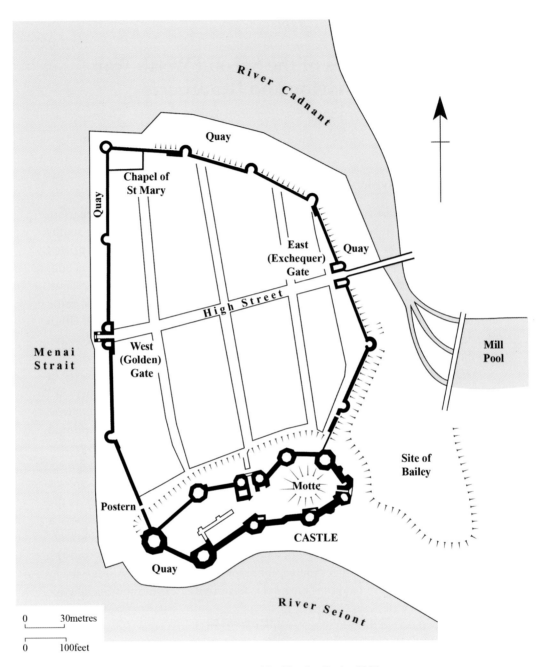

Figure 7.1: *Caernarfon. Town plan. By Nigel Dodds after Taylor 1986*

castle rose to a level approximating that of the lower wall passage floor, approximately equal to the height of the town walls.[1] Another two seasons may have been sufficient to carry the south and east curtains to their full height.[2]

The northern limits of this first phase are denoted by joints in the masonry of the curtain to the east of the Eagle Tower and in the north-west face of the

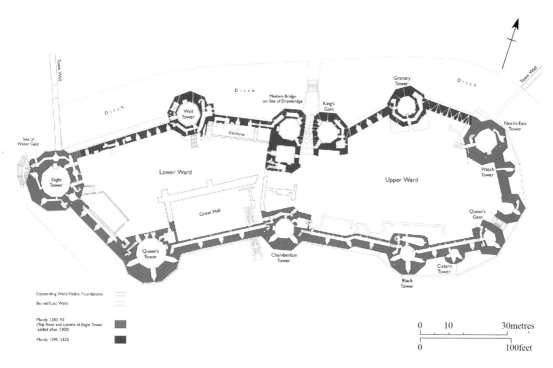

Figure 7.2: *Caernarfon. Castle plan. © Crown copyright (2018) Cadw, Welsh Government*

North-East Tower, both junctions lying within the walls linking the castle to the town walls. However, it seems that the lower courses of the rest of the north front were also laid down as part of the preliminaries, indicating that the full extent of the castle plan was known from the outset.[3] This is best attested in the western stretch of curtain between the Eagle Tower and the Well Tower, where the battered plinth, which belongs to the same structural period as the Eagle Tower and its adjoining section of the north curtain, can be seen above ground level. The greater part of this elevation, then, belongs to the second main phase of construction, which was carried out between 1295 and 1299.

After the 1287 season there was a dramatic fall in expenditure, and work can only have continued in a desultory fashion until 1292 when it came to a halt. By this time there existed a complete circuit of defences around the town and castle which, around the south and east sides of the castle, rose to at least the level of the first gallery, and probably up to parapet height. As a general rule, because the priority was to complete a defendable enceinte, only the outer facades of the towers were raised to their full height during the first phase, the greater extent of the inner walls and fitting out of the interior being reserved for subsequent building programmes. The principal exception to this was the Eagle Tower, the three lower storeys (basement, ground, and first floors) of which were built in their entirety, and temporarily roofed at the level of the current second-floor string course.

By 1292, then, despite the castle's unfinished state, it wore the appearance of a powerful fortress in concert with the town defences, which adjoined it to the north. This defensive circuit was largely surrounded by water, the only landward approach being from the east. Access to the town and castle on this side was via the Exchequer Gate and Queen's Gate respectively. Like the main entrance to Conwy, the Queen's Gate, at the east end of the castle, was at a very elevated level and must have been approached by a ramp somewhat similar to that of Conwy. It too had a drawbridge, its trunnion housings accommodated in semi-circular recesses cut into the stonework, like those of Conwy. Architecturally, however, the Queen's Gate is the antithesis of the diminutive outer gatehouse of Conwy, being a bold and unconventional edifice, its two irregularly polygonal towers joined at second-floor level by a great arch, emphasising the deeply recessed entrance and fusing the components into a single entity. It was a technique that had been used in the twelfth-century cathedral screen fronts of Lincoln and Peterborough (Figure 7.3).

The principal building of the castle was the Eagle Tower, which spearheaded the west end, and provided the main focus from the Menai Strait. Apart from Flint and possibly Builth, Caernarfon is the only one of Edward's castles in Wales to incorporate a great tower or keep. In its very thick walls containing small chambers linked by wall passages, it appears to owe something to the design of the great tower of Flint, which, incidentally, has a diameter equalling that of the Eagle Tower. Mural passages are a feature of all the residential towers along the south and east fronts, which, together with those of the intervening stretches of curtain wall, form two tiers of almost uninterrupted galleries from the Eagle Tower to the North-East Tower (Figure 7.4).

The intra-mural galleries of the curtains are rather unusual. As we have seen, a similar feature evolved at Caerphilly, during the main building period of 1268–71. At Caernarfon, however, the galleries were a systematic and prominent feature, reminiscent of similar features at Chastel Pèlerin (Athlit, Israel), the castle built by the Knights Templar from *c.* 1218 on the Mediterranean coast some 25 miles to the south of Acre. Chastel Pèlerin was linked to Acre by the coastal road or by sea and was well within Edward's reach during his time in the Holy Land, although if he did not visit it personally there is a strong possibility that it would have come into his conversations with the nobility of crusader states. Tiers of arrow loops were also a characteristic of some crusader castles, for example, the Templars' Tortosa (Tartus, Syria) and the Hospitallers' Crac des Chevaliers (Syria).

A more general point is that the coastal fortresses of Outremer were interesting examples of how sea communication allowed a colonising power, in this case the crusader states, to survive a crushing defeat on land. Despite the military disaster of 1189, when the crusader army was annihilated and the King of Jerusalem captured, coastal footholds such as these had enabled a continuing

Figure 7.3: *Caernarfon. Queen's Gate from the south east.*

Figure 7.4: *Caernarfon. Mural gallery in the south curtain.*

European presence into the late thirteenth century and kept alive the dream, however impractical, of re-establishing control over the Holy Land. Well might they have served as an example to Edward when considering his strategy in Wales.

Whilst there is no doubt that the castle was designed as a formidable fortress, the greater element of ostentation found here, compared with Edward's other castles, has given rise to suggestions that the building embodies a high degree of symbolism, although the message it was intended to convey, other than one of power by conquest, is far from certain. To Taylor it was an evocation of Constantinople and representative of Roman authority from which the princes of Gwynedd traced their legitimacy, now arrogated by Edward.[4] Alternative interpretations include Edward's appropriation of the place in Welsh legend and tradition afforded by the nearby Roman fort of Segontium, and a reference to Arthurian legend.[5] The supposed association of the Roman Emperor, Magnus Maximus, with Segontium, half a mile to the south west of the castle, may be nothing more than a piece of Welsh mythology, but imperial Rome was still a powerful source of entitlement, and Maximus was the supposed founder of the royal house of Gwynedd; it was after all the ancestors of the Welsh who had inhabited Britannia and the English who were the usurpers, so the site may have been a place of special significance to the inhabitants of Gwynedd.

It is certainly possible that some reference to Roman architecture lies behind the horizontal banding, which may indeed derive from the Roman practice of interspersing masonry courses with bands of tiles, the most celebrated example of which is embodied within the Theodosian walls of Constantinople. Despite the fragmentary remains of Roman architecture in Britain several examples of prominent tile coursing survive to this day at, for example, the Roman forts of Burgh Castle (Suffolk), Pevensey (Sussex), and Richborough (Kent); there is also some evidence for the use of the technique at Segontium, though not, so far as we know, in such an exterior display. It is also true that polygonal towers, which were a rarity in thirteenth-century Britain, and which in their clustering at Caernarfon must have produced a rather exotic appearance, were associated with a number of Roman sites including, in Wales, the defences of Cardiff (Glamorgan) and Caerwent (Monmouthshire), though not, apparently, at Segontium. There is, then, some reason for believing that the character of Caernarfon was intended to recall Roman exemplars, but, if so, there was no slavish adherence to authenticity, and the models were adapted rather than revived.

Regarding Constantinople itself, how great a part might it have played in determining the character of Caernarfon? The city of Constantinople was sited on a peninsula with the Sea of Marmara to the south, the Bosphorous to the east, and the estuary known as the Golden Horn to the north. The fifth-century landward fortifications extended a distance of some 4 miles from the Sea of Marmara to the Golden Horn, thereby cutting off the peninsula to the west. They comprised multiple lines of defence: firstly, a stone-revetted moat, with a low wall rising above the inner revetment, then a berm, then a higher wall, then another berm, and, finally, an even higher wall. The inner wall was strengthened by interval towers, mostly square, but with a number of polygonal towers as well. Even in their present incomplete state, these fortifications are an arresting sight and must have impressed themselves forcibly on the mind of the thirteenth-century observer, unused, perhaps, to such military extravagance. There is little doubt that they would have been a topic of conversation for those who had witnessed them at first hand. The horizontal banding of the tiles is prominent and the polygonal towers stand out against the uniformity of the square towers; both are features that would have been unusual enough to have been retained in the memory as characteristic of the city, and therefore elements to be reproduced as recognisable references to it.

That such a reference was being made in the design of Caernarfon is, as Taylor noted, suggested by one of the names by which the west gate of the town was known in the seventeenth century: the Golden Gate.[6] This epithet is perhaps derived from the Golden Gate of Constantinople, the Roman triumphal arch that had been incorporated into the defences to form the principal entrance to the city from the West.[7] It straddled the Via Egnatia, the Roman road leading from Dyrrhacium (Durrës), the gateway to the Byzantine Empire from the West, on what is now the coast of Albania. Interestingly, the site chosen for Caernarfon has some similarities with that of Constantinople, albeit on a miniature scale, being a peninsula between the Menai Strait to the west, the River Seiont to the south, and the River Cadnant to the north, with extensive wharfage provision for sea-borne trade.

How direct a source Constantinople might have been is open to question; we should bear in mind that there were several medieval precedents for the use of horizontal banding patterns much closer to home including Richard I's Château Gaillard of 1196–8, the west front of Windsor Castle as rebuilt by Edward's father, Henry III, in the 1220s, and its near contemporary, the French royal castle of Angers, where, owing to the strongly contrasting characteristics of the building materials, the scheme is particularly emphatic. It is true that these examples may also have been based on Roman models, but, unlike Caernarfon, none is combined with polygonal towers, and Caernarfon, therefore, seems more pointed in its allusion.

Arthurian associations are less tangible, although it is pertinent that Edward, like his uncle, was an Arthurian enthusiast, and may, therefore, have been well-disposed to draw on a legend that loomed large in Welsh folklore. Symbolism has to be recognisable to be effective as propaganda, a truism that has been cited as reason for scepticism regarding the Constantinople theory.[8] However, the symbolism of raising the most magnificent of Edward's castles at the mouth of the Arfon would have been recognisable to those with a knowledge of Welsh folklore, whatever its physical form, provided it was striking enough, because Arfon was the greatest of the castles that Maximus, in his mythological guise of Macsen Wledig, built for his British bride, Ellen. If Segontium was raided for building stone, as has been suggested, then the symbolism would have been even more potent, and on a par with the removal of Aberconwy Abbey and the remains of Llywelyn Fawr. The added value of this particular site was the pre-existing motte and bailey, another older centre of power, the incorporation of which reinforced the notion that the king of England was justifiably reclaiming his inheritance.

Excavation and soundings of the ditch separating the castle from the town have shown that it was at least 50ft wide and 24ft deep, flat bottomed, and with a stone-revetted steeply sloping counter scarp.[9] On the opposite side, the north curtain of the castle rose vertically from a battered plinth. What we know of the dimensions and character of this ditch is that it was broadly comparable to that around the outer ward of Rhuddlan Castle, and as such, a very formidable obstacle, far more substantial at these two sites than any other such feature amongst the royal Welsh castles.

The castle ditch, together with the town walls to the north of the castle, enclose an area of some 10 acres (4 ha); the enclosed borough was therefore half the size of Conwy, but its character was determined by the defensive capabilities of the site, the walls following the lines of the Menai Strait to the west and north and the River Cadnant to the east, with wharves all around the navigable sides. There were two gateways (east and west) linked by High Street and eight mainly D-shaped towers. Both gateways were flanked by D-shaped towers. As at Conwy, some of the towers retain helicoidal putlog-hole patterns.

In the autumn of 1294 the King's works in Wales were disrupted by a widespread and probably co-ordinated Welsh uprising. The most serious effects of which were felt in the north, where the rebels were under the leadership of Madog ap Llywelyn, who kept the spark of rebellion aglow until his defeat in March 1295. Caernarfon and Denbigh were both captured early in the insurgency. By December the English had regained Denbigh, but Caernarfon remained in rebel hands for the almost the entire duration of the revolt, giving the Welsh ample time to inflict some serious damage on the new buildings. The town and castle were fired and a good deal of effort was put into demolishing the newly completed town walls. One immediate consequence of the rebellion was a decision to proceed with the construction of a new castle at Beaumaris on the east coast of Anglesey in order to secure the north–east end of the Menai Strait and the island. It was the final link in the chain of royal castles along the northern coast. Beaumaris and the resumed works at Caernarfon constituted the King's works in Wales during the last few years of the thirteenth century.

When construction resumed at Caernarfon, on 5 June 1295, it was under the direction of Master Walter of Hereford, one of the most significant architectural figures of the later thirteenth century. For thirteen years (1277–90) he had been the mastermind behind the construction of the King's foundation of Vale Royal Abbey (Cheshire), a project that was brought to a shuddering halt in 1290 when Edward cut off the funding.[10] In 1278, soon after work had begun on Vale Royal, Master Walter was engaged by Winchcombe Abbey (Gloucestershire) for life, and a 1295 reference in the royal accounts to him as 'Walter of Amesbury' suggests that in the interval between Vale Royal and his appearance in the records for Caernarfon, he may also have been at Amesbury Priory (Wiltshire).[11] The Queen Mother, Eleanor of Provence, who had been a resident of the priory since 1285, died in June 1291, being buried before the High Altar three months later. There is a strong possibility, therefore, that Master Walter had been entrusted with her tomb and/or some other significant work.[12] There is also reason to suspect that Walter of Hereford was involved in the design and construction of Maenan Abbey, the replacement for Aberconwy (the site of which had been commandeered for Conwy Castle and its accompanying fortified town).[13]

Regrettably, the buildings of Winchcombe Abbey, Vale Royal Abbey, Amesbury Priory, and Maenan Abbey have almost entirely disappeared, so further insights into Walter of Hereford's work and significance are unlikely to be forthcoming. What we can say, however, is that he was evidently a man held in royal esteem, though not, so far as we know, as a castle builder, so it is somewhat ironic that of all the architectural projects for which he is known to have had responsibility, the sole survivor, and the building on which he is likely to be judged, should be a castle. Caernarfon, however, was far from being the average castle, having something of the quality of a great church in its scale, architectural quality, and symbolism, its special nature giving reason to believe that Master Walter may have been involved in the project from the start and that much of the architectural character of the building is owed to him. This is a viewpoint that Taylor himself favoured initially.[14] However, subsequent consideration brought him round to the idea that, given his responsibilities at Vale Royal, Walter of Hereford's influence on Caernarfon was unlikely to have been felt prior to 1295, and that James of St George was more likely to have been the mastermind behind the plan, owing to affinities between Caernarfon and some of the other Edwardian castles, and Master James' dominant position over the Welsh project.[15]

In re-examining the case for attributing Caernarfon largely to Walter of Hereford, we need, first of all, to consider how practical such an arrangement would have been during the period when he had charge of Vale Royal. To get to Caernarfon from Vale Royal and vice versa would probably have involved a journey of some 100 miles by land, lasting for up to a week. This seems onerous, but it was a shorter distance than that between Vale Royal and Winchcombe, and such arrangements were not unknown.[16] Besides, sea transport was always a possibility, and the port of Chester, at a distance of around 17 miles from Vale Royal, was less than a day's journey, and a sea trip to Caernarfon no more than two days away. Medieval master builders in demand were accustomed to being on the move, and, with a trusted deputy permanently on site, such a responsibility would have been feasible.

Secondly, we need to take account of the architectural evidence. As we have seen, one of the most distinctive and visible aspects of Caernarfon Castle is the use of polygonal towers. There had been a vogue for polygonal great towers in the late twelfth and early thirteenth centuries, notably in the royal castles of Tickhill (Yorkshire, *c.* 1179–8), Chilham (Kent, 1170s), and Odiham (Hampshire, 1207–16). Another example is Richard's Castle (Herefordshire), and the fashion extended to the enceinte of Warkworth Castle (Northumberland) where the south-west corner tower and the flanking towers of the gatehouse were polygonal. However, there were few precedents closer in date than the beginning of the thirteenth century, and those that did exist were Continental rather than British. Frederick II's Castel del Monte might be considered a possible source of inspiration for Holt; it was certainly remarkable enough to have been the subject of travellers' tales amongst the upper echelons of society. One of these Continental precedents was, of course, the castle of Saint-Georges-d'Espéranche, which, as Taylor implied, must be included amongst the more likely sources of the concept.[17]

There are, however, profound differences in the way the idea was developed at Caernarfon, for, whereas the towers of Castel del Monte and Saint-Georges-d'Espéranche were uniform and of regular form, those of Caernarfon vary considerably in size and plan.[18] Here too the main figure was the octagon, but the Eagle Tower and the Queen's Tower are both based on the decagon and others were based on the hexagon. One interesting aspect of the south front, which demonstrates the way in which Caernarfon transcends the bounds of convention, is the hierarchy of the towers which gradually diminish in size and significance from the Eagle Tower at the west end to the diminutive Cistern Tower next to the Queen's Gate (Figure 7.5). Whether this was deliberately intended to create a false perspective in order to overemphasise the length of the elevation is uncertain, but it is a possibility. Neither can we be certain as to the

Figure 7.5: *Caernarfon. The castle from the south west across the Seiont.*

extent to which these attributes are owed to the King, on the one hand, and the master builder, on the other, but, whilst the assumption must be that the general vision was that of the King and his lay advisors, the final appearance must to a great extent be that of the master builder.

Apart from the polygonal towers, which are otherwise found only at Denbigh, Caernarfon also contains a good deal of distinctive detail, its generally richer character compared with the other castles being an indication of its special status. First amongst the distinguishing elements is the shouldered lintel, a detail that had been used in the English royal works since the 1240s, but which appears at Caernarfon in such profuse quantities for doorways, windows, and wall passages that the form took on the name of the castle in which it was used most widely, and with which it was most readily identified. It also appears in other castles of the Second Welsh War but not in such quantity nor as creatively as it does in Caernarfon.

In the wall passages the form is refined to take on a double-ogee, or S-shaped, profile, a pattern that is repeated in the fireplace corbels of the Eagle Tower, suggesting that it was a primary aspect of the design perhaps dating from as early as 1283. The ogee became one of the defining attributes of architectural embellishment in the Decorated style of the first half of the fourteenth century. The earliest datable ogee arches in England are those over the niches of the Eleanor Crosses, the first of which date from 1291. A year later they were being incorporated into the design of the window tracery of St Stephen's Chapel in the Palace of Westminster, by the London-based mason, Michael of Canterbury.[19]

The Caernarfon ogees, then, are early examples of the form in Britain, and probably predate the Eleanor Crosses.

A number of different contractors worked on the design and construction of the ten Eleanor Crosses. Michael of Canterbury was entrusted with the Cheapside cross, but five others, including that of Hardingstone (Northamptonshire), one of the three surviving crosses, were made by John de la Bataille and Simon Pabenham. The relationship between the Eleanor Crosses and Walter of Hereford, and, by extension, Caernarfon, is an interesting one. In 1278–80 John de la Bataille had been the undermaster at Vale Royal Abbey under Walter of Hereford, and in 1287 Simon Pabenham, a London mason, acted as a guarantor for Ralph of Chichester, who, with his partner, John Doget, contracted to supply polished marble columns, capitals, bases, and cornices for Vale Royal Abbey according to a specification supplied by Master Walter.[20] Such personal relationships, the evidence for which is so often lost to us, lie behind the often anonymous transfer of ideas and diffusion of style.

Another sinuous form used at Caernarfon from the beginning was the wave moulding, which was used to decorate various doorways (Eagle Tower, Queen's Tower, Chamberlain Tower) and the outer orders of the King's Gate arch. Again, this was amongst the earliest applications of the form, which is more normally associated with the first half of the fourteenth century. Moreover, it was used at Vale Royal, and was probably part of Master Walter's repertoire, though which came first is uncertain.[21] Something of the same spirit is captured in the inverted-wave profile of the great hall plinth, another early feature, and in the ogee-profile scroll mouldings of the parapet strings.[22] These are further instances of the advanced character of the architecture at Caernarfon, and the style of its neoteric designer.

The first season of the second phase of work at Caernarfon was devoted to the reconstruction of the town walls, which had been severely damaged by the Welsh. Then, for three more years, work on the castle was carried on steadily until the autumn of 1299 when major constructional work ceased and the scheme was mothballed for the next five years, as the King diverted his resources to Scotland (see Chapter 9). A progress report compiled by Walter of Hereford and Hugh of Leominster, Chamberlain of North Wales and clerk of works at Caernarfon, dated 25 February 1296, just before the start of the second season, tells us something about the state of works at this point. This account, which almost certainly relates to the north front, tells us that four towers (the Well Tower, Granary Tower, and the two towers of the King's Gate) had been begun and that of the 18 perches (297ft/90.52m) of walling 8 perches (132ft) had risen to a height of 12ft (3.65m), whilst the other 10 perches (165ft/50.29m) had risen to 24ft (7.31m).[23]

The priority for the 1296 season and the ensuing years up to the end of September 1299, when work was again curtailed, would have been the continuation of the north front in order to make the castle secure, even though the internal buildings were unfinished. The principal feature of this elevation is the King's Gate, the entrance to the castle from the town. Because the King's Gate was never completed in its intended form, it is only partially understood, and any interpretative description is to some extent conjectural. Essentially, it was to contain three storeys above basements, though only the north front survives to its full height. Two semi-polygonal flanking towers flank a central entrance passage. At the front of the gateway, the two lower floors each contained two octagonal rooms which flanked the gate passage at ground-floor level and a chapel at first-floor level. On the second floor there was to be a hall extending across the full width of the gatehouse (Figure 7.6).

A rearward (southern) continuation of the west tower, known as the Prison Tower, contains a rectangular room, and, in the south wall, a staircase (the only one within the King's Gate) ascending to the upper storeys of the gatehouse. That this arrangement was to be replicated on the other side of the gate passage is evident from stubs of walling and toothing on the rear (south) of the less complete east tower. It also seems that, as originally planned, the central gate passage was to lead to an octagonal entrance hall, now represented only by one canted side at the south-east corner of the Prison Tower. From here another defended passageway led into the Lower Ward. It is to be presumed that there was to be a corresponding entrance to the Upper Ward on the east side of the entrance passage.

The King's Gate has been justly noted for its formidably defended main entrance passage containing a series of obstacles that would, properly managed, have been impregnable to a manual assault. A drawbridge, four portcullises, five lines of murder holes, and numerous loops on both sides of the passage show that defence was taken very seriously indeed. Whether such extreme measures were planned from the outset cannot be verified but as the gateway dates from after the Welsh revolt during which Caernarfon was captured and badly damaged, it is not unreasonable to surmise that these multiple hurdles might have been the result of a heightened awareness of the castle's potential vulnerability.

Beginning with parallel side walls, the gate passage widens from the midway point, as the side walls start to splay outwards to the south, until, towards the end of the passage they straighten out again to either side of a small rectangular vestibule or ante-chamber. This gives access to the Prison Tower, and, via a portcullis-controlled archway, to the putative octagonal entrance hall. After the grimness of the gate passage the entrance hall would have been something of a relief. It was to be an open space covered with a rib vault, elements of the wave-moulded wall ribs surviving at the south-west angle of the Prison Tower where they form a blind arch. The keystone of the arch is also the springer for a rib that would have extended to the apex of the vault. The gateway from here to the Lower Ward was also rib-vaulted, scars of the arched wall ribs surviving on the south wall of the Prison Tower (Figure 7.7).

Quite apart from its defensive attributes, the gate passage is a well-considered architectural device comprising a carefully regulated sequence of spaces: first the

Figure 7.6: *Caernarfon. King's Gate from the north east.*

Figure 7.7: *Caernarfon. King's Gate from the south east showing the main gate passage (behind the glazed ticket office), the canted side of the putative polygonal entrance hall (centre), and the abortive passage to the Lower Ward (left) with arched wall rib scars above the door and window.*

constricted entry, then the gradual opening out, first into the rectangular vestibule and next into the unusual vaulted entrance hall in which the accent was on architectural display rather than defence, and, finally, into another, but more aesthetically agreeable passageway (albeit defended at each end by a portcullis) that led into the splendours of the Lower Ward.

The profiles of the portcullis grooves in both the King's Gate and the Queen's Gate, which are semi-circular, represent another distinctive aspect of Caernarfon. Semi-circular grooves had indeed been the norm in the royal works from the second quarter of the thirteenth century, but this characteristic didn't extend to the other Welsh castles under the charge of James of St George, all of which incorporate portcullis grooves of square section.[24] This very much suggests that the latter were Master James' choice. The more elegant Caernarfon profiles may, of course, be another example of the higher specification to which the builder of this the premier castle was adhering, but, equally, they may represent the hand of a different designer.

The same may be said of the hooded principal fireplaces of Caernarfon's thirteenth-century phase, which differ from those of Conwy in three major respects. Firstly, the jambs are either sunk-chamfered or wave-moulded; secondly, a frontal fillet extends up each jamb and around the soffit of the corbelled head; and, thirdly, instead of segmental-arched heads there are flat, joggle-jointed lintels (Figure 7.8). Lesser, non-hooded fireplaces, which are found in both the early and later phases of Caernarfon also make use of joggling, having several (up to five) tiers of joggled lintels.

Figure 7.8: *Caernarfon. Eagle Tower, ground-floor fireplace.*

Beaumaris (Anglesey)

After Caernarfon, Beaumaris, the last of Edward's Welsh castles, was the most ambitious, but it provides a powerful visual contrast. Far from the intimidating grandeur of Caernarfon's lofty ashlar walls, here at Beaumaris, the tranquil moat and low outer curtain with its small-scale towers, exude a sense of homeliness that belie the castle's purpose and the circumstances in which it was built. For there is no doubt that it was intended as a serious fortification, a point that is inferred by the greater scale of the inner ward defences, which loom over the outer enceinte, and verified by a perusal of its martial provisions. However, Beaumaris was also intended to contain domestic accommodation of princely character, and more than at any of the Edwardian castles, there is sense here of a scientific approach to planning unhindered by a challenging topography. Like Caernarfon, Beaumaris was never completed, and therefore fell short of its early promise as a *beau idéal* of castle design, but, notwithstanding the eventual abandonment of the project, enough was accomplished to appreciate its scale and the intentions of the builder.[25]

The new castle of Beaumaris was sited on marshland next to the Menai Strait, to which it had direct access, being provided with a water-filled moat fed by the sea and a dock conveniently sited next to the outer southern gatehouse (the 'Gate-next-the-Sea'). The castle comprises two concentric wards, the rectangular inner ward having the most symmetrical plan of all Edward's north Walian fortifications. It has cylindrical corner towers, D-shaped mid-wall towers to the east and west, and, in the middle of the north and south fronts, two massive gatehouses with twin D-shaped flanking towers (Figure 7.9).

The slightly less evenly proportioned outer curtain consists of straight lengths of walling delineating an irregular octagon, the angles of which correspond with the positions of the inner ward gatehouses and wall towers. This outer enclosure is punctuated by twelve round mural towers and twin-towered gatehouses to the north east (Llanfaes Gate) and south west (Gate-next-the-Sea). The dock was to the east of the Gate-next-the-Sea, enclosed on its east side by a wall (Gunner's Walk) that extended southwards from the curtain, and to the west by the foundations of the abortive town wall which joined the Gate-next-the-Sea.

Work on the castle began very soon after the collapse of Madog's rebellion, and, during the first season (18 April–29 September 1295), when over £6,000 was spent, construction advanced rapidly under the personal direction of James of St George. Like Conwy, then, Beaumaris is another castle in which the influence of James on the design and construction is likely to have been strong. Indeed, a rare echo of Master James' voice is heard in the progress report dated 27 February 1296, issued by James and his clerk of works, Walter of Winchester, two days after Walter of Hereford's statement regarding the state of progress at Caernarfon.[26]

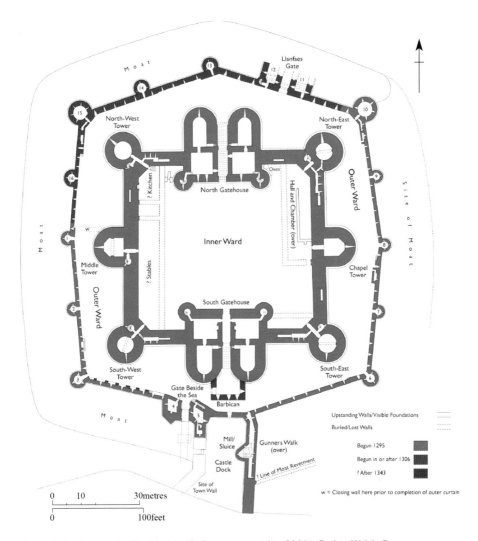

Figure 7.9: *Beaumaris. Castle plan. © Crown copyright (2018) Cadw, Welsh Government*

By this time the ditches had been excavated and the stone foundations for the entire castle had probably been laid. The inner curtain had been raised to heights of between 20ft and 28ft. Progress on the twin towers of the north and south gatehouses was sufficiently advanced to allow the gates to be hung and locked so that the inner ward at least could be secured, even though the mural towers had yet to be started. It was here, in the inner ward, that the workforce was living in timber buildings, only too aware of the hostile environment in which they found themselves.

The outer curtain was less complete, but a start had been made on about two-thirds of the circuit including the five eastern towers, the three most southerly western towers and the Gate-next-the-Sea. Building breaks to the west of the

Figure 7.10: *Beaumaris. Gate-next-the-Sea and harbour from the south.*

north-east corner tower and north of the western mid-wall tower denote that the
north curtain and the northern half of the west curtain belong to a subsequent
phase. The dock had also been created, which allowed a fully laden 40-ton vessel
to come right up to the castle gate (Figure 7.10).

After this heroic effort of the first season, however, the works were rapidly
scaled back. Over the following twelve months another £4,185 was spent
on Beaumaris, which, despite amounting to considerably less than had been
requested to maintain the rate of progress achieved in the first season, must
nevertheless have allowed the work to be carried on at a reasonable pace. The
following year, however, expenditure nosedived, and thereafter the building
works were only continued in a desultory fashion until 1300. By that time it is
probable that the inner curtain had been completed to its full height, and that the
section of the outer curtain described as having been begun in 1296, had risen to
about first-floor level. The height of the outer curtain at this stage is denoted on
the southern, eastern, and south western sides by a horizontal line a couple of feet
above the arrow slits. This is particularly noticeable on the eastern and southern
sides, where the contrast between the earlier and later materials is more marked.

Beaumaris incorporates and develops a number of ideas that had already
appeared in its Edwardian predecessors, thereby indicating continuity of design.
One of these is the principle of concentricity, a system that had been deployed
at both Rhuddlan and Harlech. At Beaumaris, the outer curtain, which is best
preserved of this group, is pierced systematically with arrow loops backed by
segmental-pointed arched embrasures (Figure 7.11), and the outer ward was

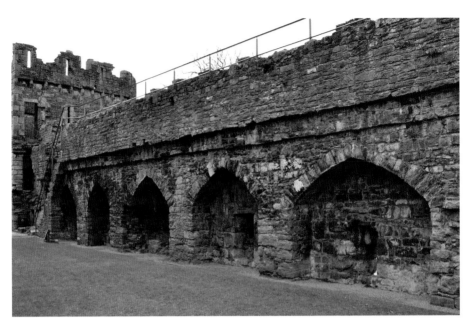

Figure 7.11: *Beaumaris. Outer curtain with an arcade of arrow loop embrasures set beneath the allure, the Gate-next-the-Sea in the background.*

overlooked by the higher inner curtain. The concept is very similar to the arrangements of Rhuddlan and Harlech. Another aspect of Beaumaris that supplies an architectural link with Harlech, but also Conwy, is the stair turrets which extended above the tower parapets of the inner ward. In addition, inclined patterns of putlog holes, which appear on the inner face of the west curtain and elsewhere, testify to the continued influence of Savoy.

The principal features of the castle were the two inner gatehouses, which, in general plan, follow in the footsteps of Caerphilly, Aberystwyth, and Harlech in having bow-fronted flanking towers and twin staircase turrets at the rear corners (Figure 7.12). The Beaumaris gatehouses, however, are the largest of all, representing the ultimate expression of this type. Neither was destined to be finished, but both were intended to rise through three storeys with the principal domestic accommodation on the upper levels, in common with Harlech. Some measure of the scale and quality of the proposed apartments can be gleaned from the North Gatehouse, where the first-floor rooms were completed. As at Harlech there was an internal division between the flanking towers beyond the curtain and the rectangular half of the gatehouse to the rear. At Harlech this rear section was sub-divided into a hall and chamber, but at Beaumaris the equivalent space was occupied entirely by a hall over 70ft in length.

Just as the north and east curtains of Caernarfon were pierced by mural galleries, so did the inner curtain of Beaumaris contain passages at first-floor level, linking the rooms in the wall towers and gatehouses in a continuous

Figure 7.12: *Beaumaris. North Inner Gate from the north west.*

Figure 7.13: *Beaumaris. Mural passage in the inner curtain.*

circuit, opening out into rooms with high, pointed barrel vaults when they reached the two gatehouses. Otherwise, the flat slab ceilings are supported on corbels, a general principle also utilised extensively at Caernarfon, but, at Beaumaris, the square-sectioned corbels, and their deployment in multiple tiers, represent a particular interpretation of the type, which only rarely occurs elsewhere (Figure 7.13). The mural passages were liberally supplied with latrines, and lit by occasional windows with large embrasures containing a single stone side bench, large enough for a servant or man-at-arms to sleep in. However, there were no arrow loops as such, and the primary purpose of the passages seems to have been to allow internal communication between the different parts of the castle.

Another connection with Caernarfon is the widespread use of the shouldered lintel, which was employed in window embrasures and in the most common type of doorway. Here at Beaumaris, however, they are simplified versions, the surrounds plain and unmoulded. This simplicity is one of the characteristics of Beaumaris, even though it was not universally applied, and is at one with the austerity of the corbelling to be found in the corridors and elsewhere, which contrasts so markedly with the elegance of the thirteenth-century work at Caernarfon. Indeed, Beaumaris contains something of the make-do attitude that can be encountered at Conwy. Here too there are rough monolithic lintels (in the Inner North Gatehouse), and, in the early phase of the outer curtain, the character of the arrow loops might be described as 'basic'. Although they are consistently provided with jambs of dressed stone blocks, the lintels, and sometimes the sills, are of the same material as the surrounding walls and no attempt has been made to ameliorate the appearance of the openings with, for example, a chamfer. Such perfunctory workmanship may have been owed to the initial haste with which the castle was thrown up, but budgetary considerations are also likely to have played their part. The best work at Beaumaris dates from the fourteenth-century (see below, Chapter 10).

Chapter Eight

Baronial Castles of the Second Welsh War

The Baronial Castles in the North

In 1282, in the aftermath of the Second Welsh War, several new marcher lordships were created from captured Welsh territory, and in each of these a new castle was raised. Lower Powys, or Powys Fadog, was carved up between the lordships of Chirk (Denbighshire) in the south and Bromfield and Yale in the north. The former was granted to Roger Mortimer (*c*. 1256–1326), a younger son of Roger Mortimer of Wigmore; the latter was bestowed on John de Warrene, sixth Earl of Surrey (1231–1304), who built his castle at Holt (Denbighshire). The third new marcher lordship, which incorporated Dafydd's former territory of Rhufoniog and was centred on Denbigh, went to Henry de Lacy, fifth Earl of Lincoln (1249–1311). Documentary evidence for the construction of these castles (Chirk, Holt, and Denbigh) is either minimal or non existant, and, although it cannot be corroborated, there is a general assumption that they were all begun soon after the grants of land. All three were interesting buildings of considerable architectural merit.

Chirk

Chirk Castle is prominently sited on a hill from which there are broad sweeping views of the surrounding countryside. Eminently visible from below, it has a squat appearance owing to the towers and connecting ranges being of uniform height, an anachronistic arrangement for a thirteenth-century castle.[1] The look reflects either an unfinished building or subsequent remodelling. It is probable that the intention was for the towers to rise at least one storey higher than the curtain. Chirk is a rectangular courtyard castle approximately 180ft (55m) x 197ft (60m) with round towers at the two northern corners, three D-shaped towers extending from the north, east, and west curtains respectively, and a gateway located between the north and north-east towers (Figure 8.1).

To the south of the west tower, the thirteenth-century curtain continues for a short length before terminating in a near vertical building joint, beyond which it has been buttressed in masonry of a different character and later structural phase. This later phase extends to the south curtain and the eastern end of the south range which date from the late fourteenth or fifteenth centuries.

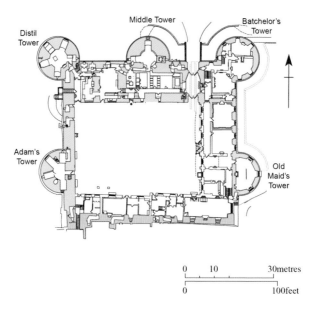

Figure 8.1: *Chirk. Castle plan. By Nigel Dodds after Brooks* et al. *2017*

The south range, then, represents a change of plan, and it is probable that Mortimer's castle was intended to extend further to the south. In view of the large degree of regularity that characterises Chirk it is not unreasonable to suppose that the objective was a symmetrical plan and that, like the north tower, the east and west towers were also intended as mid-wall structures. If that is correct, had it been realised, the main body of the castle would have measured 247ft (75m) x 197ft (60m). To put that into context, the inner ward of the royal castle of Beaumaris (Anglesey), with which Chirk is often compared, measures 220ft (67m) x 200ft (61m).[2] It seems that Mortimer may have overreached himself.

This early change of plan is symptomatic of Chirk's complex building history. Subsequent alterations and additions are wide ranging, but a sense of the degree to which the late thirteenth-/early fourteenth-century castle survives can be gained by tracing the extent of the large squared and coursed masonry blocks that constitute the primary fabric. This material is most conspicuous in the north and west curtains, but elements are to be found in the east curtain as well, and in all five towers, notably in the battered plinth that extends around the exterior. The north and west curtains are approximately 13ft (4m) thick, the walls of the Middle, Distil, and Adam towers even thicker, and they contrast with the considerably thinner-walled eastern side. The extent to which the eastern curtain, together with the north-east and east towers, represent a remodelling or a reconstruction is uncertain, but it is possible that the reduced dimensions are the result of alteration and that the fabric of the towers and curtain contains a substantial proportion of original material.

Within the courtyard, at first glance, only the west curtain appears to be of early date, but, despite it having been remodelled in the seventeenth century, patches of primary masonry are also to be found in the north range. These patches are simply the tip of the iceberg, because a more considered evaluation of the range suggests that there is substantial medieval survival. Evidence for the primary character of the north range is to be found in the very thick south wall and internal transverse walls. At approximately 3m (9ft 9ins), these walls are far thicker than structurally or defensively necessary, and it is to be presumed that, like the curtain walls, they were designed to contain mural rooms, passages, and staircases, traces of all of which survive.

The cross-walls, which extend through the full height of the range, define three main spaces, measuring (from east to west) 22ft (6.75m) x 61ft (18.5m), 22ft (6.75m) x 19.5ft (6m), and 22ft (6.75m) x 19.5ft (6m). The larger space is big enough to have accommodated a hall, the latter may have housed either the usual offices associated with a great hall, for example pantry, buttery, and kitchen, or the elements of a more private domestic suite. At first-floor level, two large medieval window embrasures survive at the west end of the putative hall looking towards the courtyard.[3]

The internal face of the west curtain contains no indications to suggest that there was a western range. Nor is there any visible structural evidence to suggest that there was an eastern range either, the current east range being entirely nineteenth-century in date. The domestic accommodation would appear to have been concentrated in the north range and in the wall towers.

The east range blocks two late thirteenth-century traceried windows within the north wall of the south range (Figure 8.2). This part of the range is occupied by the chapel, a building with large late fourteenth- or early fifteenth-century windows placed high in the south and east walls. The affinities of the two blocked windows are with Valle Crucis Abbey, some 8 miles to the west, where the great west window contains near identical tracery patterns of two trefoil cusped lights surmounted by a central oculus comprising an encircled sexfoil. The west window of Valle Crucis is usually dated to the

Figure 8.2: *Chirk. Blocked window in the chapel.*

mid-thirteenth century, but, although its hierarchical tripartite arrangement would have been rather unusual, stylistically, there is really no reason to preclude a later thirteenth-century date.[4]

Other than the towers, a major architectural and defensive feature to have maintained something of its primary character is the north-east gateway, which comprises a pointed two-centred drop arch of two continuous chamfered orders deeply recessed beneath a similar, but much loftier, outer arch with unmoulded jambs (Figure 8.3). A portcullis groove of semi-circular section extends between the two arches; when raised, the greater part of the portcullis must have been exposed to view as there would have been insufficient height to withdraw it into the building unless the north range originally rose higher than it does now. The gate passage itself has been considerably altered, but it had gates at either end, both opening inwards. An idiosyncratic aspect of the plan is that the walls of the northern half of the passage splay inwards towards the entrance. It is an unusual feature, though splayed entrance passages have also been noted at Castell-y-Bere, the Upper Gate of Conwy town defences, and the King's Gate at Caernarfon Castle.

There are also a number of external and internal masonry details that are worthy of mention: they are representative of the kind of work that was

Figure 8.3: *Chirk. Gateway from the north west.*

being done at Chirk in its primary phase, and they contribute towards a consideration of the construction date. Few primary windows survive; those that do are mostly small rectangular loops with chamfered surrounds, for lighting small mural chambers including latrines. More diagnostically useful is the courtyard-level opening to a light shaft in the west curtain; this has a monolithic trefoiled head and appears to be of thirteenth-century date. A window of similar form, but with a two-stone head, is to be found in the north range, immediately east of the Middle Tower (Figure 8.4).

The courtyard entrance to Adam's Tower and the west curtain is one of a number of two-centred pointed doorways at Chirk in which the arch is made up of two voussoirs, one forming

Figure 8.4: *Chirk. Light-shaft opening to Adam's Tower from the east.*

each side of the arch; it is an unusual form of construction, particularly for doorways of substantial width, as here in Chirk (Figure 8.5). A segmental light-shaft opening in the basement-level Lower Guard Room of Adam's Tower displays the same structural characteristic. The other main type of doorhead to survive is the shouldered lintel, which is generally unmoulded and used in subordinate positions (Figure 8.6).

Window embrasures, which mostly survive in the towers, are unusually wide, have parallel side walls and pointed (Adam's Tower, Distill Tower, North Range) or segmental (Distill Tower, Middle Tower) rear arches and vaults. The rear arches are unmoulded, but, in architectural terms, the overall impression is starkly effective. Although the embrasures could have been used as stations for archers, they are large enough to have served as small semi-private rooms, and may have been used as such, possibly as bed chambers. These embrasures are highly reminiscent of the embrasures in the western towers of Windsor Castle built for Henry III in 1227–30 (Figure 8.7).

The central areas of the three upper storeys of Adam's Tower were each heated by a fireplace; the one that survives intact has a segmental-arched head.[5] Each of these rooms was also served by a latrine in the northern angle between the tower and curtain.[6] The three upper rooms, then, were residential. There were two further storeys below courtyard level, the lower one being partly cut into the natural bedrock and lacking any facilities other than light shafts placed high up

Figure 8.5 (above left): *Chirk. Adam's Tower, first-floor Muniment Room entrance from the north west.*

Figure 8.6 (above right): *Chirk. Adam's Tower, Guard Room, doorway to basement stairs from the north west.*

Figure 8.7: *Chirk. Adam's Tower, Guard Room window embrasure from the south west.*

in the walls. The upper one has a segmental-arched fireplace and more refined light-shaft opening, but no access to a latrine.

Two mural chambers at the north end of the west curtain, one above the other at first-floor and attic level, each have a primary corner fireplace with flat lintel, an ogee and convex quarter-round moulded surround, and a stop with ogee tongue and bar stop. These mouldings are consistent with a late thirteenth- or early fourteenth-century date. The two rooms were entered from the north range, although a passage was later created within the west curtain to link the lower chamber to Adam's Tower.

The other interesting structural feature at Chirk is the use of continuous corbelling to support the stone slab ceilings of the wall passages. This expedient is found in a number of Edwardian castles in Wales, notably Caernarfon and Beaumaris where there are large expanses of mural passages. At Chirk a number of different techniques have been used: large, roughly formed blocks; slate; and small squared blocks (Figure 8.8). The two former are peculiar to Chirk, but the latter is a particular feature of Beaumaris, and indicates the presence of masons with experience of the royal works in north Wales, particularly Beaumaris, which was begun in 1295. Examples of the technique survive both in the west curtain, and the north range.

The general resemblance of Chirk to the inner ward of Beaumaris has already been touched upon, but this likeness is a partial one, based mainly upon the rectangularity of the plan, the three-quarter round corner towers and the D-shaped mid-wall towers. In fact, rather than being D-shaped the mid-wall towers of Chirk are really semi-circular. Chirk has no gatehouse as such, whereas the inner north and south gatehouses are one of the main elements that contribute to the character of Beaumaris. Nevertheless, the correlation of the two castles in general layout is enough to imply that there was some form of collusion between the respective builders, and the similarities in the corbelling are close enough to suggest that at least one of the contractors worked at both sites. The shouldered-lintel doorways, unmoulded as they are, provide another link with Beaumaris, where this particular (and unusual) form is also to be found.

Figure 8.8: *Chirk. West curtain, former latrine passage from the south.*

These correspondences are significant in that they tend to imply that Chirk is broadly contemporary with Beaumaris, even though other aspects of the design suggest a high degree of independence.

Holt: The Castle of the Lion

The second of the baronial castles to be considered is the Earl of Surrey's Holt (Denbighshire).[7] This was first mentioned in 1311.[8] Lying some 15 miles to the north east of Chirk, the scanty remains of Holt Castle lie on the west bank of the River Dee, where the river crossing it was built to control is now represented by the fourteenth-century Farndon Bridge. The bridge crossed directly into the main street of the accompanying medieval borough, which then led southwards to the castle.[9] Regrettably, the castle has largely been quarried away, including the curtain wall and everything above courtyard level, so that the only stonework to survive is the lower (basement level) part of the inner wall that encircled the courtyard (Figure 8.9). Within this wall is the only architectural detail to survive in its original state, namely, a doorway with a segmental-pointed arch,

Figure 8.9: *Holt. The remains of the castle from the south.*

situated at the north end of the east elevation. This opening is at the foot of a staircase descending from the courtyard into the basement. Just inside, the roof of the vestibule was carried on two-tier quadrant corbelling of the type found at Caernarfon from 1295 onwards.

This is all we can ay about the details, but the broader character of the castle has been established from several written surveys combined with a number of sixteenth- and seventeenth-century drawings.[10] Like Chirk, it had a regular plan, but of great originality, and it is evident that it was designed for a patron with a well-developed aesthetic sense, by an architect of considerable ability. Holt was a tightly planned courtyard castle in the form of a regular pentagon with integral two-storey domestic ranges lining the courtyard, four-storey cylindrical towers projecting from the five corners, and spiral staircases in each of the towers and in the angles of the domestic ranges. The geometry of the design was based on a circle, within which the pentagon was constructed; smaller circles representing the towers were set out at the angles. The castle was surrounded by a moat, fed by the Dee (Figure 8.10).

On the north side, a bridge crossed from the borough to a freestanding rectangular outer gate tower or barbican, with its own drawbridge and a portcullis at each end of the gate passage. A second bridge crossed to the main gateway in the centre of the north range, also protected by a drawbridge and portcullis. Above this entrance, apparently set beneath a pointed relieving arch, was a carving of a lion said to have been in the attitude passant guardant, although no detailed representation of the sculpture survives. It is for this reason that the building was known variously as *Castrum Leonum*, *Chastellion*, and *Caerlleon*, that is to say, the Castle of the Lion, although the significance of the symbol is unknown.

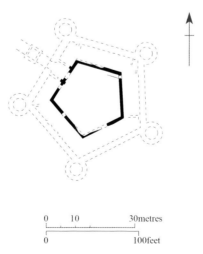

Figure 8.10: *Holt. Castle plan. By Nigel Dodds after Butler 1974*

There are some analogies with the royal works, notably cylindrical stair turrets rising from the roofs of the corner towers, reflecting those at Conwy, Harlech, and Beaumaris, and the understated entrance, which has something in common with the gateways from the east and west barbican to the inner and outer wards of Conwy. On the other hand, the integrated nature of the building seems more advanced than at any of the Edwardian castles, which might suggest a date nearer the turn of the thirteenth and fourteenth centuries than 1284. Sadly, the remains are too insubstantial to make a more fruitful comparison.

Nevertheless, despite the loss of the building, the drawings allow us to assert that Holt was a rather extraordinary building for its time, foreshadowing the symmetrical integrated courtyard castles that, in England, are more usually associated with the later fourteenth century.[11] It would not be outlandish to suggest that the inspiration behind it might be Castel del Monte, the emperor Frederick II's octagonal castle of *c.* 1240 in Puglia, where, interestingly, sculptured lions are also associated with the gateway. Holt is not such a regular building, but, it is difficult to imagine that it was not designed according to strict geometrical principles. However, in translation from the tracing house to the realities of the site, the proportions seem to have gone awry; not sufficiently so as to mar an appreciation of the intent, but enough to suggest that the difficulties presented by the circumstances of construction prevented a scrupulous adherence to the plan. In spite of the discrepancies, it is still a remarkable building, surpassing Goodrich (which has been noted as an early exemplar of the integrated castle both in symmetry and in the depth of integration between the defences and the domestic accommodation[12]). The earls of Surrey had a history of original architectural projects. In the late twelfth century, John de Warenne's grandfather, Hamelin Plantagenet, had erected a highly unusual great tower at Conisbrough Castle (Yorkshire), strikingly modern and stunningly effective in appearance. John de Warenne himself had been instrumental in completing the reconstruction in stone of the twelfth-century motte and bailey castle at Sandal, near Wakefield (Yorkshire), a work carried out over the years *c.* 1240–72. Like Holt, the great tower of Sandal, which occupied the top of the twelfth-century motte, seems to have been another centrally-planned building. Circular in plan, it had a gateway with twin flanking towers balanced by two additional wall towers on the opposite side of the circuit. Concentric inner and outer walls contained the domestic accommodation and there was a central area, *c.* 18ft (5.5m) in diameter, containing a courtyard or a central living space. The possibility that Sandal acted as a model for the great tower of Flint has already been mooted (Chapter 4), but despite being on a smaller scale, it is also possible that it suggested some of the attributes of Holt.

Denbigh

Both Chirk and Holt lay close to the English border, but the third of these new marcher lordship castles, Denbigh, was in Gwynedd. Denbigh had served as the centre of the Welsh cantref of Rhufoniog, the rulers of Gwynedd having had a residence here by 1230.[13] Now, on 16 October 1282, Edward granted Rhufoniog, as well as the adjacent cantref of Rhos to the north west and the commote of Dinmael to the south east, to the Earl of Lincoln.[14] These territories made up the lordship of Denbigh where building began on the castle and town defences very soon after the grant, possibly within the next couple of weeks, with the assistance of royal craftsmen, including James of St George. The King took a personal interest in its construction, being present at Denbigh between the 23 and 31 October.[15] Amongst the new castles engendered by the Second Welsh War, then, Denbigh may have been the first to be begun.

The medieval fortifications enclose a hilltop site of roughly triangular shape, the base to the north and the apex to the south, this latter containing the high point of the defended area on which the castle is situated, and from which point the ground falls away markedly to the north and east. There is therefore a degree of similarity between the topography of Denbigh and that of Caernarfon, where the walled town was also laid out on sloping ground below the castle. The entire enclosed area has a circuit of around 3,000ft, an area of approximately 12 acres (4.9ha), and the castle itself contains 1.6 acres (0.7ha), making the length of its circuit and the greater area almost the same as the corresponding enclosure at Caernarfon, although Caernarfon Castle itself contains about half an acre (0.2ha) less than its Denbigh counterpart. Whether these correspondences denote some form of collusion or are simply fortuitous is a matter of conjecture, but the two castles are certainly related architecturally (Figure 8.11).

The construction of the castle and town walls has generally been considered to fall into two main phases.[16] The earlier comprised the main circuit of the town walls which formed a continuous circuit around the edge of the hill, and doubled as the southern and western walls of the castle; this outer circuit is characterised by a relatively narrow wall and largely round-fronted towers. The second phase comprises, firstly, the north and east walls of the castle facing the town, which are characterised by thicker walls and polygonal towers; secondly, a mantlet, or outer enclosure, that extended around the south and west sides of the castle; thirdly, an elaborate postern gate complex on the south side of the castle; and fourthly, an addition to the town walls at the north-east corner of the enclosure, where a salient was thrown out, including a polygonal tower known as the Goblin Tower and the two town gatehouses, the Exchequer Gate to the west (of which only the lower courses survive), and the Burgess Gate to the north west.

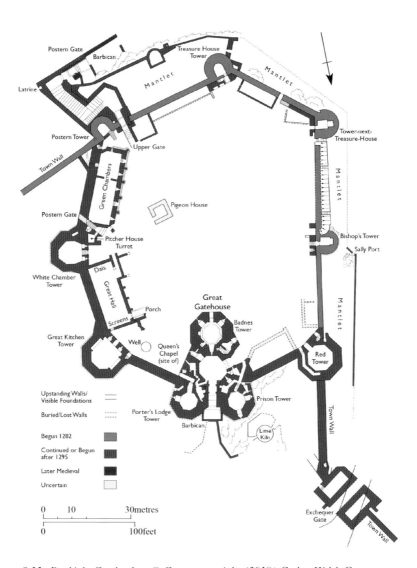

Figure 8.11: *Denbigh. Castle plan. © Crown copyright (2018) Cadw, Welsh Government*

These two phases have been dated to either side of the Welsh rebellion of 1294–5. The dates, however, are conjectural, and if the pattern of construction followed at Caernarfon was to have been replicated here, the foundations of the entire castle are likely to have been laid down at the same time as the town walls. Indeed, recent archaeological research on the castle suggests that the construction sequence was not as straightforward as implied by the traditional chronology. Structural analysis of the castles's north and east defences points to a first-floor level hiatus in construction, encompassing the gatehouse, curtain, and wall towers; there is also reason to believe that the back of the gatehouse post-dates the front, and that the initial work on the gatehouse was confined to the facade, a sequence that is paralleled at Caernarfon.[17] The lower courses of the castle's northern and eastern sides then, may also predate the capture of the town and castle by the Welsh in 1294, by which time it is possible that twelve consecutive seasons of building work had been carried out.

The general resemblance of Denbigh to Caernarfon has long been recognised, and there are reasonable grounds for assuming that Caernarfon provided the model for the north and east fronts of the castle. This assumption is partly based on the use of polygonal towers, which, prior to Caernarfon, were a rarity in English castle building. Taylor saw their adoption at Caernarfon as a symptom of the castle's special status in Edward's scheme, which is a reasonable inference, and the logical corollary to it would be that Denbigh followed Caernarfon rather than the other way round. The reason for the appearance of polygonal towers at Denbigh, then, is not necessarily because it too had a special status, but because it was designed to emulate an esteemed exemplar. Be that as it may, there is plenty of divergence from the model. The Red Tower, at the north-east angle of the castle, is the closest in form to some of the wall towers at Caernarfon, though it has greater projection beyond the curtain, a trait that is replicated by the Kitchen Tower and White Chamber Tower on the east side, but the rear walls of all three towers are coterminous with the inner elevation of the curtain, in contrast to Caernarfon where the towers project inwards as well as outwards.

This divergence in approach extends to the relationship between the great gatehouse of Denbigh and the King's Gate at Caernarfon (Figures 8.12 and 7.6), which is often at the centre of a comparison between the two castles. Both buildings make use of octagonal towers. In the case of Denbigh these comprised the two towers flanking the entrance and a third tower to the rear separated from the others by an octagonal space enclosed by linking walls giving a broadly triangular layout to the whole complex. It isn't quite so obvious what was intended in respect of the King's Gate, but it clearly took a different form, appropriate to its site and intended function. However, as has been suggested, here too the plan may have been to incorporate a vaulted polygonal chamber behind the entrance passage from which at least one and probably two obliquely aligned passages gave access to the castle's interior.

Both gatehouses were given a high outer arch of four orders in red sandstone to contrast with the lighter coloured stone of the walls; at Caernarfon the three outer orders are wave-moulded, whilst the innermost is sunk chamfered; at Denbigh, the two outermost mouldings (the only ones to survive) are sunk chamfered; apart from the innermost order at Caernarfon, none of these moulded orders extends to the jambs, instead, they die into the walls at springing level. Above the arch, in both instances, there is a horizontal string course surmounted by a niche containing a statue.

Whilst the concept of these frontages is similar, there are also pronounced differences in the interpretation of the theme, to the extent that Caernarfon seems

Figure 8.12: *Denbigh. Great Gatehouse from the north.*

staid beside the more flamboyant Denbigh. The architect of Caernarfon achieved an imposing and tightly knit frontage with a relatively narrow and shallow entrance recess. Compare this with Denbigh where the depth of the recess, and the widths of the flanking splays, portal and proscenium-like over-arch are all twice the size of their Caernarfon counterparts, an aspect of the design that has resulted in a more generous and inviting frontage, and endowed the gatehouse with a vitality that is absent from Caernarfon. The approach taken at Denbigh is closer to that of the Queen's Gate, which also has a more generous splay and deeper recess than the King's Gate.

The treatment of the Denbigh gatehouse above the arch is more restrained than the ground floor; the statue niche is plain compared with that of the King's Gate and whereas the latter is physically connected to the upper gate arch and emphasises the verticality of the building, at Denbigh, where the vertical element is less pronounced, the separation between entrance arch and the arrangement overhead is absolute. A string course extended right across the entrance recess between the two flanking towers; below it, hanging like a starched flag upon a line, is the rectangular panel containing the niche, which extends to just above the upper gate arch.

The string and frame are studded with ballflower decoration, a sculptural embellishment mostly falling within the date range 1300–30 and having a particular association with the western English counties, even though its distribution is more widespread. An early example is the central tower of Hereford Cathedral, underway by 1307. The Denbigh form is slightly unusual, in that the ballflowers are linked by trailing stems, a combination also to be found at Salisbury Cathedral, on the central tower begun *c.* 1310, and on the tomb of Bishop Ghent of *c.* 1315 in the same building. The presence of this decorative motif certainly suggests that work on the first floor of the gatehouse continued into the fourteenth century, and may perhaps denote a designer with a West Country background, this being the only detail of its type to ornament the Edwardian castles of Wales.

Further embellishment is to be found in the targeted use of red sandstone; this has already been mentioned in respect of the upper gate arch, but it occurs elsewhere in the building too: at the angles of the flanking towers where the quoins are picked out in red, a treatment extended to the wall towers, and some evidence for horizontal banding. Above the string, red sandstone blocks alternate with lighter masonry to create a chequered pattern. Less formal distributions of similar character have been noted at Beaumaris where the towers of the inner ward are so decorated, and it is possible that they inspired the more regular scheme of the Denbigh gatehouse.

The quality of spaciousness that pervades the frontage extends to the interior of the gatehouse, the gate passage giving access to an octagonal entrance hall, an unusual and unexpected feature, calculated to induce surprise and admiration. Rising through two storeys, it was covered by an octpartite rib vault of which only partial outlines survive within the walls. Wall ribs rose from the angles of the room to the ridge ribs, which probably extended to a central boss rather than a column. Whether there was any practical purpose to this room is uncertain, but it may have served as a waiting room or a place of business for suppliants. In structural principle (but not in complexity) the vault was similar to those of the octagonal chapter houses of York, of *c.* 1290, and Southwell Minister (Nottinghamshire), of *c.* 1293, the latter being only slightly larger than the entrance hall (Figure 8.13).[18]

The great gatehouse is the pre-eminent feature of the castle, but another noteworthy aspect is the elaborate south entrance, or postern. This secondary entrance gives access to the castle from a rock-cut ditch that extends around its south side. A sub-rectangular outer gatehouse with a turning bridge and portcullis led to a rectangular space at the foot of a broad staircase, which, after a right-angled turn, led under an open arch and then up the rock to a landing where the stairs took another right-angled turn and ascended to a sloping road in front of an inner gateway (Figure 8.14). This second gateway was also protected by a turning bridge and portcullis, in addition to which there was a single flanking

Figure 8.13: *Denbigh. Great Gatehouse entrance hall from the north.*

tower (Postern Tower). During the creation of the postern complex the Phase 1 Postern Tower was modified by the addition of a rectangular block in front of its rounded prow; this supported a platform, or alure, defended by a parapet from which the approach could be monitored. The enclosing wall on the west side of the main flight was also provided with a defended wall walk that communicated with the upper floor of the lower gatehouse. The Denbigh postern is unusual but not unique, bearing comparison with the water gate of Conwy, now no longer extant, which incorporated a long flight of stairs extending between lower and upper gateways.

Unlike the royal foundations of Conwy and Caernarfon where the town walls are augmented by towers at fairly regular intervals, at Denbigh the wall towers are to be found in two clusters, the main one comprising a group of five, all with rounded prows, around the south end, four of which form part of the castle enceinte. The other group lies to the south east and consists of the round-nosed North-East Tower and the square Countess Tower. All these towers are unexceptional in their architectural interest.

More interesting is the salient situated on the east side of the enclosure towards its northern end. This addition to the initial stone defences comprises an outer curtain, enclosing an irregularly triangular area beyond the cliff face, at the apex of which is the two-storey Goblin Tower (Figure 8.15). Built to a polygonal plan,

Figure 8.14: *Denbigh. Postern Gate steps from the south.*

like the two eastern towers of the castle, the Goblin Tower contained a well and the main purpose of the fortification was to defend this water supply. The base of the tower is protected by a steeply sloping talus. The salient and the Goblin Tower represent one part of the fortifications at Denbigh that can be assigned with confidence to a later phase.

Of the two gateways to the town, the Exchequer Tower had disappeared by the mid-nineteenth century, but excavation has shown that its ground plan was broadly similar to that of the Burgess Tower.[19] The Burgess Gate, which is the main element of architectural note within the town defences, is a two-storey building with a central entrance passage flanked by a pair of D-shaped towers (Figure 8.16). The interest of these towers lies in the fact that they sit on rectangular bases, the angles of which are carried up the towers as spurs. Such features are found nowhere in the royal castles of the Edwardian period in Wales, but, as has been noted above, they are a regional characteristic of the Welsh Marches, notably at Caerphilly, Chepstow, and Goodrich. At Caerphilly they were applied to polygonal towers, but at Goodrich to round towers. The spurs flanking the gate passage rise to roughly half the height of the first-floor window. The other aspect of architectural interest is that here too different coloured masonry was used to create a chequerboard pattern as seems to have been the case in the great gatehouse of the castle, the upper storey of which dates from the first quarter of the fourteenth century.

Figure 8.15: *Denbigh. Goblin Tower from the north.*

Figure 8.16: *Denbigh. Burgess Gate from the north east.*

Powis

During the First Welsh War, the Earl of Lincoln had played a major role in reinstating Gruffudd ap Gwenwynwyn as ruler of Upper Powys. In 1286, the estate passed to Gruffudd's eldest son and principal heir Owain (d. 1293), who adopted the title of Baron de la Pole, thereby reinventing himself as a member of the English nobility. The principal castle of the erstwhilst principality was Powis, near Welshpool (Montgomeryshire), which is doubtless to be identified with the castle of 'Pola' that Gruffudd ap Gwenwynwyn prepared for attack in 1274, and which was subsequently burnt by Llywellyn ap Gruffudd. Following Edward's victory in 1277 Powis was rebuilt.[20] Gruffudd may have begun the work, but it may have been completed by Owain.

The castle sits on a ridge to the west of the River Severn. It is approached from the south west, where a ditch preceded a rectangular north-east to south-west aligned outer ward, with a pair of small round towers at the two angles of the entrance front, the south-western one of which survives.[21] The predominant medieval feature of the outer ward is a large D-shaped tower that projects from the centre of the north-west curtain. However, the main point of note in respect of the outer courtyard, given its Welsh ownership, is perhaps its rectangular plan, which has analogues at Dinas Brân and Dolforwyn, of the 1260s and 1270s respectively. Moreover, the little corner turrets that framed the entrance front are reminiscent of the dainty gatehouse turrets at Brân. Dinas Brân is 23 miles to the north, and Dolforwyn only 7 miles to the south west of Powis. The three make up an interesting regional and chronological group, but the affinities of the main feature of Powis, as rebuilt after the Edwardian conquest, is predominantly with English rather than Welsh antecedents.

At the north-east end of the outer ward, formerly separated from it by a ditch, and at a slightly higher level, is the inner ward, transformed internally from the sixteenth century onwards, but retaining a good deal of exposed medieval masonry on the outer elevations. The principal thirteenth-century element is the great gatehouse, which faces the outer ward, its imposing closely-set twin drum towers recalling Harlech, which was obviously the major influence (Figure 8.17). The Powis gatehouse, however, is more a facade than a building, and is used

Figure 8.17: *Powis. Great gatehouse from the south west.*

here to take advantage of the confined nature of its site to generate a more concentrated impact than at Harlech. There is greater emphasis on the entrance, which comprises a segmental-arched opening of four rounded orders recessed beneath a similar arch also of four orders, each with a rounded arris. Above this, the gap between the towers narrows; it seems that the designer of Powis had taken note of the narrow space between the twin towers of Harlech and had emphasised the feature in order to make the towers loom larger. It's an effective tweak of an existing format, although the slightly awkward transition from the wider entrance is not entirely successful.

As we have seen, multi-ordered arches of a more grandiose fashion appear over the gateways of Caernarfon and Denbigh, so they too may be sources for the design of the Powis gatehouse, but the rounded arris is a particular feature of Goodrich Castle, where it is found in a number of late thirteenth-century window and door surrounds, and of the gatehouse of St Briavel's Castle (Gloucestershire), which dates from 1292–3. In addition, in common with the Exchequer Gate at Denbigh, the towers are provided with spurs, which is a feature associated with the castles of the Welsh Marches, including Goodrich.

The Baronial Castles in the South

Chepstow

The defeat of Llywelyn also encouraged further building activity amongst the marcher lords of South Wales. Chepstow Castle was one centre of activity. In 1270, it had been inherited by Roger Bigod, fifth Earl of Norfolk, who was to take part in all Edward's major campaigns in Wales and also serve in Scotland. Substantive works were carried out at Chepstow in his time including the Gloriette in the Lower Bailey, Marten's Tower, which projects from the south-east angle of the Lower Bailey, the remodelling of the great tower, including the addition of a gallery on its north side, and the Upper Gatehouse at the west end of the castle (Figure 8.18).

The earliest of these projects was the Gloriette, a suite of rooms occupying the north side of the Lower Bailey, on which work was progressing in 1282–4 under a Master Ralph, although the complex had probably been begun somewhat earlier.[22] The Gloriette is an interesting example of thirteenth-century integrated domestic planning, which heralds the more extensive schemes that are characteristic of the later fourteenth century; one of its attributes is the utilisation of space at several different levels in response to the topography of the site. Ranged along the north curtain were (from west to east) a cellared ground-floor great hall with a two-storey porch; pantry and buttery with chamber above; full-height kitchen; and larder with first- and second-floor chambers over.

There is some unusual fenestration in which two trefoil-headed-light windows are surmounted by single quatrefoil oculi and set beneath relieving arches shaped

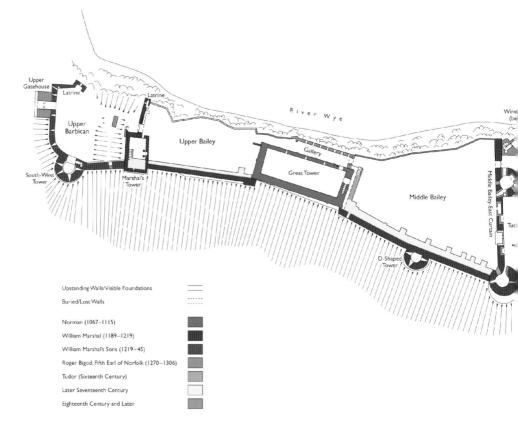

Figure 8.18: *Chepstow. Castle plan.* © *Crown copyright (2018) Cadw, Welsh Government*

to the shouldered profile of the ensemble (Figure 8.19). Surviving examples lit the kitchen and second-floor chamber at the west end of the range, and there were probably further windows of this type in the hall.[23] Two windows of identical form are to be found in the keep at second-floor level, where they lit the north side of a two-bay chamber block that is said to have been raised over the west end of the keep during the second quarter of the thirteenth century.[24] If the dates are correct they suggest an extended longevity for this design and perhaps an insularity of

Figure 8.19: *Chepstow. Gloriette kitchen window from the south east.*

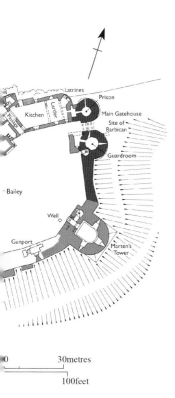

Latrines
Prison
Kitchen
Larder
Main Gatehouse
Site of
Barbican
Guardroom
Bailey
Well
Gunport
Marten's
Tower

0
30metres
100feet

masonic practices. The type was used again in the South–East Tower of Caldicot Castle, some 5 miles to the south west of Chepstow, on which basis the building has been assigned to the late thirteenth century.[25]

Somewhat later than the Gloriette is Marten's Tower, a large three-storey residential wall tower built in 1288–94 under the supervision of Master Ralph (Figure 8.20).[26] This structure, which, at 52ft (16m) x 42ft (12.8m), is unusually large for a wall tower, is built to a D-shaped plan on a square base from which spurs rise to clasp the front of the building. This arrangement is reminiscent of the even larger North Tower, or keep, built some forty years earlier at Cardigan Castle. The similarities are more than superficial: in addition to the ground plan, spurs, and the degree of projection beyond the curtain, both towers have the same regular arrangement of three loops at basement level, and both had an integral spiral staircase situated towards the rear. Further comparison is hampered by the differing degrees of survival, but it seems reasonable to suppose that Cardigan's North Tower may have served as the principal model for Marten's Tower. If so, it is another indication that south Walian building traditions were independent of the royal works in the north, although use of a royal model would tend to support the theory that Marten's Tower was built as a royal lodging to be reserved for the use of the King in the event of a visit to the castle.[27]

Another prominent aspect of Marten's Tower is the sculptural decoration, notably the five figures that adorn the battlements, but also the carved rosettes around the internal frame of the chapel window. The statues bring to mind the sculptural crestings of the merlons at Caernarfon, the most extensively applied example of this general type of adornment. Unfortunately, it is impossible to say for certain which came first, but it has been argued that similar statues to those at Chepstow were to be found at the Tower of London in the 1270s, which, given that the Caernarfon sculptures are mostly heads, rather than figures or demi-figures, suggests that the Tower may well have been the source.[28]

From *c*. 1292 to *c*. 1300 Bigod also made substantial alterations to the great tower (Figure 8.21). A single-storey gallery was added to the north side, which extended to the edge of the cliff and provided a defended passageway linking the Middle and Upper baileys. The main alteration, however, was at second-floor level. Prior to reconstruction work, the Great Tower was a two-storey building, except at the west end, where a second-storey room had been built above the first-floor chamber. Bigod extended the second floor over the entire building by

Figure 8.20: *Chepstow. Marten's Tower from the north east.*

adding another room above the first-floor hall. The fenestration of this room is different from the earlier thirteenth-century work, for, although they conform to the format of twin lights beneath a pointed arch, the lights themselves have shouldered lintels, and in place of the tracery there is a blind tympanum above.

Finally, the Upper Gatehouse is less well dated than the buildings of the Lower Bailey, but it is an addition to the early to mid-thirteenth-century curtain,

Figure 8.21: *Chepstow. Great Tower from the north east.*

and is attributed to the fifth earl's tenure. It is a plain rectangular building, and its main interest lies in the drawbridge and portcullis mechanisms. Unusually, the portcullis grooves did not extend to the floor of the gate passage. Also unusual is the character of the drawbridge mechanism – the axle was fitted into cranked grooves like those at Caerphilly but angled upwards rather than downwards. When Clark visited the castle in the late nineteenth century he noted holes in the masonry for the drawbridge chains, although the masonry above the outer portal is now depleted and the evidence for his observations no longer extant.[29] However, there is no pit for a turning bridge so it must be assumed that despite the existence of superior technology the drawbridge was raised by manual labour. This drawbridge was rebuilt in 1298 so the assumption must be that Caerphilly influenced Chepstow rather than the other way round.

Master Ralph, the earl's mason, is first mentioned at Chepstow in 1282 in connection with the new kitchen, and he died in 1293 soon after work had begun on the remodelling of the Great Tower.[30] It is believed that he was the mastermind behind the greater part of Bigod's work at Chepstow. He is identified with the earl's mason who was working at Bosham (Sussex), where, in 1283–4, he was referred to as Ralph Gogun, and, in 1292–3, as Ralph, mason of London. On these grounds Master Ralph has been seen as an outsider, who brought to south Wales the benefits of a metropolitan savoir faire. There is some support for this view of a cosmopolitan interloper with experience of the royal works in the figure sculptures on the battlements of Marten's Tower, which may have been based on similar features at the Tower of London, and in the introduction of shouldered lintels into the great tower, but, as has been suggested above, there is also reason to believe that some of the sources for Bigod's Chepstow are to be found within the region. What we can be sure of, however, is that the earl's master builder was a highly skilled professional, and that the two main additions of the period, the Gloriette and Marten's Tower, were masterly accomplishments, the former for its sophisticated internal planning, and the latter for its general and monumental effect.

Kidwelly

Towards the west, in Carmarthenshire, Kidwelly was one of two major projects that were undertaken in the aftermath of the Second Welsh War. The castle stands on a ridge above the west bank of the River Gwendraeth, where it forms a semi-circle, its base towards the east where the steep slope down to the river offers a degree of protection. A ditch arcs around the landward side to define a fairly compact enclosure containing two wards, the inner one roughly square, its east wall forming part of the outer enceinte on this side (Figure 8.22). The castle was substantially rebuilt in the later thirteenth century, a project generally thought to have been instigated by Payn de Chaworth between 1275 when he returned from

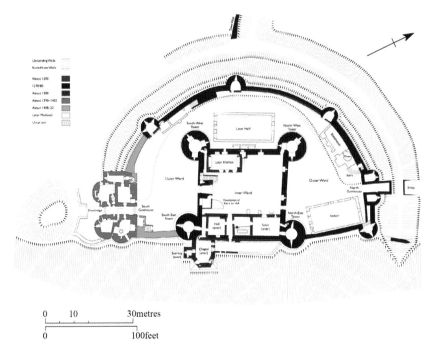

Figure 8.22: *Kidwelly. Castle plan © Crown copyright (2018) Cadw, Welsh Government*

crusade with King Edward, and 1279 when he died, although there is no direct evidence to support the attribution.[31] Payn de Chaworth was succeeded as Lord of Kidwelly by his brother Patrick. When Patrick died, in 1283, the castle came to William de Valence, Earl of Pembroke, who held it until his death in 1296.[32] Either or both may have contributed to the rebuilding. On William's death, the castle reverted to Patrick de Chaworth's daughter and heiress, Matilda, who, the following year, married Henry of Lancaster, the King's nephew. Matilda and Henry may also have added to the castle.

The reconstruction of Kidwelly Castle probably began with the creation of a new inner ward inside the existing enclosure, hard up against the east side, its curtain wall on this side replacing the old one. Built to a nearly square plan, it was given four cylindrical corner towers, the southern ones projecting slightly beyond the outer curtain. There are two gateways, the main one to the south, and a smaller one to the north; both were protected by a portcullis and a gate, but were otherwise simple passages through the curtain walls. Then, the existing outer curtain was rebuilt and provided with a number of D-shaped wall towers, and a twin-towered gatehouse on the north side; there may have been a second gatehouse on the opposite side of the castle where the present late medieval South Gatehouse now stands. Later, *c.* 1300, a semi-polygonal chapel tower, with a prominently spurred base, was added to the outer face of the east curtain, and the domestic apartments of the inner ward were rebuilt.

One of the main interests of Kidwelly is the resemblance of the inner ward to the inner ward of Conwy, which was also built to a square plan. A comparison of the dimensions is intriguing in that both are approximately 100ft square (30.5m²). Is this coincidence or does it indicate collaboration, and does it help to refine the chronology of Kidwelly's inner ward? If this similarity is the result of consultation between the builders of Conwy and Kidwelly, it can have amounted to little more than the rudiments of the plan, perhaps no more than verbal or written advice. Apart from the round corner towers, which are not uncommon features, the only other similarity is in the understated gateways, which are rather unusual, and which, at Conwy, may hark back to the simple entrances of many Savoyard castles. Conwy was under construction from 1283, which is one reason for thinking that Kidwelly may have begun in the 1280s rather than the 1270s.

However, other details of Kidwelly are independent of the royal works in north Wales, and are more indicative of the south Walian region. This is particularly true of the Chapel Tower, the polygonal plan, and spur buttresses which are clearly related to Caerphilly and Carreg Cennen; another sign of regional practice is the use of domed vaults in the North-West Tower, a technique that stems ultimately from the great tower of Pembroke, and of which there are other thirteenth-century examples in south Wales.

Carreg Cennen

Kidwelly is situated near Carmarthen Bay. Carreg Cennen lies 16½ miles north east of Kidwelly, as the crow flies, where the castle is ostentatiously sited on top of an 883ft (266m) mountain. Originally a Welsh castle, it was the stronghold of the commote of Iscennen. First mentioned in 1248, the castle was captured by Payn de Chaworth in 1277 during the First Welsh War, briefly recaptured by the Welsh in 1282, but, in the aftermath of the Second Welsh War, Edward granted Iscennen along with Carreg Cennen to John Giffard (d. 1299), one of his followers, who had played a leading part in the skirmish during which Llywelyn was killed. The castle was captured during Rhys ap Maredudd's uprising of 1287, but was in Giffard's possession again by 1289. Giffard was probably the builder of the greater part of the existing castle, the first two phases of which can probably be dated to the 1280s and 90s.

Three main structural phases are evident at Carreg Cennen, the earliest being the sub-rectangular inner ward which surmounts the hill. The inner ward was entered via a gatehouse in the centre of the north curtain. The entrance is recessed between a pair of semi-polygonal towers on rectangular bases; short broach spurs rise from the outer corners of the rectangular base to die into the canted angles of the towers. A tower projects from each of two northern angles of the enclosure, one square with canted angles and spurs like the towers of the gatehouse, the other circular. A square chapel tower projecting from the centre of

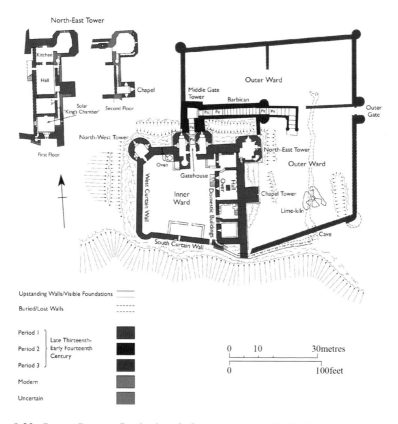

Figure 8.23: *Carreg Cennan. Castle plan. © Crown copyright (2018) Cadw, Welsh Government*

the east front was associated with the main domestic range which extended across the east side of the enclosure (Figure 8.23).

Subsequently, but perhaps only a little later, an elaborate barbican was built to form a defended approach to the main gateway. This elongated structure, which protected a steeply ramped passage, was entered from the south, and after the first few steps turned 90 degrees towards the west to meet the barbican gate tower. This entrance was protected by a turning bridge pivoted on the threshold of gateway; near the head of the ramp was another turning bridge which controlled access to the nearly rectangular Middle Gate Tower, which was itself built against the front of the inner gateway. There was a third turning bridge between the Middle and Inner gateways. All three drawbridges spanned an inner and outer pit, being pivoted between the two; when the drawbridge was raised its inner end swung down into the inner pit, whilst the outer pit was exposed. At a still later date, possibly in the fourteenth century, an outer ward was added on the east and north sides of the inner ward. It had a gateway on the east side with twin D-shaped flanking towers and round corner towers. Regrettably, this section has been reduced to its foundations.

The domestic accommodation in the inner ward is an interesting piece of integrated planning taking in not only the east range but also the North-East Tower and Chapel Tower. The range is divided by transverse walls into four compartments, which, at first-floor level are occupied (from north to south) by a kitchen, hall, and two private chambers, entered independently of one another. The ground-floor rooms were principally for storage. Access to the hall was from the courtyard via an external staircase. The door opened to a screens passage, from which there was access to the kitchen on the left (north) and hall on the right (south). At the far (east) end of the passage a doorway led to mural staircases which descended to the basement of the North-East Tower and ascended to the chapel in the North Tower and a chamber in the North-East Tower. This latter could also be entered from the gatehouse.

In considering the architectural analogues, let us begin with the inner ward, the earliest part of the complex. Here, the canted and spurred towers suggest a link with Caerphilly, that is to say, the phase generally dated to the last quarter of the thirteenth century, which includes the Outer Main Gatehouse, North Gatehouse, and the towers of the North Dam.[33] The relationship between the Inner Gatehouse of Carreg Cennen and Outer Main Gatehouse of Caerphilly is particularly close, suggesting that the first was modelled on the second. The stylistic connection between this phase of Caerphilly and the inner ward of Carreg Cennen is

compounded by two other details. One is a very distinctive cruciform arrow loop, in which each arm terminates in a circular oillet (Figure 8.24); the other is a doorway with a continuous quarter-round profiled surround (Figure 8.25), both of which are features that appear in the Outer Main Gatehouse of Caerphilly (Figures 5.11 and 8.26). This combination of attributes suggests that Caerphilly was the principal source for the builder of Carreg Cennen and that he may have worked on both castles. The theory is made all the more plausible since Giffard was an adherent of the Earl of Gloucester.

Two further characteristics hint at the influence of the royal works. One of these is to be found in the first-floor chamber at the south

Figure 8.24: *Carreg Cennan. Arrow loop in the North-West Tower.*

Figure 8.25 (above left): *Carreg Cennen. Doorway in the Inner Gatehouse.*

Figure 8.26 (above right): *Caerphilly. Doorway in the Outer Main Gatehouse.*

end of the east range where there is a pair of shouldered two-light windows (Figure 8.27). There has been some restoration but the form appears to be authentic. Shouldered lintels are most often associated with the castles of the Second Welsh Wars: Caernarfon in particular, and, to a lesser extent, Conwy and Harlech, but the twin form used here at Carreg Cennen is a particular feature of Caernarfon, and it is plausible that this is the ultimate source for both Carreg Cennen and the similar features in the great tower of Chepstow.

The second feature is the gatehouse to the barbican, now reduced to its lower courses, the remains of which suggest a rather interesting and recognisable design, with a flat front and rounded

Figure 8.27: *Carreg Cennen. Twin carnarvon-arched window in the chamber block.*

ends, a type that has its origins in the royal castles of Henry III's time, between *c.* 1220 and 1250.[34] In the case of Carreg Cennen, however, the nearest parallel both geographically and chronologically is the gate tower of Monnow Bridge over the Wye at Monmouth. Monnow Bridge Tower is probably associated with a grant of murage made by Edward I on 27 August 1297 at the request of his nephew, Henry of Lancaster, Lord of Kidwelly, who, in March that year, had been granted livery of castle and town of Monmouth and his father's lands beyond the Severn.[35] Given the limited and largely royal distribution of this type of gateway, one wonders whether a royal mason was involved at Monmouth, and, if so, whether he also made his way to Carreg Cennen.

The baronial castles of the Second Welsh War form a disparate group of buildings, each with its own personality, and architecturally independent of one another. However, three of the four northern castles discussed here can each be linked stylistically to a royal counterpart: Chirk to Beaumaris, Denbigh to Caernarfon, and Powys to Harlech (Holt, owing to the scale of its destruction is something of an unknown quantity). In each of these instances the builder focused on a key aspect of his royal model in order to capture something of its essence, and incorporated it into his own plans. Whether this was a tribute to the quality or novelty of the design, or whether it represented the presence of royal craftsmen on site, or, indeed, whether it was a reference to royal authority and the brave new world that it represented, can no longer be calculated, but there is a suspicion that all three motives may have made their contribution to a greater or lesser extent. In contrast, the castle architecture of south Wales was only marginally affected by Edward's building programme for the subjugation of Gwynedd, maintaining its own traditions, but nevertheless cognisant of developments in royal circles.

Chapter Nine

The Edwardian Castle in Scotland

Summary Narrative

During the 1290s, and more particularly after the pacification of Wales in 1295, Edward's attention was increasingly drawn to Scotland in an effort to find a satisfactory resolution to a succession crisis within the northern kingdom following the untimely death of King Alexander III in 1286, followed by the demise of his young granddaughter and heir, Margaret, in 1290. Invited to preside over the court that was assembled to decide upon the succession, Edward accepted on the condition that the claimants recognised him as superior lord of Scotland with legal authority to judge the case; the custody of Scotland was temporarily assigned to him. In November 1292 judgement was given in favour of John de Balliol, Lord of Barnard Castle and Bywell in Durham and Northumberland respectively, but also Lord of Galloway. Balliol swore fealty to Edward.

In 1295 Scotland made an alliance with France against England; the following year, Edward invaded Scotland, and in a lightning campaign deposed Balliol, apprehended the principal antagonists, and subdued the country. It was during this episode that the coronation stone of the Scottish kings was removed from Scone Abbey, near Perth, and taken to Westminster. Edward did not seek a successor to Balliol, but appointed an English administration under the military leadership of Balliol's father-in-law, John de Warenne, Earl of Surrey. On 28 August 1296 Edward received the homage of the Scots at Berwick.

Subsequently, many Scots remained loyal to Edward, but substantial numbers would not be reconciled to the new order, and, in 1297, William Wallace sparked off a widespread revolt with the assassination of the English Sheriff of Lanarkshire, an act that was followed a few months later by a decisive victory over an English army at Stirling Bridge, severely damaging Edward's hold on Scotland, and leading to the loss of most of his castles. The following year, England invaded Scotland again and defeated Wallace's army at Falkirk. English power was enhanced by the recovery of a number of castles: Bothwell, Edinburgh, Linlithgow, Jedburgh, Stirling, and the capture of the Bruce castles of Lochmaben and Dumfries.

Scotland, however, was far from pacified, the King's control being confined to areas south of the Forth–Clyde line, though even here the grip was tenuous. In 1299 Stirling Castle was recaptured by the Scots. So too was Bothwell, which was regained by the English the following year, only to be retaken by the Scots. Further to the south, Caerlaverock Castle, whose lord, Sir Herbert Maxwell, had been killed at Falkirk, had, by 1299, become a centre of Scottish resistance once again and a thorn in the side of the English garrison of Lochmaben.

The process of re-establishing English control over Scotland began slowly in the summer of 1300, with the capture of Caerlaverock, which was now taken over by Edward's man, Robert de Clifford, to whom the castle had been granted following the victory at Falkirk in 1298. The following year Bothwell was recaptured, and Aymer de Valence, now Lord of Bothwell, to whom the castle and barony had been granted, made the castle his headquarters.

The King spent the winter of 1301–2 at the royal manor house of Linlithgow, where work was carried out on the King's camera and a peel was erected around the complex. In January 1302, a truce was concluded, and Edward took advantage of a period of calm to set in motion a more serious programme of construction at Linlithgow under James of St George, who took charge in April. Also during 1302 a new peel was begun at Selkirk.[1]

In January 1303, in anticipation of a major invasion of Scotland, Richard the Engineer was summoned from Chester to Windsor to consult with the King on the construction of three fortified bridges with which to cross the Forth. He then returned to recruit carpenters from Chester and bring them to the Norfolk port of Lynn (King's Lynn) where the bridges were to be made. Master Richard's deputy, Henry of Ryhull, followed with another contingent of carpenters, and the bridges were completed by 23 May, the master smith Walter de Barton having undertaken the ironwork.[2]

The bridge components were loaded onto a flotilla of 30 ships, which, together with 2 pilot vessels, set sail for Scotland, taking with them Henry of Ryhull, 30 carpenters and 4 blacksmiths, ready to assemble the bridges once they reached their destination. Fitted out with pennants, its principal ships bearing long streamers and standards emblazoned with the Cross of St George, the little fleet must have presented an engaging sight as the wind filled its sails and it made its way up the coast in the early summer of 1303.

Meanwhile, the English army had assembled at Roxburgh, from where it set out at much the same time as the ships left Lynn.[3] On 4 June the King was in Edinburgh, and at Linlithgow two days later. The army must have met the fleet near Stirling, the river being navigable up to here, so that the ships could have transported the bridges all the way to the crossing point where they were assembled. By 10 June, the army had crossed the river and a temporary headquarters had been established at Cambuskenneth Abbey. Stirling Castle was left in peace for the time being and the English moved on to Perth, reaching the town by 20 June, and remaining there until the end of July. From Perth the army advanced to Arbroath, and then to Aberdeen, which it reached by 14 August, taking Brechin Castle on the way.

At Aberdeen, Edward was within the orbit of the loyalist Cheyne family. Henry Cheyne, Bishop of Aberdeen, also administered the sheriffdom of Aberdeen, whilst his brother, Reginald Cheyne of Inverugie near Peterhead, where he had a castle, was a former Sheriff of Inverness. Edward was still at Aberdeen on 23 August but by the 4 September had reached Banff, and by the 10th was at Kinloss where he stayed for three weeks, and where he no doubt took up residence at the abbey. Some 8½ miles to the north east of Kinloss is the site of Duffus, another castle held by Reginald Cheyne in 1303; it is feasible that Edward visited it and discussed its refortification with Cheyne; it was certainly under repair in 1305 (see below, this chapter).

In September Edward occupied Lochindorb, the castle of John Comyn of Badenoch, now guardian, or governor, of Scotland in the name of King John, and by 8 October was at the castle of Kildrummy, then probably in the keeping of Robert Bruce, Earl of Carrick and the future King Robert I, and here there is reason to believe James of St George raised a new gatehouse (see below, this chapter). By 17 October Edward had reached Dunfermline where he overwintered.

In February 1304 John Comyn submitted to Edward, and the stage was set for the final act of the campaign: the siege of Stirling. It began on 21 April, and the castle was captured on 20 July; other than a few pockets of resistance, the rebellion had been put down and Edward took over the government of the realm. William Wallace was captured and executed the following year, and, shortly afterwards, in the September of 1305, Edward set out his Ordinance for the Settlement of Scotland in which the administrative arrangements for the government of the country were set out and appointments confirmed.[4]

Scotland's future course seemed set, but, only a few months later, in February 1306, just as the years of conflict appeared to be over, and the country reconciled to the new regime, Robert Bruce broke out in rebellion, murdering his powerful rival, John Comyn, and having himself crowned King of Scotland. This uprising was short-lived, the rebel army being routed at Methven near Perth, and victory was followed by executions and arrests. Bruce, however, remained at large and the insurgency lived on. Edward made his way north to take charge, but his health was failing and he was forced into a lengthy recuperative stay at Lanercost Abbey (Cumberland). The rest cure proved unsuccessful, and, on 7 July 1307, at Burgh by Sands (Cumberland), he died. By this time, however, both James of St George and Walter of Hereford had returned to Wales and resumed their positions at Beaumaris and Caernarfon respectively.

Castle Building by Edward in Scotland, 1296–1307

Large numbers of building craftsmen accompanied or followed the King to Scotland. Some had been employed on the royal works in Wales, including James of St George and Walter of Hereford, although little is known of their movements in Scotland. Master James was in Linlithgow by the autumn of 1299, and was undertaking the fortification of the site in 1302.[5] He may have worked at Kildrummy in 1303, and was present at the siege of Stirling in 1304. The first mention of Walter of Hereford in Scotland was in 1300, and, in 1304, following Edward's major invasion of the previous year, he was working on the town wall of Perth and making artillery ammunition for the siege of Stirling. Both men probably undertook, or were consulted about, other projects, but, if so, the details have not survived. There were a number of other craftsmen whose names are familiar from the Welsh accounts, but there are many more who seem to have had northern origins, and it is probable that the greater part of the workforce came from the northern counties, notably Cumberland, Westmorland, and Northumberland.

There is little evidence that Edward built any new castles in Scotland, but a number of existing castles are known to have been re-fortified, or had their defences strengthened, including Aberdeen, Berwick, Dundee, Dumfries, Edinburgh, Forfar, Jedburgh, Kirkintilloch, Linlithgow, Lochmaben, Oban, and Selkirk. Town defences were also constructed at Perth and Dunfermline. However, the scant detail of the documentary evidence, the poor survival of the buildings, and the limited amount of archaeological fieldwork conducted mean that only at a handful of sites is there much idea of the nature or scale of the English work.

Exceptions in this latter respect are the Bruce castles of Dumfries and Lochmaben. The former in Nithsdale, and the latter in Annandale (Dumfriesshire), which, in the aftermath of the 1298 campaign, were given into the custody of Robert Clifford who, on 25 November, was appointed warden of Annandale. On 4 and 5 September Edward himself had been at Lochmaben, probably reviewing the defensive possibilities of the site, and, by the end of the year, work was underway on the construction of a peel.[6] Following a siege by the Earl of Carrick in August 1299, the peel was strengthened.[7]

In early October 1299, the constable of Caerlaverock Castle was slain and his head displayed by the English on the 'great tower at Lochmaben', suggesting, perhaps, that the motte and bailey castle, at the north end of Castle Loch, was still occupied.[8] However, Edward's peel was probably built on a promontory at the south end of the loch, although it is unclear whether this was a new site.[9] A ditch dug across the base of the promontory isolated it from the mainland and tapped the waters of the loch. Inside the ditch, sited on a low, partly artificial, platform and separated by another, formerly water-filled ditch are an inner and outer enclosure, arranged north and south respectively.

Archaeological excavation at the south-west corner of the outer ward has revealed possible indications of a timber palisade on the north side of the great ditch, suggesting that the outer ward might represent the Edwardian peel.[10] The inner ward now contains the remains of a quadrangular stone castle, the most conspicuous element of which is a pair of wing walls, each pierced by an arch, which extend at right angles from the south front and cross the ditch between the two wards, where they probably connected with the timber defences of the peel. The arches allowed boats to sail through the ditch and load or unload at the castle gate under cover, an arrangement that brings to mind the protected harbour at Beaumaris that allowed ships to dock next to the gateway (Figure 9.1).

Figure 9.1: *Lochmaben. One of the two wing walls straddling the ditch between the inner and outer wards.*

The first mention of the stone castle here dates from 1365, and the masonry has accordingly been dated to the English occupation of 1333–85, when at least some stonework was carried out.[11] However, the date of the remains is far from certain, and it is not impossible that at least some aspects of the masonry work belong to the Edwardian occupation of 1298–1313. The earliest phase uncovered by excavation around the site of the centrally placed south gateway to the inner ward consisted of foundations for a south curtain, set back from the later curtain, with two roughly rectangular projections extending from it on either side of the gateway. This scheme may have been abortive, for it was soon modified by the addition of a barbican, and then a new curtain wall was built next to the ditch.

If the details of work at Lochmaben are sparse, there is slightly more information about Dumfries, where, in 1300, substantial building operations were carried out at the pre-existing motte and bailey castle.[12] The strengthening of the site included the construction of an outer peel around the castle under the supervision of the carpenters, Brother Robert of Holmcultram Abbey (Cumberland) and Adam of Glasson (probably Glasson, Cumberland), one or both no doubt overseeing the felling of the timber in Inglewood Forest (Cumberland). The presence of a large contingent of diggers suggest that the timber defence was complemented by a substantial earthwork, and the presence of a party of masons under Master Edward of Appleby (Westmorland), demonstrates that there was also a stonework element. Edward of Appleby's appearance is of interest in that the Lord of Appleby was Robert Clifford, a notable builder at his castles of Brough and Brougham, and possibly at Appleby too, but also active in south–west Scotland; it is a possiblity that Master Edward had worked on Clifford's castles.

Perhaps the most interesting aspect of the building work at Dumfries, however, is the attention paid to the wet moat system. The use of natural and artificial water features in defence and transport is a recurrent theme in Edwardian castle building in Scotland, and was perhaps a development of the significant use made of the sea in the Welsh castles. At Lochmaben it was presence of the loch that was turned to advantage, but, at Dumfries, it was the proximity of the River Nith that allowed water to play an important part in the defensive scheme. The ditch network around the castle and peel was completed and modified by Master Adam the Fleming, a specialist in water engineering, based in Bury St Edmunds, who was tasked with ensuring that the dykes were so prepared to enable them to contain water to a depth of 10ft (3m) and a width of 20ft (6m).[13] The capacity was important if the castle and peel were to be supplied by sea, and the ditching was no doubt intended to carry the transport vessel themselves.

The remains of the castle and peel are situated in Castledykes Park, to the south of the town, on the left bank of the Nith, and at a bend in the river. Significant landscaping has obscured the medieval earthworks, but the truncated motte of the castle is close to the north bank of the river, and the probable site of its associated bailey lies to the south east. A larger raised earthwork to the east, partially demarcated on its the east and south sides by a large ditch (formerly containing a stream), is probably the site of Edward's peel.[14]

Lochmaben and Dumfries were the precursors to Edward's principal building project of 1302, which was the strengthening of Linlithgow (West Lothian), the royal manor house at which the King had established his headquarters at the end of 1301, and fortified by surrounding the manorial complex with a timber peel. The fortified manor, or castle, was situated on the elevated promontory site, now occupied by Linlithgow Palace, which juts out into Linlithgow Loch to the north, sloping down to the water on the north and west sides, and to a flat open area to the east, which has probably been reclaimed from the loch. The landward approach ascended from the borough to the south. The transformation of the site in the years ensuing the dismantling of the peel in 1313 has obliterated any sign of the Edwardian defences, so that their exact configuration cannot, at present, be verified, although something of their nature is to be gleaned from an indenture drawn up between King Edward and James of St George on 20 May 1302. It is a document that gives a rare insight into the interchange between patron and master builder and the vacillations that might characterise a major building project.[15]

In essence, the King's original plan for the strengthening of Linlithgow, which had, apparently, been discussed with Master James, had been to cut a ditch across the neck of the peninsula, thereby isolating it from the borough and allowing it to be filled by the waters of the loch. Behind the ditch there was to be a peel, or palisade, augmented by a stone twin-towered gateway and two stone towers, one at each end of the peel and standing within the waters of the loch. Further consideration prompted the King to change his mind and to have the planned stone elements built in timber instead. In addition, the church, which occupied a prominent position between the borough and the manor house on the high ground at the south end of the promontory, was to be fortified, and to form part of the line of defence separating the castle and the borough. This landward entrance front represented the first phase of construction. In the second phase the perimeter of the promontory, which was less vulnerable to attack, was to be enclosed by the construction of a ditch and a less substantial, but nevertheless defensible, palisade.

Working under Master James at Linlithgow were the master carpenters, Thomas of Houghton and Adam of Glasson, the latter having already been mentioned in connection with the strengthening of Dumfries.[16] Master Thomas had made his mark as a royal carpenter at the palace and abbey of Westminster and later at Beaumaris.[17] His provenance is unknown (there are numerous Houghton place-names) but Adam de Glasson's name hints at a north-eastern origin, and he first comes to attention in 1300 during the Scottish war, working his way to Linlithgow via the fortification of Dumfries and the siege of Caerlaverock.[18] Another craftsman at Linlithgow with experience of the Welsh castles was the mason Ralph de Ocle. He had previously worked at Conwy (1285–6) and Harlech (1289).[19] He may have been a relation of John of Ocleye, the principal mason at Aberystwyth in 1283, in which case, he too may have been a Gloucestershire man. In September he was working on a wall beneath the gate, surmised to be a revetment of the ditch. Thus, there was indeed some stonework, despite Edward's decision to build the gatehouse and terminating towers of the main defensive line in timber, and there is a strong possibility that elements of this survive.

One other castle that is known to have had elements of stone was Selkirk, some 40 miles south west of Edinburgh, the surviving remains of which lie to the south of the town within the eighteenth-century landscaped park of the Haining, and immediately north of Loch Haining.[20] They comprise a motte and bailey, the bailey lying to the south of the motte. The refortification of the castle in 1302 included the erection of a peel around it, and the construction of 'the tower of the fortalice of Selkirk', probably also of timber and sited on the motte. The masonry works included a stone-faced postern with a turning bridge, portcullis, and brattice, and some work, possibly a bridge, connected with the main gateway, which also had a turning bridge.

More visible stone remains are to be found at Lochindorb (Moray), a castle of the Comyn lords of Badenoch, which was probably built *c.* 1260–80.[21] It was certainly in existence by 1302, when John Comyn the Competitor died there.[22] Sited on an island within the eponymous loch, it has a slightly irregular quadrilateral plan with semi-circular towers at the two southern corners, and towers of slightly greater arc at the northern angles. There were gateways on the south, east, and west sides, of which the eastern one was probably the main entrance. Within the courtyard are the remnants of an eastern range, backing onto the curtain (Figure 9.2).

A large outwork, enclosing a wide strip of previously exposed land on the east side and eastern end of the north side, has been tentatively attributed to Edward I.[23] It screens the main (eastern) entrance, which lies closest to the shore, and also the domestic apartments of the east range, thereby giving the castle some protection against stone-throwing engines and against a hostile landing on the spacious berm on this side. The entire eastern arm of this outwork, which survives almost to full height, presents a blind front, except for a ragged gap towards the right-hand (south) end which denotes the position of the gateway. This was an arched opening, protected by a barred gate and portcullis, the latter being operated from a rectangular gatehouse building situated behind (west of) the wall, and rising to at least two storeys (Figure 9.3).

There is little to say about this purely functional defensive structure, except to observe that, if it is Edwardian, it is one of the most tangible remnants of Edward's works in Scotland. There are, however, few, if any, clues, other than historical circumstance, that can confirm this attribution, though there are certainly none to discount it. Seeking for parallels with Edward's castles is relatively fruitless. The structure could be said to have performed a similar function to the barbicans

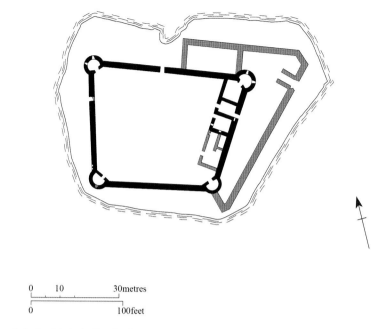

0   10   30metres

0   100feet

Figure 9.2: *Lochindorb. Castle plan.*

Figure 9.3: *Lochindorb. The screen wall from the south east.*

at Conwy, but it doesn't seem to have had the same hierarchical relationship in respect of relative height, perhaps being only slightly lower than the curtain wall. The retracted gatehouse has something in common with the inner gate of Flint, but is not a distinctive enough arrangement to rule out mere coincidence. In any case, the nature of the building is a result of its particular function, and should not, therefore, be expected to fit into a pre-existing template.

However, the opposite is true of Kildrummy (Aberdeenshire), one of Edward's subsequent ports of call during his 1303 perambulation. The plan of Kildrummy forms an irregular triangle, and has a round tower at each of the basal angles, two D-shaped internal towers, and a twin-towered gatehouse at the apex (Figure 9.4). This gatehouse, however, has long been of interest with regard to the Edwardian contribution to the castellated architecture of Scotland.[24] Edward's presence here from the 4–9 October 1303, together with a payment of £100 made to James of St George five days later, suggests that James may have undertaken some reasonably significant work here. This latter is considered to be the gatehouse, the design and dimensions of which have a high degree of correspondence to the inner gatehouse of Harlech raised by James of St George between 1282 and 1290.

Although the Harlech gatehouse largely survives, its counterpart at Kildrummy has, maddeningly, been reduced to its lower courses, so that a full comparison is no longer possible. However, there is no doubt that the plan has similarities with Harlech that are too intimate to have occurred by chance. In both instances the

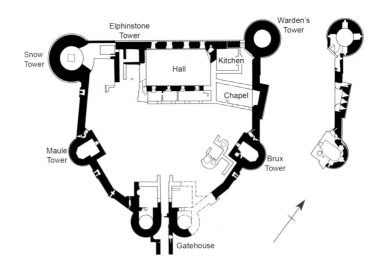

Figure 9.4: *Kildrummy. Castle plan. By Nigel Dodds after Apted 1962–3*

flanking towers extend in a semi-circle from the curtain to the entrance passage, a rectangular residential block extends into the courtyard, the two sides of the gatehouse at ground-floor level were divided internally into an apsidal-ended room at the front and a rectangular room at the back, access to the ground storey was from the gate passage into the rear rooms, and latrines were situated at the junction between the curtain and the gatehouse.

Comparing a number of key measurements produces some interesting results: the width (across the residential block), depth (from the bowed fronts to the rear walls of the residential block), total width across the bows, and the projection of the bows in front of the curtain are, in each instance, within one foot of one another.[25] The foundations of two walls continuing the line of the gate passage into the courtyard may have formed the base for a platform in front of a first-floor entrance, as existed at Harlech.

A final piece of evidence is to be found in the remains of a hooded fireplace in the north-west room. The hood has gone but the jambs have wide chamfers, and curve forward as corbelled heads with squared faces; this is a design particularly associated with Conwy Castle, and, in concert with the evidence of the plan, one which supports the contention that James of St George built the gatehouse (Figure 9.5). One modification of the Harlech plan is the absence of the two stair turrets attached to the rear angles, but complete replication is not to be expected and the correspondence of the other aspects enumerated here is more than enough to identify Harlech as the source.

Figure 9.5: *Kildrummy. Gatehouse fireplace from the north east.*

Another probable sign of the English occupation at Kildrummy are two twin lancet windows on the upper floors of the Warden's (north) Tower, of which only the lower one survives in its entirety; irregularities in the surrounding masonry suggest that they are insertions (Figure 9.6). These windows are deeply set within rectangular chamfered frames with steeply inclined sills. The general form of the frame, apart from the head is not unlike those of the adjacent chapel lancets, but the ends of the one surviving lintel are supported on double-cusped corbels, a modification of the usual shouldered lintel, but one that might have been derived from Caernarfon, where a similar adaptation survives (Figure 9.7). The embrasures originally had flat ceilings carried on double rows of corbels, a characteristic shared with the (now arched) ground-floor loop embrasures.[26] This is a form found in the wall passages of the later work at Caernarfon.

In considering why it was felt necessary to build a new gatehouse at Kildrummy, Simpson speculated that by 1303 the castle was yet to be completed even though construction had probably started by the second quarter of the thirteenth century.[27] An alternative explanation is that, like many other thirteenth-century Scottish castles, the entrance consisted of little more than an opening in the curtain, and that the gatehouse constituted a major strengthening of the defences.

One of Edward's last castle-building projects in Scotland was intended to secure the Forth. To this end a new castle was begun early in 1304 at Inverkeithing

Figure 9.6 (above left): *Kildrummy. Warden's Tower, inserted window from the east.*

Figure 9.7 (above right): *Caernarfon. Double-cusped carnarvon arch.*

(Fife), a royal borough south of Dunfermline, at the narrowing of the Firth. In the spring of 1305 orders were issued for two more castles, one on each side of the Forth to the east of Stirling, at Tullibody (north) and Polmaise (south) near Fallin. Work on Tullibody was curtailed by the Bruce rebellion after no more than one building season, and it is unlikley that any of these castles was completed, although it is possible that there are below-ground remains to be excavated.[28]

The Castles of Edward's Scottish Supporters, 1296–1307

The South West

If the remains of Edward's castle-building activities in Scotland are disappointingly few, those of his Scottish supporters are in greater evidence. The earliest of these to be recorded is the construction of Tibbers (Dumfriesshire) in Nithsdale. Built by Sir Richard Siward, Tibbers was described as 'just begun' on 27 August 1298, and, in 1302, Edward made a contribution of £100 for its repair.[29] In 1291–2 Siward had been keeper of 'the three castles of Galloway and Nithsdale' (Dumfries, Kirkcudbright, and Wigton).[30] A supporter of King John during the 1296 campaign, he was imprisoned in the Tower and elsewhere, being released in the summer of 1297 and his lands restored to him on his promising to serve Edward in the Flemish campaign of that year. Work on Tibbers was begun immediately after the expedition returned in the spring of 1298. In April 1299 Robert Clifford was empowered to appoint 'Richard Syward or other fit person as warden of Nithsdale'.[31] Later the same year Siward was jointly charged with strengthening the palisade of the close of Lochmaben Castle, and in 1302 seems to have been keeper of both Lochmaben and Dumfries.[32] In 1304 he was Sheriff of Fife and in 1305 Sheriff of Dumfries.[33]

The remains of the castle are situated on a headland, which rises from the west bank of the River Nith, and shadows the course of the river. They comprise a series of baileys extending from south to north in a lateral sequence to terminate in the inner bailey, which is situated on a mound isolated from the main body of the bluff by the enlargement of a natural ravine, and creating what was, in effect, a motte. This inner bailey was built in stone, and although only the lower courses of masonry survive, the recording of the ground plan allows a degree of comparative analysis (Figure 9.8). The inner ward consisted of a sub-rectangular enclosure with external measurements of

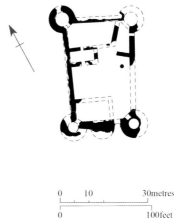

Figure 9.8: *Tibbers. Inner ward plan. By Nigel Dodds after Dixon* et al. *2015*

approximately 125ft (38m) x 75ft (23m) and four three-quarter round corner towers approximately 29½ft (9m) in diameter, being entered via a portcullis-protected gateway between the south-east corner tower and a semi-circular gate tower that projected from the middle of the south curtain. The gateway opened to a courtyard covering much of the eastern side of the enclosure; on the western side a hall range extended along the west curtain with kitchen and chamber wings to the north and south respectively, both projecting beyond the east wall of the hall. At the north end of the hall range was a small rectangular room with central doorway, probably to contain the pantry and buttery. A door in the north wall, directly opposite that from the hall, is a doorway to the kitchen block.

It is interesting to note that Richard Siward's new 'house' at Tibbers had much in common with his former charge of Kirkcudbright (Figure 9.9), including the rectangular enclosure, round corner towers, substantial entrance block with twin gate towers, the postern at the opposite end of the enclosure, and a near correlation in size. These parallels are close enough to suggest that Siward took Kirkcudbright as his exemplar, modifying its characteristics to suit his own requirements. The Kirkcudbright elements of great tower and staircase tower were not replicated at Tibbers, omissions that resulted in a more regular and rational plan.[34] Despite Siward's allegiance to Edward, then, nothing remains at Tibbers that attests to English influence, nor indeed is there any evidence to suggest that it is anything other than a purely regional development.[35]

The same cannot be said of Morton, another Dumfriesshire castle which lies on the slopes of the Lowther Hills above Nithsdale only 2 miles to the east of Tibbers, being sited on a triangular promontory jutting into Loch Morton, which is an artificial reservoir of unknown origin (Figure 9.10). The historical record is vague as to the construction date of the surviving stone structure, but, in 1307, the manor was held by Sir Thomas Randolph, a nephew of Robert Bruce, and it may well be that Randolph was the builder.[36] In 1306 Randolph had supported Bruce in his bid for the Crown and was captured at the Battle of Methven.[37] He changed sides, thereby saving his neck, but, in 1308, sided once more with King Robert.[38] In 1309 he was described as Lord of Nithsdale, later becoming first Earl of Moray and eventually Guardian of Scotland.

The main building is a first-floor hall house with an unvaulted lower storey and a three-quarter round tower projecting from one corner. The hall range cuts across the centre of the promontory, thereby creating an inner and outer ward to the north and south respectively. There is a corner tower at the south-east angle and a five-storey gatehouse at

Figure 9.9: *Kirkcudbright. Castle plan. By Nigel Dodds after Robison and Curle 1913–14*

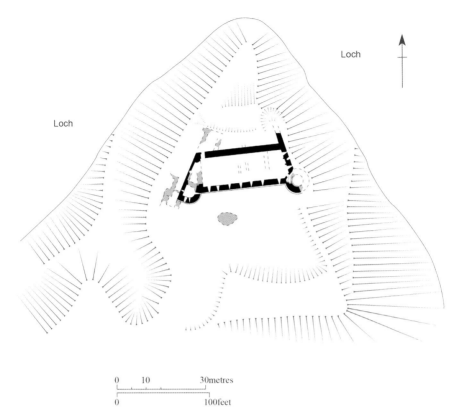

Loch

Loch

0   10   30metres

0   100feet

Figure 9.10: *Morton. Castle plan. By Nigel Dodds after RCAHMS, Canmore catalogue no. DP 163572*

the south-west angle. This latter is rather unusual, seeming to have comprised two D-shaped towers (of which only the eastern survives) placed back to back, flanking a central entrance (Figure 9.11). As we have seen (above, Chapter 8), this is a thirteenth-century English type first developed at Dover in the 1220s and subsequently found at the royal castles of Newcastle and Scarborough, but, more pertinently, perhaps, at Carreg Cennen Castle in south Wales, and at Monnow Bridge, Monmouth, under Edward I's murage grant of *c.* 1297.

The only direct access to the basement of the main block is from an inserted doorway at the west end of the north wall, and it is probable that it was originally entered from above. The basement is lit by small rectangular windows placed high up in the wall (to the south and east) (Figure 9.12), a type that is encountered elsewhere in late thirteenth-century Scotland (see below), but also in the upper storey raised by Robert Clifford on top of the keep at his castle of Brougham (Cumberland), *c.* 1300. At Morton, these windows have deep embrasures with stepped sills and shouldered corbelling supporting slab ceilings (Figure 9.13), this latter aspect being found in the embrasures to the ground floor of Hawarden keep.

Figure 9.11: *Morton. East gatehouse tower from the south east.*

Figure 9.12 (above left): *Morton. Ground-floor window from the south west.*

Figure 9.13 (above right): *Morton. Ground-floor window embrasure from the north.*

The entrance to the first-floor hall was at the west end of the north elevation through an elaborately-moulded doorway with three orders of convex quarter-round quasi-shafted jambs and a two-centred arch of two orders of double-hollow chamfers beneath a hood mould, the mouldings of the arch dying into the jambs (Figure 9.14). The quasi-shafting of the entrance was certainly being used in the English west midlands by the later thirteenth century, notably at Dudley Castle (Staffordshire), where it is to be found around both the main gateway and the entrance to keep.[39] The technique is related to the broad rounded finish of openings found in buildings of the Welsh Marches, e.g. Goodrich, Caerphilly, and Carreg Cennen (see above, Chapter 8).

Immediately to the right (west) of the entrance there was a pair of large shouldered-lintel windows, now only partially surviving. Paired openings of this type are a particular feature of Caernarfon Castle, and it is likely that this was the source of the Morton examples. In addition to these windows, and the rear arches of the ground-floor windows, shouldered lintels were also used for a number of internal doorways, and for first-floor embrasures. Other internal details include segmental-arched window embrasures with stone benches, and the remains of three hooded fireplaces. Of these latter the one on the first floor of the gate tower survives sufficiently well to show that it is a version of the type in the Kildrummy gatehouse described above and similarly derivative of Conwy.

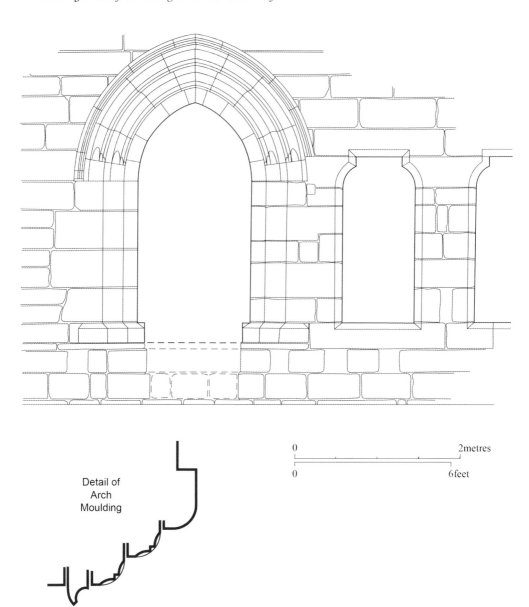

Detail of
Arch
Moulding

0   2metres

0   6feet

Figure 9.14: *Morton. First-floor doorway and windows. By Nigel Dodds after RCAHMS 1920*

Although the history of Morton is obscure, the architectural analogues of the castle are so suggestive of Wales and the Marches that it is difficult to avoid the conclusion that the craftsmen concerned had had recent experience of that region. This, therefore, gives us a reason to surmise that it was built under the aegis of the English occupation, and that English craftsmen were involved in its design and construction. The large shouldered-lintel windows adjacent to the first-floor doorway are best compared to the courtyard openings to the mural galleries and window embrasure openings in the Eagle Tower at Caernarfon. Corbelling of similar form within the ground-floor window embrasures is also a technique that is found at Caernarfon, notably in the second-floor wall passages of the Well Tower.

The North East

Aspects of the Morton plan are to be found far to the north east in the fortified manor house of Rait (Nairnshire), approximately 2½ miles south of Nairn. This building was probably raised either by Gervase de Rait, constable of Nairn Castle in 1292, who, in 1296, made his submission to Edward I, or, by his younger brother, Andrew, also an Edwardian loyalist, who succeeded Gervase in 1297.[40] The castle is sited on the side of a hill, above rolling countryside sloping down towards Nairn and the coast. The element now standing is a two-storey hall house aligned north east to south west, and facing north west towards the rising terrain of the hill. When William Douglas Simpson visited the site in the 1930s he discerned traces of an enclosure and ancillary buildings, but these are no longer evident apart from the existence of some undulations to the north east, and the hall house is largely hemmed in by trees and undergrowth.[41] The main block measures about 60ft (18m) x 27ft (8m), and, as at Morton, there is a cylindrical corner tower which, in this case, projects from the south corner. In addition, there are the fragmentary remains of a narrow rectangular latrine turret at the south-west end of the north-west elevation (Figure 9.15).

The ground floor was lit by a combination of small lancets and rectangular, nearly square windows (Figure 9.16, cf. Morton, Figure 9.12), and the first-floor hall was provided with tall two-centred arch windows with chamfered surrounds and Y-tracery. Similar tracery is also found in a first-floor window in the tower, but this is set beneath a flat lintel and deeply recessed within two chamfered orders, apparently to effect a transition between the curving face of the tower and the flat face of the window (Figure 9.17). The entrance to the building is at first-floor level, towards the north-east end of the south-east elevation, being flanked on its east side by a small pointed window. Here too, special emphasis was placed on the main entrance, but, instead of being heavily decorated, as at Morton, it was exaggerated in size (Figure 9.18). It has a chamfered surround, segmental-pointed arch and hood mould, and was protected by a portcullis and barred door.

Access to the ground storey was either from the first floor, in common with Morton, or from the east, where there is now a large gap in the wall. This space

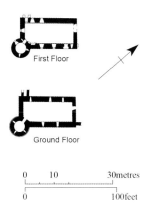

Figure 9.15: *Rait. Ground-and first-floor plans. By Nigel Dodds after RCAHMS, Canmore catalogue no. SC 1300403*

Figure 9.16 (above left): *Rait. Ground-floor window from the north west.*

Figure 9.17 (above right): *Rait. South tower, first-floor window from the west.*

Figure 9.18 (left): *Rait. First-floor entrance from the south.*

was unheated and plain in character, the window embrasures and doorway into the south-west tower being provided with simple flat lintels. The first-floor entrance led into a screens passage and/or servery at the lower end of the hall. The hall window embrasures, which were provided with stone seats, have double-chamfered, segmental-pointed rear arches. At the upper end of the hall a doorway in the north wall led into the latrine turret, whilst the south wall contained a hooded fireplace with twin sconce brackets next to a doorway giving access to the tower, which contains a room covered by a hemi-spherical dome (Figure 9.19). The dome is a rather unusual feature, perhaps best paralleled with that of Pembroke Castle keep, another (much larger) dome of hemi-spherical form, built a century before Rait.

The analogues with Morton (basement windows, emphatic first-floor entrance, and cylindrical corner tower) are interesting, but, although the general concept is similar and may have had a common source, there are considerable differences in the architectural detailing. Here at Rait there are none of the features by which Morton can be linked to English practices. This argues for an independence from the royal works to match that of Caergwrle, Chirk, and other baronial castles of the Welsh wars.

Some 23 miles to the north east of Rait, 3 miles north west of Elgin and 3½ miles south west of Lossiemouth, is the castle of Duffus (Moray). Duffus is a

Figure 9.19: *Rait. Domed vault of the tower.*

twelfth-century motte and bailey castle, which, in the early fourteenth century was rebuilt in stone (Figure 9.20). The one date we have for the reconstruction of the castle is 1305, when Edward I granted Reginald Cheyne 200 oak trees 'to build his manor of Dufhous', which suggests that it was carried out during the English occupation.[42]

The earthworks comprise a raised, roughly U-shaped bailey about 1 acre (0.4ha) in area, with the top towards the north, and a large motte at its north-west corner. At the level of the surrounding low-lying and formerly marshy plain, these elements are surrounded by a water-filled ditch forming a roughly oval outer enclosure of approximately 8.5 acres (3.5ha). This outer ditch was bridged on the west side, from whence a causeway led to the inner bailey.

The fourteenth-century stone remains comprise a curtain wall surrounding the bailey, and a rectangular great tower *c*. 70ft x 30ft (21m x 9m) surmounting the motte (Figure 9.21). This two-storey tower is aligned north–south with the cardinal points; subsidence has caused its northern end to break away and it now rests part way down the motte at an oblique angle determined by the slope of the motte, its upper storey little lower than the ground-floor level of the standing

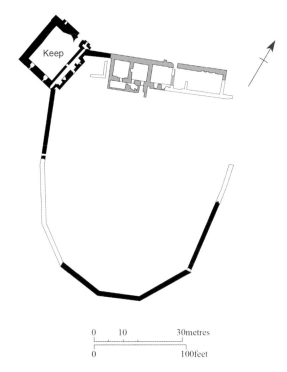

Figure 9.20 (above): *Duffus. Castle plan showing the great tower as built. By Nigel Dodds after Cannell and Tabraham 1994*

Figure 9.21 (below): *Duffus. Great tower from the east.*

portion of the tower. Narrow rectangular projections extend from the north and east sides, the former to contain latrines, the latter to accommodate a staircase.

The great tower sits on a chamfered plinth, plain, heavy, and of rubble construction on the south side, but three-tiered, elegant, and of ashlar on the east and west sides. Towards the east, the entrance block, which breaks forward from the main building, extending across roughly two-thirds of the elevation, breaks up the frontage in a simple but effective manner, adding depth to what could otherwise have been a tedious two-dimensional expanse. Otherwise, the main feature of the elevation is the simple square-headed doorway with chamfered surround. The fenestration on this side relates mainly to the mural staircase and wall passages and consists of small lancets with chamfered surrounds, which can be compared to corresponding features at Rait. The windows of the main rooms, however, are rectangular, those of the ground storey nearly square, reflecting the proportions of similar features in the basement of Rait (Figure 9.22); the first-floor windows are tall and comparatively narrow. All these rectangular windows are of two orders, the inner one deeply recessed, and both with unusually wide chamfers (Figure 9.23). This chunky style, which extends to the single-order lancets, is one of the defining characteristics of the tower.

The eastern entrance, which was protected by a portcullis, gives access to an entrance passage leading to the ground storey. To the left (south) a straight mural staircase ascends to the first floor, and on the right (north) there is a porter's lodge with a latrine at its north end. The stair well was ceiled by flat slabs carried on two-tier quadrant corbel courses, very much like the ceilings of the mural passages of the later work at Caernarfon (i.e. from 1295) and the keep of Hawarden. In the main body of the tower, the internal width of the ground storey is 36ft (11m), quite a broad span when considering the practicalities of

Figure 9.22 (above left): *Duffus. Great tower ground-floor window from the south.*

Figure 9.23 (above right): *Duffus. Great tower first-floor window from the south.*

flooring and roofing. Joist sockets in the side walls and a central beam socket in the south wall at a slightly lower level imply that there was a central arcade or row of piers supporting an axial beam, which itself carried the ends of the joists. The first floor contained the main apartments, notably a hall entered at its south end. The presence of an arcade at the lower level might suggest a similar structural contrivance at first-floor level in order to carry a twin-span roof.

This structural arrangement at Duffus has been seen as an anomaly in Scottish architecture, and rather within the Norman keep tradition.[43] Spine walls serving a similar purpose to the former timber arcade at Duffus were certainly to be found in a number of eleventh- and twelfth-century English keeps, and timber spinal arcades are known to have existed in the eleventh-century Scolland's Hall, in Richmond Castle, and in the twelfth-century keeps of Bridgnorth and Portchester. The idea that Duffus might have been influenced by the Norman keep tradition is compounded by its entrance arrangements, which, in essence, reflect those of Bamburgh and Carlisle in that they have a ground-level entry giving access to a portico and a staircase leading to the ground and first floors respectively.[44] At the two English castles this arrangement could be accommodated in the massive walls, but at the less substantial Duffus a localised thickening of the wall had to be provided. Finally it is also pertinent to mention the stepped plinth of the Duffus tower, because it was a recurrent form in northern England from the twelfth century onwards, the most elaborate example being at Bamburgh, where the steps were interspersed with mouldings.

Of course, Duffus is a smaller building than most twelfth-century keeps, and in that respect is better compared to thirteenth-century Welsh keeps, or, indeed, some of the English towers that were being raised along the Welsh border in the late thirteenth/early fourteenth century at, for example, Clun and Hopton, both in Shropshire, which measure 66ft (20m) x 41ft (12.5m) and 49ft (15m) x 38ft (11.5m) respectively. A third Shropshire building pertinent to Duffus is Acton Burnell, not a tower, but a hall house, which was divided longitudinally by a stone arcade. Acton Burnell, which is discussed below (Chapter 11), is a particularly apposite analogy, partly because it was probably designed and built by royal masons, and partly because it too contains the unusual feature of rectangular windows of two chamfered orders. There are also twin-light lancet windows which bear comparison with the Y-traceried tower window at Rait, and it is possible that Acton Burnell is the source for both (see below Chapters 11 and 12).

Tulliallan

Next, let us examine another building that has been considered to have English traits. This is the defended hall house of Tulliallan (Clackmannanshire), on the border between Fife and Stirling, which may have been built by Sir William Bisset of Upsettlington, now Ladykirk (Berwickshire).[45] Bisset made his submission to Edward in 1296 and served with the King in Flanders. By 17 April 1304 he was Sheriff of Clackmannanshire and was in possession of Tulliallan, having been ordered by Edward to strengthen its walls.[46] Immediately following the capture of Stirling Castle on 20 July that year Bisset was made Sheriff of Stirling and constable of the castle, being confirmed in these positions in the Ordinance for Scotland in September of 1305.[47]

The strong house is set within a ditched and banked enclosure and built with ashlar blocks (Figure 9.24). The main rectangular block is roughly 75ft x 35ft, and thus slightly larger than the great tower of Duffus, but the two are generally of a comparable scale. At Tulliallan, rectangular wings extend northwards from the two northern corners. The north-east wing is entirely secondary, having been rebuilt in two phases, so the primary plan at this angle is obscure. However, the lower storey of the north-west wing appears to be primary, although the building has been heightened at a later date. At the junction with the east gable of the main block and the north-west wing a semi-polygonal turret contains a service stair. At the south-west corner, forming the western termination of the main entrance block and incorporating the main staircase, is another semi-polygonal projection.

This entrance block breaks forward from the west end of the south front. The pointed doorway was protected by a drawbridge, a portcullis, and a barred door. A second entrance at the east end of the south front also had a drawbridge and two barred doors. The ground storey was lit by small square windows like those encountered at Morton and Rait; there are also two larger windows, one at the east end of the south front and one in the east gable, both of which appear to have been trefoiled monolithic heads. At first-floor level the west end retains a large rectangular window of two orders with chamfered and moulded surround.

One of the main interests of Tulliallan is the elaborately vaulted ground storey. There were two rooms at ground-floor level, a large western room and a smaller eastern room both of which were vaulted in double quadripartite

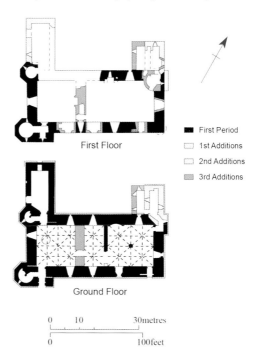

First Floor

First Period
1st Additions
2nd Additions
3rd Additions

Ground Floor

0   10   30metres
0   100feet

Figure 9.24: *Tulliallan. Ground- and first-floor plans. By Nigel Dodds after RCAHMS 1933*

bays, three to the west and two to the east, with octagonal pillars at the centres. The western vault is much plainer than that of the eastern room where the wall ribs, responds, vaulting ribs, pillar base, and capital are all moulded with profiles of late thirteenth-/early fourteenth-century character.

Also in this room are the remains of a hooded fireplace of similar date. It has very broad jambs, decorated with a bold central roll moulding, which angle forward at the head as brackets. It is a particular and emphatic interpretation of the same general type that is found in the Edwardian castles of Wales. The same may be said of the moulded sconce brackets, which are similarly assertive in character. Additional architectural features from the primary phase of Tulliallan include segmental-pointed window rear arches, two-centred pointed doorways and a shouldered lintel, all of which have parallels in the Edwardian castles of Wales and the Marches.

Access to the first floor was from the main entrance passage via a generously proportioned spiral staircase. A lesser staircase, probably a service stair, is located in the north-west turret, being entered from the passage between the main block and the north-west wing. Later alterations are too extensive to be certain of the primary first-floor plan, but, to judge from the relative sizes of the surviving windows, in common with the ground-floor, the east end contained accommodation of higher social status than the west, though the fireplace here is smaller than the one at ground-floor level.

Many of the architectural features would be at home in an English manor house. The polygonal turrets also provide a link with the hall house of Edlingham Castle in Northumberland, which is considered to date from the period 1297–1300, the builder of which also made use of polygonal turrets.[48] Here, only the lower courses of walling survive, but they show a three-cell, east–west aligned main block with octagonal corner turrets and, on the same alignment, a contemporary east wing with diagonally disposed corner buttresses. The east wing was self-contained with its own entrance and fireplace. The hall was at first-floor level, and entered independently of the ground storey by an external staircase.

The Edlingham hall house is attributed to Sir William Felton (d. 1327), who, prior to serving in Scotland, had worked his way up through the royal service to become constable of Beaumaris Castle (1295–1301). He fought at Falkirk at the head of the Anglesey contingent, losing a horse in the process.[49] Subsequently, he was warden of Linlithgow Castle (1302–5). Felton completed the purchase of Edlingham in 1296, and the house was probably begun soon afterwards.[50] Polygonal towers in the later thirteenth century are principally associated with north Wales, that is to say, Caernarfon and Denbigh. It is not unreasonable to suggest that the form of Felton's Northumbrian hall house is related to his service in north Wales, and that Edlingham was influenced by the royal works in progress during his sojourn at Beaumaris.

Bothwell

In this discussion of the architectural impact of the Edwardian occupation, mention needs to be made of Bothwell, the construction of which has generally been attributed to Walter of Moray, between his acquisition of the barony in 1242 and his death in 1278, or to his son, William (nicknamed 'the Rich'), between 1278 and the confiscation of the barony by Edward I in 1296.[51] There was certainly a residence at Bothwell by 1278, though not necessarily a castle, but a castle did exist by 1298, when it was besieged by the Scots, being captured the following year. After the recapture of Bothwell in 1301 the castle came into the hands of Aymer de Valence, titular Earl of Pembroke, to whom the barony had been granted. It remained in his tenure until 1310.

All this sounds straightforward, but Bothwell is, in fact, one of the great enigmas of medieval castellated architecture in Scotland. Despite later alterations and the castle's ruinous state, it is clear that the thirteenth-century layout bears a resemblance to the more regular plan of Kildrummy, with a twin-towered gatehouse at the basal (north) point and a cylindrical great tower close to one of the upper corners (south west) (Figure 9.25). However, it is also evident that the greater part of the castle, as planned in the thirteenth century, never rose higher than foundation level.[52] The present enclosure is a revised, late fourteenth-century scheme, comprising a much smaller rectangular courtyard than was originally intended. The only part of the primary phase to survive above ground level is the four-storey keep known as the Valence Tower (Figure 9.26) and the attached section of curtain ending in the Prison Tower; it may be that little else of the original plan was ever completed.

The keep is unusual in a number of respects, but particularly for its great size, which, at 65ft (19.8m) in diameter and 90ft (27.4m) in height, makes it amongst the largest great towers in Britain.[53] Generally, little if any consideration has been given to the idea that Aymer de Valence may have made a contribution to the castle's fabric during his nine-year tenure, but, in 2018, archaeologist Neil Ludlow, made an interesting case, on architectural grounds, to support the contention that Aymer may well have been builder of the great tower.[54] This theory is based on apparent affinities between Bothwell and buildings of the Welsh Marches of *c.* 1280–1320, and related structures of the same period.

Diagnostic details referred to in this analysis include bold chamfered surrounds of two orders, raised chamfered door sills, shouldered lintels, cusped windows without sunken spandrels, wall passages with corbelled slab ceilings, triangular or steep segmental-pointed arches, plain cruciform arrow loops, heavy chamfered vault ribs, the central column in the keep, and filleted shafts and roll mouldings. The existence of comparable features in Wales and the Marches, and in other buildings connected with Aymer de Valence, is contrasted with their rarity elsewhere in Scotland. Interestingly, aspects of Robert de Clifford's late

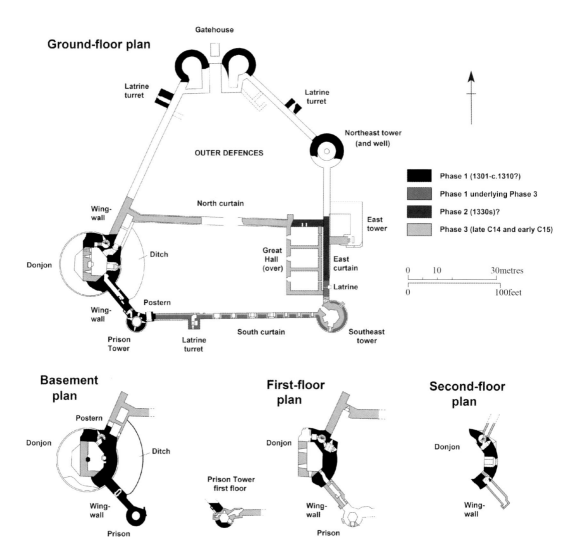

Ground-floor plan

Gatehouse

Latrine turret

Latrine turret

Northeast tower (and well)

OUTER DEFENCES

North curtain

Wing-wall

Donjon

Ditch

Great Hall (over)

East tower

East curtain

East curtain

Latrine

Postern

Wing-wall

Prison Tower

Latrine turret

South curtain

Southeast tower

	Phase 1 (1301-c.1310?)
	Phase 1 underlying Phase 3
	Phase 2 (1330s)?
	Phase 3 (late C14 and early C15)

0   10   30metres

0   100feet

Basement plan

Postern

Donjon

Ditch

Wing-wall

Prison Tower

First-floor plan

Donjon

Prison Tower first floor

Wing-wall

Prison Tower

Second-floor plan

Donjon

Wing-wall

Figure 9.25: *Bothwell. Castle plan.* © *Neil Ludlow*

thirteenth–century work at Brougham Castle (a building that itself appears to have been influenced by the royal works in Wales, see below Chapter 11) are also cited as parallels.

Ludlow compared the general form of the Bothwell keep to the great towers of Hawarden and Flint, both cylindrical, like Bothwell, with external diameters (60ft/18.3m and *c*. 75ft/22.9m respectively) that exceed most keeps of this form. Hawarden is a large example of its type, but is exceeded in diameter by Bothwell. Flint's dimensions exceed those of Bothwell, but, as we have seen, Flint had an inner cell and is therefore atypical; nevertheless, both buildings may have acted as exemplars for outward appearance and scale. To take this particular theme further,

Figure 9.26: *Bothwell. Valence Tower from the east.*

the same might well be said of the Eagle Tower at Caernarfon, the most ambitious of the great towers raised in the aftermath of the Welsh wars. The width of this irregularly decagonal tower from side to side is the same as the diameter of the Bothwell keep (though its greatest width from angle to angle is *c.* 73ft/22.3m). The thickness of the wall ranges from 16½ft (5m) to 18½ft (5.6m), compared to the 16½ft (5m) thickness of Bothwell. The two towers, then, were built on a comparable scale, although, in 1301, only the first three storeys of the Eagle Tower had been completed. In its final form it would rise to a height of about 80ft (24.4m), but would surpass Bothwell by dint of its three roof-top turrets which bring the total height to *c.* 110ft (33.5m).

Overall, the analogues between Bothwell on the one hand and the castles of the Welsh Marches on the other, make a plausible case for attributing Bothwell to Aymer de Valence, but Ludlow also introduced a more personal aspect in comparing the great tower of Bothwell to Pembroke Castle keep, that potent symbol of Aymer de Valence's patrimony as future Earl of Pembroke. Particularly, the large second-floor two-light window of Bothwell, with plain tympanum beneath a two-centred head, is likened to the early thirteenth-century second-floor window of Pembroke, and it is intimated that the Bothwell donjon was referencing (whilst outdoing) the earlier tower.[55] Further possible references to Pembroke were noted in the central column, which at Bothwell rose from basement level to support the ribs of the first-floor (timber) vault, and in the vaulting itself, an unusual feature in British great towers, the most memorable example being the high-level dome of Pembroke. Bothwell, then, might be seen as an updated and improved version of an influential icon, the impact of which had now been reduced by other, more recent developments.

Caerlaverock

Finally, we need to talk about Caerlaverock (Dumfriesshire), a castle that has also received its share of speculation. Caerlaverock is sited on the south coast at the mouth of the Nith. The plan is based on an isosceles triangle with its base towards the south, two cylindrical corner towers at the southern angles, and a twin-towered gatehouse at the northern apex incorporating a residential block cutting across the angle of the courtyard (Figure 9.27). The castle is surrounded by inner and outer moats separated by an earthen bank; it thus displays characteristics of concentricity, and even though there is no outer stone curtain, the bank was probably crowned by a palisade. Access was from the north via an outer courtyard.

By 1300, the castle seems to have acquired the general form with which we are familiar, being famously described in a lyrical account of the siege of that year, thought to have been compiled by an eyewitness. That is to say, it had a triangular plan with round towers at the three corners including the twin towers of the gatehouse (Figure 9.28).[56] Furthermore, dendrochronological analysis of

Figure 9.27: *Caerlaverock. The castle from the north.*

timbers discovered in the moat in front of the gatehouse has given a felling date of *c*. 1277 for the earliest phase of the bridge leading to the gatehouse.[57] The date of the castle, then, seems fairly secure, and on the grounds of these two crucial pieces of evidence is assigned to Sir Herbert Maxwell (d. 1298).

Although there is nothing quite like it anywhere else in Britain, it is arguable that, in an architectural sense, Caerlaverock would be quite at home amongst the

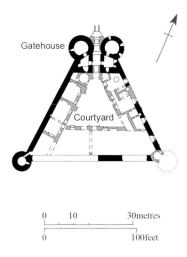

Figure 9.28: *Caerlaverock. Castle plan.*

Edwardian castles of north Wales, and has, in the past been considered to be of English origin.[58] This is evident in the essentially geometric plan, the elements of concentricity, and in the twin-towered gatehouse, a rare feature in Scotland before the late thirteenth century. The particular interest of this gatehouse lies in its integrated domestic block which seems to have housed a reasonably substantial residence. In England and Wales the type can be traced back to the De Clares' works at Tonbridge and Caerphilly, which, as we have seen, helped to shape the character of Edward's castles in Wales.

In attempting to set Caerlaverock Castle within its architectural context we are hampered by a history of destruction and reconstruction and the subsequent loss of much of the thirteenth-century detailing. It is difficult to assess how much damage was sustained by the siege of 1300, or by the 'destruction' of the castle in 1312, and to what extent its present character results from rebuilding in the 1330s, because major fifteenth-, sixteenth-, and seventeenth-century building programmes now dominate its appearance.

However, one interesting form survives within the two small chambers that flank the entrance passage, and which were entered from it. These rooms each contain a fireplace with a shouldered lintel, a detail that was also applied to the doorway leading into the western room. Such features are comparatively unusual in Scotland but closely associated with the English Crown in the thirteenth century, and were recurrent aspects of English castle architecture throughout the fourteenth century. Unfortunately, owing to the degree of alteration within the gatehouse it is impossible to be certain that these instances at Caerlaverock were part of the original build.

The tree-ring date of 1277 makes Caerlaverock a close, possibly exact, contemporary of the royal castles of the First Welsh War (Builth, Aberystwyth, Flint, and Rhuddlan). The best comparison is with Rhuddlan, another concentric castle, which also had a fairly regular polygonal inner ward and two angle-sited gatehouses, like the one at Caerlaverock. It is also the case that the Rhuddlan and Caerlaverock gatehouses both incorporated flanking towers of three-quarter round projection, and there were cylindrical towers at the other angles. Rhuddlan is built on a larger scale but one could quite readily believe that both were designed by the same hand, or that the designer of one was not working in isolation, and had knowledge of the other. It raises an interesting question about the transmission of ideas and the manner in which architectural designs were conceived and attained their final forms.

Conclusion

Of all the work on the castles of Scotland undertaken by Edward I between 1296 and 1307, the only visible remains of which we can be reasonably certain are the alterations and additions undertaken at Kildrummy. As far as the gatehouse is concerned, the correlation in the dimensions with its counterpart at Harlech are too close to be coincidental, and the design of the inserted windows in the Warden's Tower does seem to have been inspired by Caernarfon. The one other extant element that has been recognised as possibly being attributable to Edward is the outer curtain of Lochindorb, a plain structure, but one that adapts the concentric principles applied at some of Edward's castles in Wales. It is possible that there are other surviving structures, as yet unrecognised, that might furnish the broader picture more extensively. Moreover, archaeological fieldwork offers the potential for the discovery of further details of Edward's earthwork and timber defences, and their associated elements of stonework. The full story of the English royal works in Scotland is yet to be written, but we have the means to at least compile a research agenda for future reference.

Greater physical survival is to be found amongst the castles of Edward's supporters, though only at Morton is there substantive evidence of the influence of the English royal works and the employment of a master builder with experience of recent developments in Wales. This evidence, however, is no more than our experience of the Welsh baronial castles of the last quarter of the thirteenth century would lead us to expect, for their architectural relationships with the royal works suggest both emulation and independence. There are, however, some hints of affinity with the northern counties of England, something that might be anticipated because of the influx of northern English craftsmen from 1296. This relationship is also a question that might be pursued fruitfully and which might permit a more rounded perspective of the castellated architecture of Scotland during the Edwardian occupation.

Chapter Ten

Last Works: Caernarfon and Beaumaris

Following the collapse of organised Scottish resistance and the recapture of Stirling Castle in 1304, Walter of Hereford was redeployed to Wales, and work resumed at Caernarfon in September of that year. The project, however, was continued at a reduced scale and a correspondingly slower rate of progress. Taylor estimated that in the four years of Walter of Hereford's second term, between 1304 and 1309, expenditure averaged around £620.[1] Although the details of the work programme are scanty, task payments for the year 1304–5 made to two carpenters for the flooring of three towers have been cited as evidence that priority was being given to completing the three main towers along the south front: (from west to east) the Queen's Tower, Chamberlain Tower, and Black Tower.[2] In which case, the raising of the upper storeys of these three towers, with their large shouldered-lintel windows, must have been overseen by Walter of Hereford.

Henry of Ellerton

Then, early in 1309, Walter of Hereford died, and, on 13 February, his deputy, Henry of Ellerton, was confirmed as his successor. Ellerton had been undermaster at Caernarfon since work recommenced there in 1304, and probably for a number of years prior to the suspension of work owing to the war in Scotland.[3] Nothing is known about his early career but Taylor favoured a Yorkshire origin, and speculated that he was one of a contingent of Yorkshire masons sent to Rhuddlan in 1283.[4] If so, then the greater part of his working life may have been spent on the royal castles of north Wales.

In 1307 Ellerton had obtained a licence to build a chantry chapel on his Caernarfon burgage, a project that was in progress down to 1316, and which resulted in the construction of the Church of St Mary in the north-west corner of the walled town.[5] St Mary's comprises a four-bay nave and single-bay chancel with north and south aisles to both. The adjacent corner tower of the defences was incorporated to accommodate a vestry at ground-floor level and a priest's room at first-floor level, equipped with a hooded fireplace and a latrine and reached from the north aisle via a mural staircase. Following the rebuilding of the north and west walls, the main fourteenth-century survival is to be seen in the rather plain arcades in which two-centred arches of two chamfered orders spring from octagonal columns with moulded capitals. More diagnostic is the original east window, now re-set into the west wall; it has three lights with trefoil-cusped heads.

Work progressed steadily on the castle during Ellerton's tenure, and although it is difficult to link him with specific elements, one work that can be attributed to him with a reasonable degree of confidence is the uppermost storey of the Eagle Tower, which was being roofed in 1317, and at least one of its three octagonal turrets that rise above the roof.[6] The slab ceilings of the mural passages at this level are carried on plain quadrant corbelling in contrast to the more refined ogee-shouldered corbelling of the lower storeys. The latter is also found in the wall passages of the south front, all the way from the Queen's Tower to the North-East Tower and is predominantly a feature of the pre-1295 work. Quadrant corbelling appears in several areas of the later work, including the Prison Tower, King's Gate, Granary Tower, Well Tower, and the later parts of the North-East Tower; it may reflect an economy measure more appropriate to the reduced circumstances of the project, and its perhaps less ambitious objectives.

The merlons of the Eagle Tower battlements, including those of the turrets, were surmounted by sculptures, mostly badly eroded now, although those that can be identified appear to be representations of human heads, some of which are helmeted (Figure 10.1). In addition, a stone eagle is perched on each of the three turrets. These particular sculptures were erected in Ellerton's time, but many of the towers retain evidence for similar features, and it was probably the intention to treat all in like fashion. Such lavish decorative treatment is a further endorsement of the special nature of Caernarfon.

Figure 10.1: *Caernarfon. Eagle Tower, sculptured heads on the battlements of the stair turret.*

Figure 10.2: *Caernarfon. King's Gate, first-floor fireplace with cusped corbels.*

Ellerton also did some work on the King's Gate. The lower part, including the gateway itself, had probably been built during the 1295–9 campaign, given that the priority at that stage would have been to make the castle defendable. The first floor contains a type of hooded fireplace that is characteristic of the fourteenth-century work at Caernarfon, in which sunk-chamfered jambs are standard, and instead of the ogee-profiled corbels of the earlier work, the soffit fillets are cusped (Figure 10.2). By 1320 work on the north front of the King's Gate was nearing completion, having reached the stage of fixing the King's statue in position within the second-floor niche made for it.[7] The second floor of the gatehouse, then, including the elaborate niche, may be Ellerton's work, and we can reasonably presume that the external face of the King's Gate was completed during the 1320 season.

In considering the niche composition we are hampered by its heavy erosion, which means that much of the detail has been lost (Figure 10.3). The base of the niche is immediately above the string course over the gate, but a now amorphous stone projection interrupts the string and links the statue in the niche to the apex of the gate arch. The niche itself is shallow and contains a statue; the eroded lower half does not retain any detail but juts out below the upper half and forms a base (it is impossible to be more specific) for a demi-figure of a bare-headed man, presumed to be Edward II, with erect upper body, squared shoulders, and nape length hair, the ends of which are scrolled outwards. His right hand reaches across his lower body to grasp the hilt of a dagger or sword whilst his left hand probably clutched the scabbard; a recurrent attitude in thirteenth- and fourteenth-century knightly sepulchral monuments.

The proportions are wrong for a seated figure, and the bulky lower part of the sculpture suggests that the statue was shown standing within or behind the base. The niche is framed to left and right by a pair of hollow-chamfered shafts, and covered by a canopy projecting from the face of the wall; it is difficult to be confident about the form of the canopy, now considerably mutilated, but there is a suggestion of a trio of ogee arches, a line of foliate finials above, and rising above this a central engaged crocketed spirelet terminating in a finial. This latter is set between upward extensions of the flanking shafts capped by miniature crocketed spirelets.

Contemporary with the niche are the flanking twin-light transomed windows, the ironwork for which was purchased in 1320.[8] However, these are versions of the examples at first-floor level and the design may therefore be attributable to Walter of Hereford. The main difference is that the upper windows are larger and the transom is at a slightly lower level. These windows lit the hall that was to occupy the second floor of the King's Gate, extending over the full length of the building. Had it been completed, this room would have measured some 70ft (21m) long by 27ft (8m) wide internally (Figure 10.4). A horizontal line of corbels on the interior of the north wall, which are spaced at centres averaging 11ft 8in, together with corresponding tie-beam sockets several feet above them, show that the roof of the hall was designed to be of low pitch and divided into six bays by five roof trusses. The corbels, which were carved with human heads, would have carried wall posts, themselves supporting the tie beams, the ends of which were held within the wall sockets; arch braces probably extended between the two components to give extra support. This was a standard form of construction for floors and roofs at Caernarfon. How the upper part of the roof was configured is less certain, but the reconstructed roof of the Eagle Tower which shows principal rafters and a central king strut is a reasonable interpretation.

The timberwork of the hall is documented in the accounts by a series of purchases made between 1 June and 21 December 1320 in the following order: 12 great joists each 18ft

Figure 10.3: *Caernarfon. King's Gate, canopied niche and statue over the entrance.*

long, 1½ft wide and 2ft thick; another 33 great joists; 5 great 'Wyvres' (beams); another 6 great 'Wyvres' 32ft x 1½ft wide; and 83 pieces of timber (72 joists, 8 corbels and 3 laces).[9] It is not easy to reconcile all these items with the building, which, if it were stone walled, as planned, would have required little more than floors and a comparatively simple and compact roof. In fact, it would not be unreasonable to suppose that the second floors would have been installed prior to the 1320 season and the building roofed temporarily at that level so that the lower floors were habitable.

Figure 10.4: *Caernarfon. King's Gate from the north showing the position of the second-floor hall.*

The 32ft length of the great 'Wyvres' would have been ample for spanning the width of the hall, and could have been used as tie beams at the bay divisions of the roof. Above each tie beam there would probably have been a pair of principal rafters, which, allowing for a roof pitch of approximately 10 degrees, would require lengths of nearly 18ft. The main trusses may also have carried purlins to provide support for the common rafters. However, it is difficult to account for all the timber described in the records in the floors and roof alone, and it is possible that the side and rear walls were also intended to be timber-framed. Be that as it may, in 1343 it was reported that the hall remained unfinished, along with the Well Tower and Queen's Gate.[10] Henry of Ellerton died *c.* 1323 and Caernarfon came under the aegis of Nicholas Derneford, who hitherto had been solely in charge of Beaumaris.[11]

The resumption of construction at Beaumaris after the hiatus of the Scottish wars was heralded in 1306 by the appointment of John of Metfield as constable. Metfield proceeded to report on the condition of the castle, enumerating a number of necessary improvements, the most glaring of which was the completion of the outer enceinte, which still lay open on the north and north-west sides. This apart, Metfield's survey adds little to the castle's chronology, although his recommendation that a barbican be built in front of the inner south gatehouse provides a *terminus post quem* for the construction of this particular item.[12]

By 1307, James of St George was back in Wales as master of the works of the castle of Beaumaris. For reasons stated earlier (see above, Chapter 7), we can assume that, at this stage, the outer curtain and towers had been built to about first-floor level, except for the gap to the north and north west where it was yet to be raised above foundation level. It is possible that the inner curtain wall was nearly complete, but the towers are unlikely to have progressed further than the foundations. It is probable that the fronts of the two gatehouses had been taken to the same level as the curtain, but the rear blocks are unlikley to have progressed very far.

One of the first works at this stage is likely to have been the barbican that was recommended by John of Metfield (Figure 10.5). This is a plain construction of rectangular plan. A two-centred arched entrance in the west wall, protected by a barred gate, gave access to a small yard in front of the South Gatehouse. At ground-floor level, there are three large arrow loops in the south wall and one in the east wall with triangular terminations. Those to the east and centre south are cruciform, but the other two southern loops each have one arm only both pointing outwards towards their respective corners. There are indications that the merlons of the parapet were pierced by further loops, but there is nothing quite like them in any of the other Edwardian castles. Inside, the gate has a semi-circular rear arch, another indication, perhaps, of Savoyard influence, and the loop embrasures have joggled lintels akin to some of those at Caernarfon. A stone staircase led from the north-east corner up the east wall to the alure. This may be one of the last buildings that can be confidently attributed to James of St George because he died *c*. 1309 after a career spanning some fifty years, thirty of them in the royal service.

Figure 10.5: *Beaumaris. Inner South Gatehouse, west flanking tower and barbican.*

Nicholas Derneford

Just as Henry of Ellerton took on the mantle of Master Walter, so too, was Master James succeeded by Nicholas Derneford, who was appointed master of the works at the King's castle of Beaumaris on 18 May 1316 at a salary of 12*d*. per day.[13] This seems to have been formal recognition of a position that he had already filled for a number of years, probably from 1309, and proceeds from a petition sent by Derneford to the King appealing against a reduction in his wages.[14] This document informs us that he had been recruited by James of St George (thus, before 1309), and that prior to moving to north Wales, he had been retained, apparently simultaneously, at Repton Priory (Derbyshire), Burton upon Trent (Staffordshire), probably at the Abbey, and at the Abbey of St Augustine, Bristol (now the cathedral).[15] His presence at Bristol probably coincides with the rebuilding of the eastern arm (aisled choir, Lady Chapel, and Berkley Chapel) begun by Abbot Knowle in 1298, and it may well be that he served as the first master for the project. He was, then, a craftsman of substance, and it is perhaps reasonable to assume that he had been employed with a view to taking over from an ailing Master James.

To what degree, then, was Beaumaris shaped by Nicholas Derneford who served as master there for some twenty years, a considerably longer period than his predecessor? Firstly, there is no reason to doubt that the entire castle was laid out by Master James. Nevertheless, Master Nicholas would have had the opportunity to make his mark on the superstructures. To him we should probably assign the completion of the outer curtain, the towers of the inner ward, the upper stages of the inner gatehouses, and indeed the uppermost levels in most areas. His contribution, therefore, was reasonably substantial, but he must have followed the general lines of the design that had already been mapped out by Master James.

Part of Derneford's responsibility was the completion of the outer curtain, which was quite a substantial undertaking involving the raising of the walls and towers of the first phase, and the construction, from foundation level, of the entire northern section and the north half of the western section. Apart from the outer north gatehouse, or Llanfaes Gate, this simply followed the pattern of the earlier work. On the whole, the arrow loops of this second phase are of marginally higher quality than those of the first phase, in that they have lintels, clearly differentiated from the surrounding stonework. However, in the northern section, between towers 13 and 15, the lintels are actually inverted sills, complete with double basal plunges that are identical to examples at Caernarfon (Figure 10.6). The use of these sills, which were presumably excess stock from Caernarfon (Figure 10.7), would seem to suggest either a difficulty in obtaining suitable materials or masons, or budgetary constraints that necessitated such measures.

Figure 10.6 (above left): *Beaumaris. North outer curtain, arrow loop with inverted base used as a lintel.*

Figure 10.7 (above right): *Caernarfon. Arrow loop in the Queen's Gate.*

Nine of the outer towers were still unfinished in 1321. The outer north gatehouse, or Llanfaes Gate, was never completed, and the remains have a rather odd appearance (Figure 10.8). These include the rear wall, which continues the line of the curtain, and contains the (blocked) central pointed gate arch of two chamfered orders. Extending at right angles from it, into the moat, are the two sides walls of the gatehouse and the two walls of the gate passage, but all four have been truncated, or, more likely, never entirely realised, and their ends have been squared off, so that they now resemble four enormous buttresses. These walls define three deep recesses, which have been vaulted with heavy chamfered ribs, apparently a device to carry wall-walk level platforms in an adaptation of the original plan.

The central gateway, then, was to be flanked by a pair of rooms at ground-floor level, including, no doubt, a porter's lodge. These two chambers were to be entered from the outer ward by a pair of doors with quarter-round moulded surrounds and shouldered lintels. They are unusually well made and are likely to date from before the time that austerity started to bite, yet after Metfield's survey of 1306. The surrounds are of a style and quality found in Hawarden Castle keep in the doorway to the chapel, and in the wall passage opening to the first-floor vestibule (Figure 10.9). The western doorway also led to a staircase at the south-west angle of the gatehouse, which would have ascended to the planned upper storey, but which now only gives access to the alure of the curtain.

Figure 10.8: *Beaumaris. Llanfaes Gate from the north east.*

The intended form of the flanking towers is unknown. Re-excavation of the moat in the early twentieth century did not recover the foundations of their north fronts, so we can only speculate, but it may be that they were square-fronted and that the gatehouse was not intended to extend beyond its present size.[16]

Both the gatehouses to the inner ward remained unfinished too. It is unlikely that the inner (northern) half of the South Gatehouse rose any higher than the ground storey, whilst only two storeys of the corresponding (southern) half of the North Gatehouse were completed instead of the intended three. Towards the courtyard, the main feature of the North Gatehouse is a range of first-floor openings consisting of four tall windows, and, at the left-hand (west) end, a doorway. All have three-centred heads, an unusual choice of arch, but perhaps a development of the segmental-arched windows that dominate the rear elevation of the Harlech gatehouse (Figure 10.10). Each of the windows was divided by a transom positioned a little above mid-height. At Harlech the windows are connected by a sill string which extends around the flanking stair turrets; that is also a feature of the Beaumaris gatehouse, but, there is also a second string, a little above the height of transoms, which steps over the openings as a continuous hood mould.

This elevation has been built in two phases, the construction break extending across the windows immediately level with the bottom of the hood mould string. Below this line the window jambs are rebated with an outer moulding.

Figure 10.9 (right):
Beaumaris. Llanfaes Gate, doorway to the west flanking tower.

Figure 10.10 (below):
Beaumaris. North Gatehouse from the south.

Although the moulding continues into the upper halves of the windows, the rebate only rises just above the transoms, with the result that the upper openings are slightly wider than the lower. The interceding hiatus of this two-phase construction is most likely to be that engendered by the diversion of resources to Scotland. In which case the upper part of the elevation must belong to the period after 1306 and is most probably to be attributed to Nicholas Derneford. The one remaining transom appears to have been designed for a central mullion, indicating a two-light window, probably with tracery, perhaps something like the second-floor windows in the King's Gate at Caernarfon. When building resumed, the original scheme was abandoned and a plainer style adopted.

A three-centred arch was also used for the lintel of the first-floor fireplace in the west flanking tower (Figure 10.11). This fireplace is the only complete one to be found in the castle. Indeed, there is a suspicion that many were never finished; toothings for

Figure 10.11: *Beaumaris. North Gatehouse, first-floor fireplace in the west flanking tower.*

the hoods are widely evident, but of the hoods themselves there is no sign, except for this one instance. It is not entirely clear whether the lintel is primary, for although it fits well enough it doesn't look entirely at ease with the rest of the surround, despite being at one with the south windows. However, the other elements of the fireplace chime with those in the inner towers, and there does seem to have been a uniform design, broadly similar to those of the other Edwardian castles. The jambs were hollow chamfered, this moulding being carried along the heads, which were angled upwards as brackets to support the lintel. On each side there was a sconce bracket, ogee-profiled and rising to a polygonal upper edge.

It was probably Derneford who built the chapel, the interior of which is rectangular with a semi-hexagonal apse (Figure 10.12). Around the lower part of the walls is a blind trefoil-cusped arcade with pointed trefoils in the spandrels; the north, south, and east sides are divided into three-bay sections by the engaged vaulting columns, and above each section is a single lancet window within double-splayed jambs. Broad chamfered ribs spring from the columns (tripartite at the upper level) to form two-and-a-half sexpartite vaulting bays. Towards the west end, high up in each of the two side walls, is a rectangular opening allowing the occupants of two private pews to view the proceedings. There are analogues with the Conwy Castle chapel, notably the semi-hexagonal sanctuary,

Figure 10.12: *Beaumaris. Chapel from the south east, showing the west entrance and the opening to one of the viewing chambers.*

Figure 10.13: *Beaumaris. Inner curtain detail.*

the blind arcade of trefoil-headed panels, the deeply splayed lancet windows, and the elevated viewing chambers. Perhaps then, the plan of the chapel was determined from the outset, although the detailing may be owed to Derneford.

Another piece of decorative work is the wall-head corbelling that seems to have extended all around both the inner and outer wards of the castle. Although such treatment was applied to some of the turrets at Conwy and Harlech, its extension to the curtains is peculiar to Beaumaris. As at Conwy and Harlech, the corbelling of the outer enceinte is plain, but that of the inner enceinte is more ornate, in that the corbels are hollow chamfered on both sides and this moulding is carried up and along the soffits of the lintels that in turn carry the projecting parapet (Figure 10.13). These finishes are one of the unifying factors of Beaumaris. The plainer corbelling of the outer enceinte can be safely assigned to Derneford; that of the inner ward, the towers of which were built during his time, may also be his work, but less certainly so, as the curtain may have been finished before he took over from Master James.

William Emeldon's Survey and Subsequent Repairs

In 1343 the royal lands in Wales, including the castles, were granted to Edward Prince of Wales, and the King's clerk, William of Emeldon, was tasked with making the transfer.[17] Part of Emeldon's brief was to carry out a condition survey of the castles, which involved visiting all thirteen royal castles in north and south Wales.[18] The ensuing report provides an interesting record pertaining to the outstanding work needed to bring Beaumaris and Caernarfon to completion, and the dilapidations that had occurred here, and at other sites, since the main building programmes had been concluded.

Emeldon's report prompted some work at several of the Edwardian castles. At Conwy, the first on his itinerary, one of the principal undertakings to stem from the survey was the reconstruction of the roof that had been raised over the great hall in the 1280s by Richard the Engineer and Henry of Oxford. Instead of a new timber construction, the original timber trusses were replaced by a series of stone arches, which then carried the longitudinal timbers. The project had begun by 14 February 1347, when the order was given to complete the arches of the hall of Conwy Castle and repair the defects of the castle 'by the view and advice of the prince's mason, Henry of Snelleston'.[19] The roofs of the south and east ranges of the Inner Ward, which housed the royal apartments, were also carried on stone arches and it is assumed that these also date from the 1340s.

A similar expedient was used at Beaumaris, the second castle to be viewed by Emeldon. Here, single arches were made to carry the first floors in the North-East, South-East, South-West, and Middle towers and the second floor

Figure 10.14: *Beaumaris. Middle Tower, diaphragm arch at basement level.*

in the North-East Tower (Figure 10.14). The technique was also extended to Caernarfon, the third castle on the list, where Emeldon found that the timber floors of the Well Tower had rotted, and specified, therefore, that they needed to be replaced with stone arches. There are signs, in the form of arch springers, that this repair was carried out, and that here too a series of great diaphragm arches were thrown across the interior (just as they were at Beaumaris) to act as the principal supports for the floors.

Emeldon's recommendation of stone arches at Caernarfon suggests that he had already noted the technique elsewhere. It is possible that this was at Beaumaris, where there is nothing in Emeldon's report to support the idea that they stem from his survey, suggesting that the arches might already have been *in situ*, in which case, they may have been raised during Nicholas Derneford's term of office. So, it is interesting to note the relationship between these arches and the arched 'bridges' that traverse the choir aisles of Bristol Cathedral (formerly the Abbey of St Augustine, where Derneford had worked) at the main bay divisions and serve to carry the aisle vaults. Notwithstanding their outwardly contrasting characters, these two devices are structurally similar, and therefore represent a common concept, so there is a distinct possibility that they are the work of the same mind.[20]

Chapter Eleven

The Impact of the Edwardian Castle

Influence of the Royal Works Under Edward I and Edward II

The Welsh castle-building programme of Edward I comprises the most ambitious, costly, and architecturally interesting project of its kind ever undertaken by any medieval King of England. Vast numbers of building craftsmen were conscripted from large swathes of the realm to work on it, and many of the members of the nobility, particularly those who served in Wales, knew the castles at first hand or by repute. Under these circumstances it might be anticipated that the dissemination of building techniques and architectural concepts would follow fairly rapidly and that in addition to Wales and Scotland, the impact of the royal works would also be felt in England. There is certainly some reason to suppose this to be true, although the effect of the Edwardian castle has sometimes been overlooked when considering the apparent anti-climax of the aftermath.

Shropshire

A number of instances of the direct influence of the royal works is to be discerned in the border counties. A comparative study of the Upper Gate of Conwy and the Broad Gate of Ludlow, the now heavily disguised southern entrance to the walled town, has drawn attention to similarities in design, in particular, to the splayed sides of the inner half of the entrance passage, and it has been argued convincingly that these represent the influence of the King's works in Wales.[1] The reasoning is given traction, firstly, by Ludlow's border location; secondly, by the fact that Geoffrey de Geneville, Lord of Ludlow, served in the Second Welsh War of 1282–3 as assistant to the earl marshal, Roger Bigod, Earl of Norfolk; and, thirdly, because Geoffrey was a brother-in-law of Count Peter of Savoy, thereby linking him to the influential Savoyard party at court. The Upper Gate of Conwy was built in 1284–5. In 1283 de Geneville had granted his English lands, including Ludlow, to his son, Peter, so it was very probably Peter who built the Broad Gate.

Some 9 miles to the north west of Ludlow is the fortified manor house of Stokesay, built by the wool merchant Lawrence of Ludlow, who obtained a licence to crenellate his manor house at Stokesay (Shropshire) on 19 October 1291.[2] The debt owed by the designer of the great tower of Stokesay to the

Figure 11.1: *Stokesay. Great tower from the south east.*

Edwardian castles of north Wales has been discussed elsewhere.[3] In short, it follows a line of development from Caernarfon, where geometrical figures were being used in experimental ways, through to the great gatehouse of Denbigh, where the clustering of geometrical figures was taken a stage further. Stokesay represents an extended development of this tendency to subvert the rules of geometrical construction (Figure 11.1).

This may explain the line of development behind the highly original design of the tower, but it is the historical circumstance that clinches the argument that Stokesay was a consequence of the Edwardian castle-building programme. Stokesay's builder, Lawrence of Ludlow, was not only a wealthy wool merchant, but also a money lender and one of Edward's creditors. He may, therefore, have had the ear of the King and so been in a position to call upon the advice of royal craftsmen. It is a moot point as to how successful the design of Stokesay was, but, its source seems clear. Laurence died in 1294, and it is probable that the tower had been completed by then.

Another Salopian was Edward's long-time servant and friend, Robert Burnell, chancellor from 1274 and Bishop of Bath and Wells from 1275. At Wells, Burnell was responsible for rebuilding the great hall and chapel of the Bishops's Palace between *c.* 1280 and 1292, but on 28 January 1284, he obtained a licence to crenellate the manor house at his birthplace of Acton Burnell, some 17 miles north of Stokesay.[4] Burnell had been sole owner of Acton manor since 1269, and the building of the manor house had been preceded by the construction of the adjacent Church of St Mary.[5] St Mary's is unusually ornate for a parish church and reflects Burnell's high social position. Affinities with Wells Cathedral have been noted.[6]

The manor house was a rather extraordinary building for its time, being self contained with an integrated plan of unusual complexity (Figure 11.2). It is a rectangular two-storey structure, with square corner turrets flanking rectangular chamber and service blocks at the west and east ends respectively. An east–west spine wall allowed a double-span roof, and the first-floor hall (which occupied the

Figure 11.2: *Acton Burnell. The hall house from the north west.*

full width of the building) to be divided by an arcade. Parallels have been drawn with twelfth-century keeps, but, although the raised position of the hall, together with the corner turrets and crenellated parapets, hint at defence, they are no more than allusions, and even though the manor house was once surrounded by a moat it is essentially an undefended residence.

Analogues between Burnell's manor house and the royal works in Wales are not immediately apparent, but three details point to a connection with north Wales.[7] Firstly, the plinth mouldings of the turrets have been reasonably compared to that of the great hall in Caernarfon Castle, giving rise to the suspicion that the same designer may well have been responsible for both. The form of the great hall plinth appears to date from the earliest phase of stonework at Caernarfon, suggesting that it might predate Acton Burnell, but, if so, the two buildings can only be within a very few years of each other. Secondly, the hall windows surrounds are decorated with wave mouldings, another profile associated with Caernarfon. Thirdly, as we have seen, one of the unusual structural aspects of Caernarfon's Eagle Tower is the use of domical vaults which are to be found in some of the polygonal wall chambers. Polygonal domical vaulting is rare in England and Wales, so it is significant that an example is also to be found at Acton Burnell over the spiral staircase within the south west turret. These three features, together with the personal relationship between Robert Burnell and Edward, suggest the involvement of a mason from amongst the upper echelons of the royal craftsmen employed in north Wales.

Figure 11.3: *Acton Burnell. Windows in the west front.*

Acton Burnell has been mentioned in Chapter 9 as a source for the windows of the great tower of Duffus. The openings in question are located in the monumental west front, a tripartite composition of slim corner towers and wide central chamber block separated by deeply recessed links containing doorways. These buildings are lit by windows of two main forms: rectangular and lancet, a common characteristic of both being that they are recessed within two continuous chamfered orders, a style that contributes to a sense of solidity appropriate to the quasi-masculinity of the frontage, and which could very well have acted as an exemplar for Duffus. Furthermore, in the central block, a pair of twin-lancet windows might be described as a truncated version of the principal windows at Rait (Figure 11.3).

Haverfordwest

A different aspect of Caernarfon is apparent at the castle of Haverfordwest (Pembrokeshire), which, in 1289, was acquired by Queen Eleanor through an exchange of lands with William de Valence. Eleanor set about rebuilding it, and much of the present castle is attributed to her, the work having been undertaken in the two building seasons before her death in November 1290. However, it is also clear that some older elements were incorporated into the new work. Interpretation of the castle is assisted by a survey of 1577.[8]

A large outer ward lies to the west and a smaller inner ward to the east; the architectural interest of the castle rests with the latter. This inner ward is an irregularly shaped enclosure of which the north, south, and east sides survive; of the gatehouse from the outer ward there is now no trace. The principal twelfth-century elements are the sub-rectangular keep, and probably the chapel tower at the north-east and south-east angles respectively. There are thirteenth-century towers to the north west (the Brechinock Tower) and south west, the former round and the latter semi-circular.

The main thirteenth-century apartments were ranged around the south and east sides of the courtyard. Occupying the south side of the ward was the great hall, which was raised over an undercroft, the former being lit by two large pointed windows and the latter with lancets. To the east of the hall was the chapel which was also lit by large pointed windows to the south and east, the sanctuary being housed within a rectangular tower. North of the chapel was the great chamber and then a second chamber, also illuminated by large windows in the (east) curtain. In 1577 the inner ward also contained a pantry and other offices, and a kitchen with three fireplaces. Further accommodation was contained within the keep and the western towers.

To the south of the inner ward and extending westwards, was a terrace or outer enclosure, in the manner of the concentric outer wards of Rhuddlan and Harlech, but at a lower level. In 1577 it had a turret at the south-east angle and was known as the 'Queen's Arbour'; it very probably housed a garden. This terrace was reached from the inner ward via a staircase in the south-west tower which descended to a door in the east side of the tower with a shouldered lintel. This doorway, the wave-moulded surrounds of the main thirteenth-century windows, and the terrace, all point to the influence of the royal works in north Wales, a suggestion that is confirmed by the use of different coloured stone to create a banded pattern in imitation of Caernarfon. This is now most visible on the south front where two bands run across the curtain, just above the battered plinth, and in the gap between the undercroft windows and hall windows, extending over the south-west tower and around the south-eastern angle to the east front.

Episcopal Residences

There is little doubt that another, more ambitious, development in the neighbouring county of Staffordshire also stemmed from Caernarfon.[9] This was the construction, or reconstruction, of the wall around Lichfield Cathedral Close by Bishop Walter Langton (Edward's treasurer, 1295–1307, and also Bishop of Coventry and Lichfield, 1296–1321) under a licence to crenellate of 1299.[10] The close wall, which enclosed a sub-rectangular area, was built in concert with an episcopal palace integral with the north and east sides of the enceinte. Completed by 1314, the focus of the palace was a great hall, with internal dimensions of 100ft x 56ft, raised over an undercroft.[11] Mural paintings depicting the life of Edward I included scenes from his Welsh and Scottish wars and support the notion that this is a conscious emulation of Caernarfon.[12]

Subsidiary apartments to the north and south contained a chamber and a chapel with semi-dodecagonal and semi-decagonal apses respectively, both of which projected outside the close wall as turrets. At the north-east corner, an octagonal tower was also incorporated into the palace complex. In descrying the influence of Caernarfon in these forms, it is not simply that the builder made use of polygonal towers, but that he used different configurations, just as his counterpart did at Caernarfon. Further buildings, integral with the close wall, were located in the south-east and south-west corners and to the west of the south-east gate.[13] The palace was demolished in the seventeenth century, but the lower part of the north-east tower survives, albeit faced in brick, the ground storey being covered with a domed vault, which is evidently derived from Caernarfon.[14]

In this respect it is pertinent to note that the licence to crenellate coincided with the suspension of works at Caernarfon, and so a transfer of personnel to Lichfield at this date is a strong possibility.

Another of Langton's works, the now sadly depleted episcopal manor house of Eccleshall Castle (Staffordshire), situated about 7 miles north west of Stafford, is related to Lichfield close. Built to a quadrangular plan, it too was provided with polygonal corner towers, which, unusually, were nine-sided, an idiosyncrasy that chimes with the unconventional geometrical constructions at Lichfield. The principal apartments were integrated with the curtain and the two adjacent corner towers, just as the bishop's palace was integrated with the defences of the close at Lichfield.

Both Eccleshall Castle and Lichfield close and palace, then, can be considered to derive directly from Caernarfon. Another potential, but less tangible link between the Edwardian castles of Wales and Lichfield is the eastern arm of the Cathedral, the rebuilding of which was initiated by Langton *c.* 1315 under the cathedral mason William de Eyton.[15] Unusually for England, the Lady Chapel had a semi-octagonal east end, a trait it shared with the chapel depicted by Randle Holme in his plan of Ruthin Castle, which shows the chapel at the south-west end of the courtyard.[16] Assuming that the drawing is accurate in its portrayal, then Lichfield is the most likely source for the design, and this factor points to a two-way traffic in the transmission of ideas.

Caernarfon also seems to have been the source for another episcopal residence: Newark Castle (Nottinghamshire), a home of the Bishops of Lincoln, where the river (west) front of the twelfth-century castle was rebuilt in the late thirteenth or early fourteenth century on a slightly different alignment, bringing it closer to the river (Figure 11.4).[17] This remodelling retained the twelfth-century rectangular south-west tower but incorporated two new polygonal towers at the north-west angle and in the centre of the new front. The polygonal form of the towers is one reason for making a connection with Caernarfon, particularly because of the choice of the hexagon as a basis for their plans; it was an unusual figure but one that had been used at Caernarfon in the flanking towers of the Queen's Gate.

A second analogy is the use of two different colours of masonry to produce an ornamental banded effect, a rare feature, but a particular characteristic of Caernarfon, and one unlikely to have been designed independently at Newark. The band at Newark is delineated by two prominent chamfered offsets (features that are also to be found at Caernarfon), the upper one marking the floor of the courtyard buildings. These comprised two halls placed in linear succession, the great hall to the south and the bishop's hall to the north, the former straddling the position of the Middle Tower and lit by a pair of large two-centred arch windows with surrounds of three chamfered orders. It has been observed that the Middle Tower, which contained a prison, has a parallel in the Prison Tower at Conwy both in its spatial relationship to the great hall, and in the accommodation it contained.[18] That Newark can be linked with two northern Welsh castles strengthens the case for a personal connection with the royal works in Wales.

Figure 11.4: *Newark. River frontage from the south west.*

Another castle of the Bishops of Lincoln to be rebuilt around the late thirteenth or early fourteenth century was Banbury (Oxfordshire). Banbury Castle has entirely disappeared but excavations carried out in late twentieth century have elucidated some of its attributes.[19] This too was a rebuilding of a twelfth-century castle, which, like Newark, consisted of a quadrilateral enclosure with rectangular angle and mid-wall towers. The new castle comprised two concentric pentagonal wards pointing towards the south, each surrounded by a ditch. At the southern apex of each ward was a gateway with twin cylindrical flanking towers; the curtain was also set about with cylindrical angle and mid-wall towers. Whilst Caernarfon does not seem to have been a model, the concentric defences may well have been emulating the royal works. Whether this was Wales or the contemporary and much closer works at the Tower of London is a moot point, but the positioning of the gatehouses, one in front of the other is echoed at Aberystwyth and Harlech, and their siting at the apex of the enclosures is paralleled at Aberystwyth and Rhuddlan.

The North

Robert Clifford's construction work at Brougham Castle has been mentioned briefly as a possible source for the builder of Bothwell (Chapter 9), but does it have analogies with the royal works in Wales? Clifford inherited the estate in 1295, and soon set about making improvements.[20] The enceinte was rebuilt in stone with a large rectangular tower at the south-west corner, now known as the 'Tower of League', the Norman keep received an additional storey, and a singular gatehouse complex was built abutting the north side of the keep.

The rectangularity of the gatehouse and Tower of League, and the massive rectangular buttresses of the former, do not recall the Edwardian castles of Wales, but, rather, seem to herald the architectural style of the fourteenth century in northern England. Clifford's works contain some fine freemasonry, notably in the top-floor apartment he added to the keep, but the details are to a great extent quite distinct from anything in Edward's works. However, we have already seen that, even in Wales, the baronial castles could be substantially or wholly independent, although there is usually something to identify them as part of the same group.

At Brougham, despite the differences, there are indeed a few aspects that suggest a link with royal works of Wales. Firstly, the shouldered lintel is used copiously within Clifford's additions. Secondly, the latrine turret to the Tower of League is of similar type to those Taylor noted in Wales as being analogous to features in Savoy, in rising from ground level and being of slight projection, the latrine passage almost wholly within the curtain. Thirdly, on the ground floor of the Tower of League, there is a rather unusual fireplace, a mannerist rendition of the shouldered lintel, in which the arches of the shoulders are elongated and distorted and the verticals shortened (Figure 11.5); the form recalls the doorways on either side of the first-floor south window embrasure in the great tower of Hawarden (Figure 5.7).

Figure 11.5: *Brougham. Tower of League, ground-floor fireplace.*

This brings us to the fourth point of comparison, and perhaps the most striking one, which is the mural passage that extends around the top floor of the Brougham keep, the analogues of which are surely to be found in similar features in Hawarden keep and in the Eagle Tower of Caernarfon (Figure 11.6). The Brougham passage runs from the staircase in the north-east corner, to a chapel, or oratory, in the south-west corner, passing through window embrasures giving access to the central chamber; a separate passage extends from the staircase within the east wall terminating just short of the chapel, but also passing through a window embrasure. At Hawarden there is also a chapel at the farthest extremity of the wall passage from the stairs, but it can only be entered from the central chamber. In the Eagle Tower, the chapels on the ground and first floors are entered directly from the staircase; the former is independent of the central chamber and the wall passages, but the latter does communicate with the mural network.

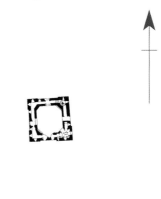

Figure 11.6 (above): *Brougham. Great tower, third-floor plan.*

Figure 11.7 (below): *Brougham. Great tower, third-floor doorway.*

There appears to be very little doubt that the Brougham scheme was inspired by Caernarfon and/or Hawarden. This being so, two other details are worth mentioning to consolidate the link with Wales. One is that, like Caernarfon and Hawarden, the passage has a slab ceiling carried on corbel courses, instead of being vaulted. The Brougham corbels have a different profile, but the principal is the same. The other pertinent detail occurs in the western window embrasure, in which the doorway to the south constitutes another curious interpretation of the shouldered lintel, which is given a bizarre twist in that only the left-hand (west) side appears to have been properly completed. Here, the inner order terminates in an angular bell capital with plain abacus stepping up to the corbel, whilst the outer order is linked to the corbel by a double-cusped line of quadrant arches (Figure 11.7). Double cusping has already been referred to as a device used at Caernarfon in connection with the shouldered lintel.[21]

There does seem to be some connection with Wales, then, and in particular with Caernarfon and Hawarden, and this implies the presence of a craftsman with experience of the royal works in Wales, who had already started to push the boundaries whilst so employed, and who, at Brougham, was able to give further reign to his innovative tendencies. The conceptual relationship between the fireplace in the Tower of League and the passage doorways in the Hawarden keep are powerful evidence that the same craftsman worked at both buildings. Clifford had an ancestral interest in Hawarden because his grandfather, Roger, had custody of the lordship from 1281, and may have had something to do with the reconstruction of the castle, but there is no direct evidence, nor reason to believe that there was any Clifford involvement at Hawarden after 4 September 1284, when the manor reverted to its heir Roger de Montalt, at which stage, Robert Clifford, who was his grandfather's heir, was only 10 years old.[22] However, Montalt was serving in Scotland by 1298, being present at Falkirk, and also took part in the siege of Caerlaverock, both campaigns in which Clifford also served.[23] It may well be that Montalt was the conduit by which Hawarden came to Brougham.

In Yorkshire, a major work was carried out between 1307 and 1312. When Edward I died in 1307, one response of the new monarch, Edward II, was to recall his friend, Piers Gaveston, from exile, create him Earl of Cornwall and begin the construction of a new great tower for his benefit at Knaresborough Castle (Yorkshire).[24] Now known as the King's Tower, it was an unconventional building breaking through the curtain wall, beyond which it presented a semi-polygonal prow like the much smaller wall towers associated with the new bishop's palace at Lichfield. The basis of this external display is surely derived from the wall towers of Caernarfon Castle, which it rivalled in scale and general character. As a symbol of royal officialdom, this imposing residence has been compared to the Great Tower of Flint and with the Eagle Tower of Caernarfon.[25] Also, based on its proximity to the main gate of the castle (which lay immediately adjacent), together with its angled profile on this side, it has been conjectured that the King's Tower might have a similar relationship to the gate as did one of the flanking towers of Caernarfon's King Gate, a theory that only excavation may confirm.[26]

The master builder of the King's Tower at Knaresborough was the London-based mason Hugh de Tichemers, whose surname indicates an association with the Northamptonshire settlement of Titchmarsh. Other than his connection with Knaresborough, little is known about him, but, given his name, it is feasible that he had something to do with Titchmarsh Castle, a moated site for which John Lord Lovell had obtained a licence to crenellate in 1304.[27] Lovell had served in Edward's military campaigns in Wales (1277 and 1287) and Scotland (1296, 1299, 1300, 1301, 1303, and 1304) and he was, therefore, part of the relevant circle, and must have been conversant with recent fashions in military architecture. In 1346–7 Titchmarsh Castle was said to have had stone fortifications.[28] In 1887, excavation revealed stone buildings on the roughly quadrangular moat platform, enclosed by a curtain wall with pentagonal towers at the angles.[29] The use of polygonal towers seems most likely to indicate the influence of Caernarfon, where building work was resumed in the same year as Lord Lovell's licence was granted.

Another figure closely associated with Edward I and his circle was his nephew Thomas of Lancaster (*c.* 1278–1322). Although he was too young to be involved in the Welsh wars, he married the daughter of a Welsh wars veteran, the Earl of Lincoln, builder of Denbigh. He also served under Edward in Scotland, taking part in the Battle of Falkirk, the siege of Caerlaverock, and on the campaigns of 1304–5 and 1306–7. In 1311 Lincoln died, and Lancaster received the bulk of his estates. In 1313, shortly after taking the leading role in the killing of Piers Gaveston, he began to build a new castle at Dunstanburgh, an isolated headland on the Northumbrian coast (Figure 11.8).[30]

The main feature of Lancaster's new castle was the great gatehouse, an ostentatious building rivalling the ambitious creations of the royal castles in Wales. The contractor for the gatehouse was a Master Elias, who has been tentatively identified with Elias de Burton, a mason who, in 1302–3, was working on 'Llywelyn's hall' at Conwy.[31] The inference is that Elias applied his experience of the Welsh castle-building programme at Dunstanburgh. Harlech in particular has been seen as a source.[32] However, although a superficial resemblance between Dunstanburgh and Harlech is provided by the bow-fronted flanking towers, given that the Harlech towers are three-quarters round and the Dunstanburgh towers D-shaped, there is a greater affinity with the inner gatehouses of Beaumaris, which are closer in date.

Like its counterparts at Beaumaris (as planned but not completed) and Harlech, the Dunstanburgh gatehouse rose through three storeys. Communication between the floors was via a pair of spiral staircases within the thickness of the rear (north) wall; despite the different treatment, these are the equivalents of the paired turret-housed stairs in the two Welsh castles and may have been derived from them. At Dunstanburgh, however, the accommodation itself was less generous. The building has a depth of only 50ft compared with 62ft at Harlech and 88ft at Beaumaris, so that whereas the Welsh gatehouses had a division between the bowed flanking towers at the front and a rectangular block at the rear, the interior of Dunstanburgh is more integrated, so that it can only be compared with the main accommodation blocks of the Welsh gatehouses. It contained three cells at first-floor level, rather than two, so that it is only on the second floor that the two-room hall and chamber layout found on both the upper floors of Harlech and Beaumaris is replicated. Nevertheless, even in this instance the accommodation was more cramped.

However, it is in a comparison of the frontages that Dunstanburgh comes into its own. The Beaumaris gatehouses exceeded that of Harlech in size, but, the

Figure 11.8: *Dunstanburgh. Great gatehouse from the south east.*

face of Dunstanburgh, with a width of some 105ft compared with 88ft and 75ft respectively, was more impressive than both. These more generous proportions give Dunstanburgh something in common with the great gatehouse of Denbigh, but even Denbigh, which had a maximum width of 97ft, was surpassed. The Dunstanburgh gatehouse was also given additional height by turrets at the two rear (north) corners and in the centres of the two bowed fronts; on the inner sides of the two south turrets, rectangular bartizans, corbelled outwards at the front, rise a little higher. This treatment of the upper reaches of the gatehouse is a highly original attempt at creating an architectural effect; the former existence of a rectangular barbican in front of the entrance added to an interesting exercise in massing and perspective.

If Dunstanburgh was derived from the King's works in Wales, the references so far are oblique. However, it is worth pointing out that shouldered lintels are as much in evidence for doorways and windows as they are at Beaumaris and Caernarfon, and although the form had been introduced to the north of England by the 1240s in the great tower of York Castle, the two-light mullioned and transomed windows to be found at Dunstanburgh represent a type that is particularly associated with Caernarfon (Figure 11.9). Also, it is not implausible that the juxtaposition of round-fronted towers and rectangular and corbelled bartizans was inspired by the concurrence of similar forms in the Gate-next-the

Figure 11.9: *Dunstanburgh. Twin carnarvon-arched window in the great gatehouse.*

Sea at Beaumaris, where the round corbelled turrets on square bases, and the attached rectangular latrine turret, present the same kinds of structural issues that are evident at Dunstanburgh. It may well be, then, that Master Elias did have experience of working in Wales and that this background is reflected in the Dunstanburgh gatehouse. This theory is supported by two other characteristic details: barrel vaults with heavy ribs (also a feature of the King's Gate, Caernarfon), which are to be found over the gate passage, mural chambers, and window embrasures, and, secondly, a gate arch of multiple chamfered orders that seems to emulate similar features at Caernarfon and Denbigh.[33]

South Midlands and South East

Reference has already been made to the building activities of Aymer de Valence, another member of Edward's inner circle, at Goodrich, and, possibly, at Bothwell. He also began, but probably never completed, Bampton Castle (Oxfordshire) for which a licence to crenellate was granted in 1315.[34] Although little of substance survives of the early fourteenth-century buildings, apart from the gatehouse, the principal (west) front was recorded in a drawing of 1664. It shows a symmetrical elevation with central rectangular gatehouse, two slim rectangular corner towers, and a linking curtain. The curtain and alternate merlons of the battlements were pierced by large numbers of cruciform arrow loops. Mid-way between the gatehouse and the two towers, two narrow shafts of semi-circular section each rose to a semi-circular bartizan with multiple corbelled base.[35]

It has been argued above that corbelled semi-circular bartizans were introduced by James of St George at Harlech and Beaumaris. The type that is depicted in the Bampton drawing seems to have the stepped corbelling of the Beaumaris type, and a reasonable assumption would be that Beaumaris was the principal source. At Bampton, the addition of the basal shafts reinforced the vertical articulation of the elevation and tied the bartizans more closely to the overall design of the frontage. This, together with a number of surviving elements, distinguishes the builder as someone with a large measure of aesthetic sensibility.

Inside, the gate passage has two bays of sexpartite chamfered rib vaulting with central bosses decorated with knobbly foliage extending over the ribs.[36] The gate jambs were embellished with bold quarter-round moulded orders, the robust character and form of which have been likened to late thirteenth- and early fourteenth-century details to be found in the Welsh Marches, including Aymer de Valence's castle of Goodrich, and in the Valence spheres of influence in Oxfordshire and Gloucestershire.[37]

The jambs of a hooded fireplace on the first floor of the gatehouse reflect those of the gateway, which comprise half-round shafts with a flat broad frontal fillet, the profile extending to the surmounting double corbels that support the lintel. Here, the fillets spread out in a pattern of cusps and arches to frame the heads of the corbels in a strap-like surround.[38] The general form of the fireplace has affinities with examples at Caernarfon, including the moulding of the jambs and the treatment of the corbel heads. It has evidently been executed by someone with experience of the style, although two tiers of corbels have been substituted for the single elongated corbel at Caernarfon.

A pointed window in the curtain, moved here from the gatehouse, is an updated version of those in the north front of Caernarfon, which are to be found at first-floor level in the curtain and at first- and second-floor level in the King's Gate.[39] They have the same combination of two transomed lights with trefoil cusped heads surmounted by a central quatrefoil. Bampton is distinguished from Caernarfon by the inclusion of ogees to produce Flowing tracery. This general form was not uncommon in the later thirteenth and fourteenth centuries, but the stylistic relationship between Bampton and Caernarfon is sufficiently close to suggest that the former might have developed from the latter.

The combination of these elements at Bampton implies that the builder had a knowledge and possibly first-hand experience of the King's works in Wales, especially Caernarfon. One possible connection is Walter of Hereford, who, in 1306, was in London, working on Greyfriars' church for Queen Margaret.[40] Such a date would not be incompatible with the details exhibited at Bampton, but, the general disposition of the building is certainly a creation independent of the Welsh works.

A building that has some similarities with Bampton is Woodcroft Castle (Northamptonshire), a quadrangular moated site, some 5 miles north west of Peterborough. The medieval complex is now represented by the north–south aligned west range, which was the entrance range, and a short rear wing at its northern end. This wing is set at an oblique angle to the west range, the list being replicated in the internal divisions of the latter. At the north-west angle is a round tower, one of a pair that formerly framed the entrance front.[41]

The west front has been much altered, but a drawing by Edward Blore, published in 1853, provides a useful reference for reconstructing its medieval appearance (Figure 11.10).[42] Essentially, the west range rose through two storeys, with three window bays to each side of a central three-storey, two-bay flush-faced gatehouse which rose above eaves level to include an additional storey. The building sits on a two-tier chamfered plinth which is carried across the north-west tower; and there was no doubt a corresponding tower at the south end.[43] Further horizontal articulation is provided by a first-floor window sill string that originally stepped up over the gateway, and by a heavier and more elaborate parapet string that also steps up in the centre in a more exaggerated fashion.

The nature of the ground-floor windows is uncertain, but the Blore drawing shows rectangular openings to the right (south) of the gatehouse. At first-floor level the windows were single transomed lights with shouldered lintels deeply recessed within broad chamfered surrounds with pierced or

Figure 11.10: *Woodcroft. The entrance front, Turner and Parker 1853*

sunken spandrels; the treatment has much in common with the windows in the great tower of Duffus as rebuilt by Reginald Cheyne *c.* 1305. The heads provide a link with Caernarfon, but the designer created an original version of the type. Nearly all these windows have since been replaced, and those shouldered-lintel lights that exist today lack the pierced spandrels shown in the Blore drawing. This more recent style has been replicated in the early twentieth-century second floor.[44] Inside, these windows have flat lintels carried on angular corbels, and on each side of the gate passage are two tiers of continuous corbelling of similar profile, a form that matches that in the Brougham and Bothwell wall passages.

The main ground-floor room, known as the Guard Room, which lies to the north of the gateway, contains a substantial hooded fireplace, possibly reset, but recognisably of the same genre as the Caernarfon group, and of late thirteenth-century or early fourteenth-century date. Chamfered jambs morph into flat-faced, ogee-profiled corbels, which support the flat chamfered lintel. Above the lintel is an ogee-moulded string. This fireplace is a variation of its Caernarfon counterparts, and likely to have been designed by a mason familiar with the type.

There is also a first-floor chapel over the gateway, with a tripartite shouldered-lintel window that incorporates the pierced spandrels that Blore depicted on the entrance front. Internally, it is set within a segmental-arched recess with an ogee-profiled roll and fillet-moulded surround; the mullions are embellished with stretched rolls which have broad fillets, also ogee-profiled.

These details suggest a late thirteenth-/early fourteenth-century date, a chronology in keeping with the other elements described above.

Further afield, in Sussex, another of Edward's intimates, John de Warenne, Earl of Surrey, veteran of the Welsh wars, and builder of Holt Castle, made modifications to his castle of Lewes by adding two semi-octagonal towers to the shell keep crowning the motte, and a barbican to the outer gatehouse. The general appearance of the towers may well have been based on similar examples at Caernarfon, although they do not have the inventiveness of their putative models. The towers are characterised by deeply splayed bases, like that of the Goblin Tower at Denbigh, and three coped offsets. They rise above the shell keep in an arrangement somewhat reminiscent of Castell Coch. The barbican took the form of a rectangular tower, placed in front of the Norman gatehouse and linked to it by a pair of walls, thus enclosing a yard. The front is framed by a pair of round bartizans corbelled out from the sides but flush with the corners of the building. Again, these features probably derive from the King's works in Wales, notably the Gate-next-the-Sea at Beaumaris.

The Influence of Caernarfon During the Reign of Edward III

In the instances discussed above, most of which can reasonably be ascribed to the influence of the King's works in Wales, it was Caernarfon, the most architectural and visually impressive of the Welsh castles, that, understandably, had the greatest impact. Some thirty years after the completion of Knaresborough, polygonal towers once again became a significant element of castellated architecture. Could these, too, be considered direct references to Caernarfon? At Wells, the Bishop's Palace was fortified during the episcopacy of Bishop Ralph of Shrewsbury (1329–63), who obtained a licence to crenellate in 1340.[45] The fortifications included a curtain wall studded with round towers and a gatehouse with octagonal flanking towers. Given that gatehouses with polygonal flanking towers at this time only existed in the royal works and at Denbigh, it is likely that one of these may have provided the inspiration, but not the model, because, in comparison, the Wells gatehouse is a rather staid building with nothing of the architectural flair that characterises the northern Welsh castles.

In the Midlands, an entirely new castle was built by William de Clinton, first Earl of Huntingdon, at Maxstoke (Warwickshire) under a licence to crenellate of 1345, although by this date the castle may have been nearing completion. Clinton's elevation to the nobility in 1337 and his acquisition of additional income to sustain his new status could have been the catalyst for initiating work on a new castle.[46] It is possible that he was in residence by 1344 when the old manor house was granted to Maxstoke Priory, Clinton's own foundation (consecrated in 1342).[47]

A quadrangular castle surrounded by a moat, Maxstoke has a comparatively low curtain wall, which, in concert with three of the four octagonal corner towers, gives

Figure 11.11: *Maxstoke. The west front.*

it a squat yet homely appearance (Figure 11.11) in the vein of the outer curtain of
Beaumaris, another castle that was surrounded by a wet moat. The fourth tower,
at the north-west angle, and known as the Lady Tower, has a larger ground plan
than the others and rises through four storeys rather than three. The only other
part of the castle to contrast with its generally low-rise character is the gatehouse,
a rectangular building twice as high as the curtain and having rather slender
octagonal turrets at the outer angles flanking the entrance. Like the corner towers,
the gatehouse lies almost entirely outside the curtain. The gateway was protected
by a portcullis and a line of murder holes in the soffit of the entrance arch.

Although the fortifications are functional, the general character of the castle
is a highly articulate exercise in geometrically engendered proportion, and the
design incorporates a good deal of high-quality decorative detail. A series of
gargoyles carved with grotesque faces breaks through the hollow-chamfered
string course at the foot of the parapet; the large traceried chapel window forms a
major feature on the west side of castle; the gate passage is covered by a tierceron
vault enriched by sculptured bosses, and the ground storey of the Lady Tower
contains a rib vault.

Direct references to Caernarfon are difficult to pin down; nevertheless, the
octagonal towers do provide one obvious connection, but they are more in the vein
of Saint-Georges-d'Espéranche than Caernarfon and the scale of the gatehouse
turrets has more in common with some ecclesiastical sites. Nevertheless, the level
of display on show at Maxstoke is very much an offshoot of the kind of architecture
that was being produced at Caernarfon, militarily functional but tempered with
an infusion of eye-catching beauty; it is a combination well suited to the Age

of Chivalry. The two castles have different emphases; if Caernarfon expresses stateliness, Maxstoke inclines towards gaiety, but both combine authority with romance and must have presented uplifting images for the knightly class.

Maxstoke was one of a number of Midlands castles that adopted the polygonal tower. Lichfield Cathedral Close and bishop's palace, Eccleshall and Newark castles, have all been considered as Caernarfon-inspired buildings. If Maxstoke was not directly influenced by Caernarfon, then local models may have acted as channels through which the influence of the King's works was communicated. Maxstoke itself probably influenced the form of Stafford Castle keep, which was raised under a contract of 1345, and which was set around with octagonal corner and mid-wall towers.[48] Warwick Castle, as reconstructed in the fourteenth century, belongs to the same group. The main gatehouse and barbican, in the centre of the east front, and the Watergate on the east side of the castle, were all supplied with polygonal towers.

Gatehouses with twin polygonal towers of more masculine character are to be found in Northumberland. At Berwick the main gateway was flanked by polygonal towers, the whole frontage being approximately 100ft wide, and therefore at a scale comparable to or at a slightly greater scale than the King's Gate and Queen's Gate at Caernarfon. In the sixteenth century this gateway was known as the 'Donjeon', a name suggestive of a substantial gatehouse with living accommodation. Caernarfon, then, would seem to be the most likely source, suggesting that Berwick may have been the conduit whereby something of the character of Caernarfon was transferred to the northern borders. The date of the 'Donjeon' is unknown, but Edward I did a substantial amount of work at Berwick, including that on an outer gatehouse leading from the town to the castle, and it is conceivable that the main gatehouse itself also received attention.

If the date of the Berwick 'Donjeon' is unclear, two Northumbrian castles have closely dated and analogous gateways which are flanked by polygonal towers. One of these is the main entrance to Bothal Castle, which was fortified by Robert Bertram (1322–62), Sheriff of Northumberland in 1344, under a licence to crenellate of 1343.[49] That this date relates to the construction of the gatehouse is corroborated by a collection of heraldic shields which adorn the front and which denote the years 1340–44, indicating that the building is a close contemporary of its counterpart at Maxstoke.[50] Be that as it may, the builder of the Bothal gatehouse produced his own distinct interpretation of the type. Unlike Maxstoke, where the turrets project from the angles, at Bothal they are semi-octagonal terminations to the main block. One of their distinctive aspects is that they project from the sides of the gatehouse, a trait that might have been derived from the rectangular gatehouse turrets of Etal Castle (Northumberland), some 50 miles to the north, which was licensed in 1341.[51]

The sculptured shields, of which there are fourteen, and which adhere to the gatehouse high above the gateway, are also a distinguishing aspect of the building's character. Three of these shields are set upon the three merlons above the recessed entrance; the central shield, which is at a larger scale than the rest, bears the arms of Edward III, in the form adopted by him in 1340 and showing the leopards of England quartered with the fleurs-de-lys of France.[52] This embellishment of the upper parts of the gatehouse is augmented by two figure sculptures, which stand on separate merlons: a piper and a wild man in the act of hurling a boulder. Such sculptural trimmings were to become a common feature of northern castellated architecture in the later fourteenth century, and, like the polygonal flanking towers, may ultimately be derived from the elaborate sculpture-clad battlements of Caernarfon.

Bothal is contemporary with the Inner Gatehouse of Alnwick Castle, one of the last elements in the castle's reconstruction by Henry, the second Lord Percy. The gatehouse bears a close resemblance to Bothal, and one would seem to have been modelled on the other. Elements of the Bothal design replicated at Alnwick include the idiosyncratic step in the sides of the building, the display of heraldic shields across the wall head, and the figure sculptures which surmount the merlons. The heraldry of the Alnwick shields has been said to indicate a date of between 1342 and 1347.[53] One aspect of Alnwick that isn't evident at Bothal is that the flanking turrets are provided with spurs emanating from square bases, a detail suggesting a connection with Wales and the marcher lordships. This same detail is to be found in the Outer Gatehouse of Alnwick, a building that is nearly identical in design to the Inner Gatehouse and which must be broadly contemporary. As at Warwick, the Outer Gatehouse is prefaced by a passage barbican, although the entrance is flanked by square, rather than octagonal, turrets.

It is impossible to know for certain whether Alnwick was preceded by Bothal or vice versa; it seems more likely, perhaps, that Alnwick, as the greater castle of a more illustrious family, would have been constructed first. However, the early form of the quartered royal arms suggests that the design of Bothal is likely to have been settled by 1340, and that it may, therefore, be the earlier of the two. What does seem probable from the degree of correspondence in both the broader aspects of the design and the structural details is that the same builder was responsible for both, or that one was copied from the other.

These gatehouses at Bothal and Alnwick post date a revival of English ambitions in Scotland following the invasion of Edward Baliol and Edward III's direct intervention in the northern kingdom in 1333. This year saw the English victory at Halidon Hill and the recapture of Berwick. Alnwick has been seen as a celebration of the Battle of Halidon Hill, but its construction coincides with a reversal of English fortunes in Scotland, which may well have been a greater impetus to fortification in the border counties.[54]

The ultimate expression of this Caernarfon-derived interest in polygonal towers was perhaps the 380ft south front of the royal apartments in the Upper Ward at Windsor as redeveloped in the 1360s. Here, the great hall and chapel complex was flanked by two twin-towered gatehouses, whilst the west end of the elevation was buttressed by the still extant Rose Tower, which, like the gatehouse towers, had a semi-octagonal prow. Some years later Edward's brother, John of Gaunt, Duke of Lancaster, made reference to it when he rebuilt Kenilworth (Warwickshire) in the 1370s.[55]

Wall-Head Embellishment

Wall-head embellishment is another aspect of the Edwardian castles of Wales that probably influenced later castellated architecture. It has been suggested above that the ultimate source of the battlement-mounted figure sculpture at Bothal and Alnwick may have been Caernarfon, where the greatest display of this form of decoration was to be found, and which, no doubt, served to popularise such ornamentation. The city walls of York, where sculpture of this type probably existed by the mid-fourteenth century, may have acted as an intermediary. At York the bars, or gateways, and their barbicans were also ornamented with cylindrical bartizans. It is probable that they were based on the corbelled bartizans of Harlech and Beaumaris, which seem to be the earliest datable examples of this feature.

At Harlech, continuous corbelling was utilised *c*. 1285 to build the outer curtain latrine turret and the bartizans flanking the outer gate. A different technique was used at Beaumaris, where stepped corbelling was employed to support the projecting turrets of the Gate-next-the-Sea, a refinement, perhaps, of the rubble-built Harlech examples. Bartizans on continuous corbelling were built at Langley *c*. 1350, Edlingham *c*. 1360, Tynemouth *c*. 1390 (all in Northumberland), and Hylton (County Durham) *c*. 1400. Bartizans on stepped corbelling appear on the barbican to Lewes (Sussex) *c*. 1330, York 1350–75 (Micklegate Bar), Belsay, and Chipchase (Northumberland) *c*. 1370. It may be significant that the appearance of these elements in England coincided with the winding down of operations at Beaumaris.

One other decorative element that was a prominent aspect of at least one of the Edwardian castles was the merlon pinnacle, which was introduced to Conwy by James and his Savoyard masons, and which also seems to have been a feature of Harlech. It is not known to have created a vogue, but such fragile appendages cannot be expected to have lasted well. However, at least one fragment has survived on the merlons of the defended precinct wall surrounding St Mary's Abbey, York, for which a licence to crenellate was obtained in 1318.[56] Such features are too specifically associated with James of St George and Conwy for us to entertain the notion that they might have been created independently, and there is a strong likelihood that this particular example takes its cue from Conwy, and was originally part of a larger scheme. It may well be that indications of other such schemes exist, but have yet to be recognised.

Chapter Twelve

The Edwardian Castle and its Builders

Taylor used stylistic analysis sparingly and as confirmatory evidence for particular historical theories. One of these was the identification of the master of the King's works in Wales as the Master James, the servant of the counts of Savoy; another was the role of the defences of Constantinople as a model for the builders of Caernarfon. Both involved the interpretation of apparent foreign influences that were otherwise difficult to explain in the context of English architecture. As we have seen, the Savoyard features that Taylor recorded in Wales, interesting as they are in denoting an international element, tell us little about the architectural development of the Edwardian castle, or, indeed, Master James' contribution to it. What has also been demonstrated in the foregoing, however, is that there are a number of common themes and lines of progression that allow us to bring a degree of order to the disparate characters of the individual buildings making up this group.

To what extent the castles of Flint and Rhuddlan were the work of Master James, on the one hand, and Master Bertram on the other is open to question. There is no record of Master James' presence in North Wales until late April 1278, but the engineers Richard and Bertram were both on the scene from the summer of 1277, when work started at the two sites. A possibility exists, therefore, that the castles of both Flint and Rhuddlan were laid out in 1277 and that when Master James arrived to take over the direction of operations he inherited a pre-existing plan. On the other hand, this doesn't rule out an involvement in formulating the initial scheme; buildings might be planned remotely, and the geometrical layouts of the inner wards of Flint and Rhuddlan give the impression of having been executed straight onto the drawing board regardless of any specific context. Nevertheless, an important part of the design process was an understanding of the terrain, its geological make up, topography, and spatial possibilities, which may be the reason that neither of the two inner wards is entirely symmetrical. Such compromises were perhaps inevitable where strategy and tactics were important factors in siting a castle, but it is interesting to surmise that ideal versions of these two castles may have served as blueprints for the modified forms that were actually built.

It has been argued here and elsewhere that Flint derives from French models. Given Edward's own connection, it is likely that the most immediate of these was Aigues Mortes and the adjacent Tour de Constance. Taylor's suggestion that the source may be found in the enlarged corner tower at Yverdon is less plausible. Edward, then, inspired by the coastal location and by his plans to build a defended town, probably suggested the arrangement (unique in England and Wales) of the detached donjon, the circular plan of which is reflected in the quadrant curve of the adjacent curtain. This unusual tower provided the castle with a distinctive architectural focus, but the internal plan is even more remarkable. Once again, the antecedents appear to be French, although great credit must be given to the designer in taking the principle of the mural gallery and creating something rather original. The unexpected complexity of the interior, which is belied by the plain exterior, is a testament to the skill in three-dimensional planning often exhibited by the medieval master builder, a point to which we will return later in this chapter. The great tower of Flint is one such example that displays the hand of the professional.

The other elements of Flint Castle were unexceptional. The gateway to the inner ward is notable for its simplicity when compared with those of the other royal castles, a characteristic no doubt owed to the proximity and overbearing presence of the great tower. It has been noted, however, that the drawbridge arrangement, as well as that of Rhuddlan, is rather interesting, as they both display a familiarity with the system used in the royal works, most recently at the barbican of the western entrance to the Tower, known as the Lion Gate, begun by 1275–6, which contrasts with the mechanisms found in the royal castles of the Second Welsh War. This too provides a suggestion that a different engineer was responsible for laying out Flint and Rhuddlan (though perhaps to a pre-ordained outline plan).

The twin-towered gatehouse, which is often considered a characteristic feature of the Edwardian castle, was being built right from the start of Master James' tenure (Figures 4.4 and 4.12). It has been emphasised that such buildings were unknown in Savoy during the thirteenth century, and that the essentials of the design may well be a directive from the King.[1] That the Rhuddlan examples were based on the Middle and Byward towers at the entrance to the Tower of London (under construction by 1277) is a possibility, but the Rhuddlan builder put his own particular slant on the design, pulling the towers closer together (a trait probably engendered by the corner positions), thereby emphasising their height and creating a striking contrast between the bulk of the towers and the narrow recessed entrance, the latter hinting at tightly-controlled access to the inner ward.

It is probable that the Rhuddlan gatehouses served as models for their counterpart at Harlech. The front elevations are essentially similar, including the narrow entrance bay (Figure 6.16), which was here a matter of choice, rather than a characteristic influenced by the nature of its siting (as at Rhuddlan). Harlech differed in that it incorporated a large accommodation block, which, as has been argued above, derives from Aberystwyth and ultimately from Caerphilly.

The affinities with Caerphilly suggest that Aberystwyth was designed independently of the northern castles and that Master James borrowed the concept for replication at Harlech, where the two separate sources of inspiration were combined to create one of the masterpieces of the Edwardian castles of Wales.

In turn, Harlech served as an exemplar for the twin gatehouses of Beaumaris begun by Master James himself, continued by Nicholas Derneford, but never completed. Had the original intention been fulfilled, the Beaumaris gatehouses would have been the ultimate expression of the type. The choice of D-shaped flanking towers is interesting. The form wasn't one that was in general use in the royal works, but had been used by Henry III at Deganwy in the 1250s and, more pertinently, by Edward himself, in the main gatehouse of Ruthin Castle from 1277, and in both the inner and outer gatehouses of Chester Castle (the former undated but the latter of 1292–3). Furthermore, a prominent example existed at Criccieth, the castle of Llywelyn Fawr, which had been captured by Edward's forces in 1283. There was, therefore, plenty of precedent in north Wales, and it is also worth remembering that D-shaped towers were a prominent aspect of the entrance front of Chillon Castle where Master James had worked in the 1260s. The D-shaped plan lent itself to the more symmetrical and integrated design that characterised Beaumaris. Here, Master James rose to the challenge of designing what might have been the greatest of the residential gatehouses, drawing on his accumulated experience of the last thirty years.

Beaumaris is a castle with which James of St George is particularly associated, in that it was his prime responsibility after 1295, Caernarfon being assigned to Walter of Hereford. So too is Conwy, where he was based for a number of years. The survival of windows amongst the Edwardian castles is patchy, and only at Conwy does tracery with much degree of complexity remain. It has been argued above (Chapter 6), on the basis of Savoyard precedents, that the patterns are to be ascribed to Master James. There is small doubt too that the fenestration of the Harlech gatehouse similarly derives from Savoy and Master James, which gives reason to presume that the simpler designs to be found at Beaumaris over the gateways, for example, were also the work of Master James.

The fireplaces at Beaumaris, and in the other royal castles of north Wales, are broadly of a similar type, hooded, with simply moulded jambs, the heads of which extend into brackets by which the lintels or arches of the hoods were supported; accompanying sconce brackets are common but not universal. The details vary between and within individual castles, but at Conwy, the brackets are mostly curved and are cut short with flat faces, an attribute that replicates that of the thirteenth-century fireplace brackets of the *Camera Domini* in Chillon (Figure 12.1). More elaborate curved brackets were used at Caernarfon, but here too we can see the abruptly curtailed flat face that is a feature of Conwy. In the later work at Caernarfon (1295 onwards) some of the fireplace brackets have cusped soffits (Figure 10.3), a version of which can also be found at Harlech

Figure 12.1 (above left): *Chillon.* Camera Domini, *fireplace detail.*

Figure 12.2 (above right): *Harlech. Fireplace in the great gatehouse north flanking tower.*

(Figure 12.2). Elsewhere at Harlech, however, in common with Beaumaris and Rhuddlan, the brackets were straight. These variations within a broad genre seem to suggest individual interpretations of a general directive rather than micro-managed specifications for different castles and rooms, and may perhaps indicate the leeway allowed to resident masters or contractors.

Another common theme is the embellishment of the battlements, with pinnacles at Conwy, and with sculpture at Caernarfon. It is possible that similar features existed at other royal castles in Wales; Taylor, for example, found evidence to suggest that they might also have adorned the Harlech battlements; in most cases, however, the battlements have been lost.[2] The pinnacles have been identified as an import from Savoy, and can therefore be ascribed to Master James. Wall-head sculptures, dating from 1276, may have been a feature of St Thomas's Tower at the Tower of London, so there may be royal precedent for the Caernarfon scheme, but the Caernarfon sculptures are unique, both in comprising heads rather than full figures, or even demi-figures, and in their proliferation. In this latter aspect they might perhaps have been inspired by the pinnacles.

Concentricity is another aspect that is considered to be a defining trait of the Edwardian castle. It occurs in four instances in the royal works in Wales: at Aberystwyth, Rhuddlan, Harlech, and Beaumaris, though only the last two are fully concentric. It appears not at all in the baronial castles that accompanied the conquest of Gwynedd. A concentric system of defence had been applied at Caerphilly from 1268 and slightly later at the Tower of London, so it was a current fashion and it would not be unreasonable to assume that the royal works, specifically those in progress at the Tower, were the source. However, the castle of Saint-Georges-d'Espérance was a concentric castle, and there were elements of concentricity in the south front of Chillon, implying that it was a theory with which Master James was familiar prior to his arrival in England.[3]

Characteristic of the later castles of Conwy, Harlech, and Caernarfon are the stair turrets that rise above the roof line of the towers. Beaumaris was also intended to have them, but they were never built. The earliest are at Conwy, where they are confined to the inner ward, a distribution that was applied to Harlech and Beaumaris as well, although at Caernarfon, in another manifestation of its singular nature, all the towers were so provided. In each case, the form of the turret imitates that of the tower. Those of Conwy, Harlech, and Beaumaris were therefore of circular plan, and those of Caernarfon polygonal. In the case of the three former, at parapet level, each turret is only partially contained within the circumference of its parent tower, resulting in a protrusion on one side. The effect is highly reminiscent of the round turrets attached to a number of early thirteenth-century marcher keeps, which must, therefore, be potential sources for this feature.[4]

The obvious kinship between these items at Conwy, Harlech, and Beaumaris, and their contrast with corresponding features at Caernarfon, is symptomatic of Caernarfon's distinct identity which sets it apart from the other castles. The difference between the stair turrets is replicated by the relationship between the twin-towered gatehouses of Aberystwyth, Rhuddlan, Harlech, and Beaumaris and the two Caernarfon gatehouses. Although the latter also have twin flanking towers, albeit polygonal, they stand outside the lines of development outlined above, and were evidently intended to be more complex and unusual. Although the Queen's Gate, which gave external access to the Upper Ward, is the earlier of the two, both may have been planned from the outset.

It is at this point that we must return to the question of the authorship of Caernarfon, for without doubt, this castle differs in many respects from the others, leading to suggestions that it might be the work of a different architect. The feasibility of Walter of Hereford having been involved at an early stage in the project has been discussed above, and has been held to be possible, but difficult to prove one way or the other, not least because Master Walter's other works have failed to survive.

Much of Caernarfon's distinctive character is owed to its special status as Edward's chief castle in north Wales, a little Windsor, designed to look different, and built to a higher specification, thus emphasising its superior standing. A comparison with Windsor is apposite in that (quite apart from any association with Constantinople) it might have been the immediate source for the coloured banding. This is not the only one of Caernarfon's distinguishing aspects to be found amongst the royal castles existing at the time. Thus, although polygonal towers were comparatively rare before 1283, some of the most prominent, and there for all to see, were in royal castles, e.g., the series of great towers built by Henry II and John (Edward's great-grandfather and grandfather respectively) at Tickhill (Yorkshire), Chilham (Kent), and Odiham (Hampshire).[5]

Another element that is particularly associated with Caernarfon is the shouldered lintel, which was used so prolifically that the form was dubbed the 'carnarvon arch'. It is especially prominent in the courtyard, including the windows of the towers and the interior openings of the wall galleries, but similar profiles are also much evident in the wall galleries themselves, where concave corbel courses carry the slabs of the roofs. Although the shouldered lintel had been used in the royal works since the first half of the thirteenth century, being particularly conspicuous in Clifford's Tower, York, of the 1240s, it was at Caernarfon that it really came into its own. It was also employed at other castles of the Second Welsh War, notably at Conwy and Beaumaris, though not in such profusion, nor so obviously. These characteristics, together with the portcullis grooves of semi-circular profile (which contrast with the square sectioned grooves of the other Welsh castles), may indicate the influence of the royal works, but the precocious mouldings described in Chapter 7 suggest the hand of someone with a background in high-quality decorative work; this is more likely to have been Walter of Hereford than James of St George. Indeed, Master Walter seems to have been in charge when the wave-moulded and sunk-chamfered entrance arch of the King's Gate was erected.

Nevertheless, despite the notable differences that put Caernarfon in a class of its own, there are also some signs of kinship with the other Edwardian castles. The general relationship of the fireplaces has been mentioned; so too has the use of the shouldered lintel in the castles of the Second Welsh War, a trait that extends to the baronial castles of Chirk and Hawarden. Moreover, reference has also been made to the kinship between the great tower of Flint and the Eagle Tower of Caernarfon, and it is this latter aspect which provides the most compelling indication of consanguinity. The relationship is not immediately obvious, but in its central chamber and encircling mural passages, the latter opening out at intervals into small rooms, the Eagle Tower yields evidence of the same thought process that conjured the great towers of Flint and Hawarden. As in the twin-towered gatehouses there is a common thread that runs through all three.

There are conflicting signs at Caernarfon, then, that complicate the task of assigning it to a particular master builder. It seems unlikely that Master James would not have been involved, at least in the initial stages of preparation and design, particularly given his credentials as a seasoned castle builder of some twenty years' standing. On the other hand, there are also good reasons for believing that Master Walter was involved from an early stage too, not least because of the use of the mouldings described above (Chapter 7), even though there is no evidence to suggest that he had previously worked on a castle. In a project of such singular nature as that of Caernarfon, which, in addition to being a fortification and a royal residence, was intended to be highly symbolic, it would have been appropriate to assemble as wide a team of expertise as possible. There is, therefore, good reason to view Caernarfon, more than any other Edwardian castle, as the product of a collaboration, with both the principal technical masters, James of St George and Walter of Hereford, making their respective contributions.

In reviewing the foregoing, it is evident that the normal relationship between patron and architect, that was outlined in Chapter 1, can be comfortably applied to the association between Edward I and his principal mason, James of St George. At Caernarfon, which may have incorporated politically motivated imagery, the King's instructions might have been more specific than they were at other castles, but, as has been suggested, design was a two-way process between patron and architect. We can only speculate about the varying degrees to which King Edward and Master James contributed to the discussion, but part of the master builder's role was to consider the implications of a patron's instructions, and to put forward his own ideas as to how the objective might be best achieved, or, indeed, modified, in order to enhance the design. James of St George was a man at the top of his profession, a highly experienced castle builder, who moved in aristocratic circles, and it has to be assumed that he was educated and articulate. He was, in short, a man whose opinion was worth seeking, and there is no reason to suppose that he was not consulted, nor that his advice was not taken into account.

Yet, latterly, Master James' value to Edward has been seen in his organisational abilities, rather than his skill as an architect, and his contribution to design has been viewed as negligible rather than central. That his organisational aptitude was an important aspect in the achievement of his dominant position can be agreed, but the downplaying of his creative role goes too far, and is less easy to take seriously; it is to be hoped that in this and the foregoing chapters, the improbability of this observation has been demonstrated. In the belittling of Master James' architectural reputation, the one aspect of his influence that has been allowed to stand is domestic planning, but the only example given is the identical sequence of hall, chamber, and chapel at both Conwy and Saint-Georges-d'Espéranche, and the broader significance of this aspect has not been followed up.[6]

In fact, shared planning concepts, such as the ones outlined above, are amongst the surest signs of a single designer's influence over buildings of contrasting outward appearance, because they tend to be hidden and are less easily imitated. Architecture is often considered in terms of external form, but, together with a grasp of structural principles, an ability to master the complexities of planning separated the professional from the dilettante, or the architect from the patron. Whilst the latter might have requirements and ideas, it was the former, by virtue of his technical training and experience, who found practical solutions to accommodate them, and in doing so, formulated the design. The common and developing themes that are to be found amongst the Edwardian castle, royal and baronial, are an indication of a powerful pivotal influence, and the specific parallels with Savoyard buildings that Master James is known to have been familiar with, notably at Conwy and Harlech, are suggestive of his close involvement in architectural detail as well as planning.

This is not to imply rigid central control (for such a system is not borne out by the facts), nor to deny the contributions of others, but it is true that no other craftsman had the same breadth of authority as Master James. Foremost amongst the significant others is Walter of Hereford, whose influence on Caernarfon has been discussed above, and who may have been responsible for much of the detail there, including the great entrance arch over the King's Gate. At Caernarfon, his salary of 1*s.* per day (half that of his pay at Vale Royal) confirms his inferior rank when compared with Master James, who drew 3*s.* Caernarfon seems to have been the limit of Master Walter's experience on the royal castles, although there is a case to be made for his involvement in some of the non-royal buildings that appear to stem from Caernarfon, including Denbigh, where he has been mooted as the designer of the north and east sides of the castle enceinte, including the great gatehouse, a building that stems from Caernarfon, but which interprets the theme in an original manner.[7] The use of sunk chamfers around the gate arch, a moulding that is also used in the King's Gate at Caernarfon, provides a degree of corroboration, even though there can be no certainty in the matter. There is, perhaps, more compelling reason to suspect Walter of Hereford's involvement in Acton Burnell.

Another major figure amongst the workforce was Richard the Engineer, or Richard of Chester, who was also paid at a lesser rate than Master James, and was, therefore, a sub-ordinate.[8] Primarily, Master Richard was a carpenter, who worked at Flint, Hope (Caergwrle), and Conwy. He wasn't resident at any site for long, and seems to have been brought in as and when necessary. At least part of his job concerned logistics, including the procurement and supply of materials, and the distribution of personnel, but his architectural role in respect of the royal castles is less certain. He was present at the start of operations at Flint, where the main group of building workers had assembled, and was probably there to take part in setting up camp by constructing the workers' accommodation and associated buildings. He may have performed a similar task at Flint in 1280, when work resumed after a period in which work had been in abeyance. In 1282, at Hope (Caergwrle), which, like Flint, was an assembly point for a large workforce, he also appeared early, and no doubt carried out a similar task. He may have had a hand in the design of two projects in the castles themselves. One was at Conwy, where he worked in partnership with his fellow master carpenter, Henry of Oxford, as contractor for the timberwork of the principal domestic apartments of the outer and inner wards, the stonework of which was undertaken by James of St George. Essentially, this amounted to the floors and roofs, but no elements survive from this time. The other is a timber superstructure that was erected on top of Flint keep in 1301, the carpentry for which was done by Henry of Ryhull.[9] His influence on the design of the castles was therefore minimal.

In contrast to these three, the other masters of whom we are aware (apart from Master Bertram, whose role has already been discussed), are shadowy figures, about whom we can say little. Most interesting is Henry of Hereford, the master mason of Aberystwyth who was, presumably, responsible for the great gatehouse there, which in turn implies a familiarity with Caerphilly. Did he work there? We cannot say for sure, but his name gives some reason to believe that he might have done so, for Hereford and Caerphilly are only some 50 miles apart. The workers for Aberystwyth, who assembled at Bristol, were drawn from the south-western counties, including Gloucestershire, which borders Herefordshire.

One of Henry of Hereford's successors as master mason at Aberystwyth was John of Ocleye, a name that may denote a Gloucestershire connection. His salary of 7*s.* per week, puts him on equal terms with Walter of Hereford. Master Thomas of Grantham, who, by the end of July 1277, was at the head of a contingent of 200 east Midlands masons at Flint, and who, a little later, may have taken charge of Ruthin, was also paid 7*s.* per week. Henry of Leominster, however, who was the master mason at Builth in 1278, received only 4*s.* 4½*d.* His undermaster, William of Winchcombe, was paid 3*s.*, so too was Ralph of Nottingham, who was master at Caergwrle in 1282; Henry of Ellerton as Walter of Hereford's deputy at Caernarfon, received 4*s.* per week. The different pay rates between the resident masters denote different levels of responsibility, but they also emphasise the gulf that separated them from James of St George.

In assessing the degree to which the characters of the Edwardian castles were determined by James of St George, it is pertinent to point out that he was actively involved at Rhuddlan and Flint, giving his full attention to first one (1278–80) and then the other (1280). There is no doubt, too, that he oversaw the repairs to Caergwrle, and was in direct charge of Conwy, where he was based. There are stylistic reasons for suggesting that Master James was the main influence on Harlech, and it is also the case that, from 1295, his principal professional interest was in Beaumaris, where he was based. Caernarfon is different, but it has been demonstrated that here, too, there is reason to believe that James of St George also made his mark, even though Walter of Hereford must also take a large slice of credit.

The accumulated evidence suggests that Master James was the guiding light of the King's works in Wales, and that he must be considered the principal architect. In circumstances in which a master had concurrent responsibility for more than one building project, the practice was to spend time at each one, to check on progress, ensure the maintenance of standards, discuss problems, and, importantly, in a situation where detailed specifications did not exist, to confer on elements of the design. Some resident masters could no doubt be trusted better than others, but it was important for the principal to maintain a close association with his staff, and a degree of control over the operations for which he was accountable to the King. Unauthorised deviations from the brief, therefore, are unlikely to have slipped through the net, for which reason, Master James must receive the lion's share of the praise.

This survey of the castles of Edward I in Wales suggests that Arnold Taylor was broadly correct in his assessment that James of St George was their principal architect. There is also evidence to suggest that Edward I supplied some of the ideas, notably at Flint and Caernarfon, though, as has been outlined above (Chapter 1), this is something that might be expected of a patron with strong views. It is also probable that Edward himself viewed the sites, discussed the layout and gave his instructions. Again, this would be nothing out of the ordinary, particularly as the castles formed part of his military strategy. However, it is not so easy to believe that he was his own military architect, because although he could have had any number of ideas, it is unlikely that he could have articulated them other than by word of mouth, or even have wanted to, given that his time was limited and he had enlisted a professional to bring form to his demands.

We can also be reasonably certain that at least one of the resident master masons, Walter of Hereford, made a substantial contribution to the appearance of the castle in his charge (Caernarfon), although Master James, as Taylor believed, probably devised the plan; it is even possible that he suggested the use of polygonal towers. Aberystwyth and Builth appear to have been largely independent enterprises until 1282, when Aberystwyth came within Master James' ambit, but, by then, its form had been largely determined by others. There is also a possibility that the plans of Flint and Rhuddlan had been confirmed before Master James took over, but it is probable that he made his mark on the superstructure of both, because what made the medieval process of design and construction different from more recent practice is that the design was not determined to the same degree of completeness prior to the start of construction, but the two stages were, to a considerable degree, carried forward together. It may very well be the case that other aspects of the Edwardian castles originated with individuals who served under Master James, or were suggested by lay colleagues connected with the project, but, if so, a general lack of evidence presents obstacles to a quantitative analysis. All great enterprises are necessarily collaborative ventures, but they need their leaders, and there is little doubt that James of St George provided the specialist leadership that was instrumental in taking charge of the visions and hammering them into reality.

Glossary

Alure	The circulatory path around the top of a wall behind the parapet, used as a fighting platform. Also known as a wall walk.
Arris	A sharp edge where two surfaces meet at an angle.
Axial wall	A partition wall extending along the length of a building.
Ballflower	A foliate decoration resembling an opening bud usually associated with the period *c*. 1300–30.
Barbican	A fortification positioned in front of a gateway.
Barrel-vault	A continuous arched vault extending between two parallel walls.
Bartizan	A small overhanging turret at the top of a wall, especially at an angle.
Batter	An external splay at the base of a wall.
Bell capital	A capital in the form of an inverted bell.
Berm	Flat area between two lines of defence, e.g. between a ditch and a curtain wall.
Box latrine	A rectangular box-like latrine corbelled out from a wall to discharge outside the building.
Brattice	See Hoard.
Buttery	A service room for the storage of beer and other liquors.
Cantref (pl. cantrefi)	A Welsh administrative division sub-divided into commotes (q.v.).
Capital	Carved feature crowning and usually overhanging a column, often decorated with mouldings or sculpture.
Carnarvon arch	See Shouldered lintel.
Cementarius	Latin word for mason.
Chamber	A more private room than a hall, used as a living room and/or bedroom. See also, **Great chamber**.
Chamber block	A structural division containing at least one chamber, and other rooms, either attached to or detached from a hall.
Chase	Recess within a wall surface to accommodate a timber.
Commote	A Welsh administrative division, one of two or more into which a cantref was divided.
Corbelled lintel	Lintel supported at each end on a convex or angular corbel as opposed to the shouldered lintel (q.v.).
Counterscarp	The outer slope of a ditch facing towards the castle.
Crocket	A stylised curling leaf moulding popular amongst Gothic architects.
Cusp	The point formed by a meeting of two foils, or lobes, typically within a traceried window.

Decorated	A division of English Gothic architecture, broadly 1290–1350.
Dog tooth	A linear decoration comprising a series of pyramidal mouldings undercut to give the appearance of being four-leaved. In England and Wales it is characteristic of the thirteenth century.
Domed vault	A vault rising from a rectangular or polygonal building to a central crown, the sections of which are separated by groins (q.v.).
Drop arch	A pointed arch with a span greater than the radii used to strike the sides of the arch.
Embrasure	The hollow space behind a window in a thick wall.
Fillet	A flat linear moulding projecting from a surface.
Finial	An ornamental (usually foliate) flourish at the apex of an arch, gable, pinnacle, spire etc.
Fortalice	A minor fortified residence.
Geometric	A division of English Gothic architecture, broadly 1240–1310, named after a style of window tracery made up of geometrical figures.
Great chamber	The principal chamber of the lord's private apartments.
Groin	An arris (q.v.) produced by the intersection of two sections of vaulting.
Hoard	An overhanging wooden gallery erected on the wall head from which the defence of a castle might be conducted. Hoard is the usual modern term for this type of structure, although brattice (q.v.) may have been a more widely used description in the Middle Ages.
Hollow chamfer	A concave chamfer.
Hood mould	A moulded band projecting from the wall face above a door or window and following its outline, the hood mould was designed to deflect rainwater from the opening and to ornament the wall surface.
Indenture	A legally binding agreement between two parties written in duplicate, the two copies being separated by cutting a jagged (indented) line between them.
Joggling	A means of jointing fine masonry in which there is a break or rebate in the line of the joint to prevent slipping or sliding. Typically used in forming a lintel out of several stones, or voussoirs (q.v.).
Keystone	Voussoir (q.v.) at the apex of an arch.
Lace	An archaic term for a free-lying beam.
Lancet	A narrow pointed window characteristic of the early Gothic style.
Light shaft	The shaft-like embrasure of a window set high above a room, typically below ground level.
Machicolation	Projecting stone gallery at the head of a wall, with slots in the base through which projectiles could be dropped.
Mantlet	A low wall surrounding or placed in front of another building, often a great tower or gatehouse. Also sometimes used for the space between the two structures.

Merlon	The solid part of a crenellated parapet.
Murder hole	An aperture in a vault, usually over a gateway, capable of fulfilling the function of a machicolation (q.v.).
Ogee	Double curved profile comprising concave and convex parts to form an S shape.
Outwork	A fortification outside, but perhaps attached to the castle enceinte.
Pantry	A service room for the storage of bread.
Peel	Fortification in the form of a palisade; also an enclosure fortified by a palisade.
Plunge	The basal termination of an arrow loop, with steeply pitched back and often enlarged end.
Postern	A subsidiary gateway, either in a different location to the main gateway or adjacent to it in the form of a pedestrian entrance that can be utilised independently.
Principal rafter	Enlarged rafter at the bay divisions of a roof, designed to carry side purlins.
Purlin	Longitudinal member in a roof structure giving intermediate support to the common rafters.
Putlog	A horizontal scaffolding pole placed across the line of a wall, and accommodated in putlog holes, allowing scaffolding to be supported on both sides of the structure.
Quasi shafting	Multiple moulding typically around a doorway suggestive of multiple orders of shafts or colonettes.
Respond	A demi-column or corbel set into a wall to carry one end of an arch belonging to an arcade or rib vault.
Revetment	A wall or palisade that buttresses and retains a body of earth like a bank or a motte.
Rib vault	Vault constructed on a framework of arches (ribs), the spaces between the ribs being infilled with stone webbing.
Roll moulding	Moulding usually of three-quarter round section.
Sally port	A type of postern (q.v.), supposedly for the purpose of making a sally against a besieger.
Scarp	The inner slope of a ditch facing away from the castle.
Sconce bracket	A bracket on which to place a sconce (lantern).
Scroll moulding	A thirteenth- and fourteenth-century moulding used for string courses and hood moulds.
Sedilia	Seats for clergy recessed into the walls of a church chancel.
Shouldered lintel	A lintel carried on a pair of concave corbels, also known as a carnarvon arch.
Soffit	Underside of a horizontal timber or stone.
Spine wall	Axial wall (q.v.) extending down the centre of a building.
Spandrel	The (roughly triangular) space between an arch and its rectangular frame.
Spirelet	A miniature spire.
Springer	The bottom stone of an arch.

Spurred base	A special form of tower plinth, stemming from a foundation of (usually) square plan which supports a rounded or polygonal tower. The 'spurs' are formed when the plinth is carried up on an incline at the angles.
Stiff leaf	A stylised leaf decoration typical of the thirteenth century.
Sunk chamfer	A recessed chamfer.
String/string course	A continuous horizontal moulding on the exterior face of a building, sometimes used to indicate a floor level, but largely decorative in intent.
Talus	The sloping face of a curtain wall, like a batter (q.v.), but rising to a greater height.
Terminus ante quem	The point before which an event happened.
Terminus post quem	The point after which an event happened.
Tongue and bar stop	A decorative termination at the base of a chamfer consisting in this case of a horizontal bar with a tongue like protrusion in front of it.
Tympanum	The infill stone between a lintel and its relieving arch over a window or doorway, sometimes a recipient of sculptured decoration.
Voussoir	One of a series of wedge-shaped stones used in the construction of an arch.
Waterholding base	Early Gothic column base containing a deep hollow between.
Wave moulding	A moulding profile forming a continuous curve convex in the centre and concave on each side, characteristic of the period *c.* 1290–1350.

Notes

Chapter 1

1. Willis and Clark 1886, 350–64.
2. See Wilson 1990, 178–80 for Westminster, and Dixon 1990 for Knaresborough.
3. E.g., Dixon 2018.
4. E.g., Dixon 1990; Ashbee 2006.
5. E.g., Taylor 1986, 77–9; Oswald and Ashbee 2007, 28; Wheatley 2010; Swallow 2019.
6. E.g. Caerphilly, Goodrich, and Castle Bolton.
7. E.g. Aberystwyth, Holt, and Rhuddlan.
8. Taylor 1986, 53–4.
9. Taylor 1950, 1958, 1963, 1977, 1986.
10. Taylor 1977, 266–8.
11. Taylor 1963, 312.
12. Taylor 1985, 82, 87.
13. Goodall 2011, 227; Ludlow 2018–19, 252.
14. Coldstream 2003, 2010. Also see Ashbee 2010, 83 and Goodall 2011, 227.
15. Coldstream 2003, 33.
16. Taylor 1978, 276.
17. Blondel 1935, 290–1; Taylor 1989, 291–4.
18. Taylor 1977, 277–8.
19. Blondel 1949, 29–30.
20. Taylor 1977, 282–3; 1986, 128–9. Taylor considered the possibility that Giles and Tassin were related to Master James, specifically, that they may have been his sons: Taylor 1977, 285–6.
21. Taylor 1963, 305–8.
22. Taylor 1985, 82–4. Master John may be identifiable with the Master John who presided over the building work at Lausanne Cathedral during the second quarter of the thirteenth century: Taylor 1977, 286–9 and 287, n. 1.
23. Taylor 1977, 272–3.
24. Although Taylor believed that a payment to *Jacquetto de Sancto Jorio* in the Chillon accounts referred to the same man, and may, in fact, identify the settlement of St Jeoire (Haute Savoie) as his origin. See Taylor 1985, 93 and footnote, and Taylor 2018.
25. Taylor 1985, 29–35.
26. Taylor 1985, 38–9 and plate 23. The Yverdon windows are no longer exposed to view.
27. Taylor 1985, 37, 42–3.
28. Taylor 1977, 275.
29. Raemy *et al.* 1999, relevés III–V.

Chapter 2

1. So named after Gruffudd's father, Madog ap Gruffudd.
2. However, see Brodie 2015, who has proposed a typology for apsidal and D-shaped towers based on size.
3. E.g. Hemp 1942–3; Avent 1983, 10–11 and 2004, 8; Butler 1974, 78 and 2010, 31; Kenyon 2010, 19.
4. Avent 2004, 9; Haslam *et al.* 2009, 650; Kenyon 2010, 20.
5. Wynne 1861; RCAHMW 1921, 112–13 and fig. 107; Butler 1974, 99 and plate XXIII.
6. Butler 1974, 99.
7. Avent 1983, 9–11; Butler 1992, 77.
8. Hopewell 2014, 2016, 2017, and 2018.
9. St John O'Neil 1944–5.
10. Avent *et al.* 2011, 9–10.
11. Avent *et al.* 2011, 19.
12. Johns 1970, 18–19 and fold-out plan.
13. See Taylor 1986, 73–5 for the figures. The extent of the expenditure was not available to St John O'Neil at the time of his exposition of the chronology.
14. E.g. Caldicot 34ft (10.4m), Dryslwyn 38ft (11.6m), Dinefwr 48ft (14.6m), Longtown 45ft (13.7m), Pembroke 53ft (16.3m), Penrice 33ft (10m), Skenfrith 35ft (10.7m), Tretower 37ft (11.3m).
15. The towers measure 43ft (13.1m) x 30ft (9.1m), 48ft (14.6m) x 32ft (9.8m) and 45ft (13.7m) x 33ft (10m) respectively.
16. 35ft (10.7m) and 30ft (9.1m) in diameter respectively.
17. H. Taylor 1922, 52–4 and n. 4.
18. Stephenson 2015, 248–9.
19. RCAHMW 1960, 59.
20. Lloyd 1912, 2: 748.
21. King 1974, 116.
22. RCAHMW 1914, 121 and fig. 43.
23. RCHME 1931; Brooks and Pevsner 2012, 678; Remfry 1998, 17–21.
24. Hopewell 2014, 8.
25. E.g. Longtown, Skenfrith, Caldicot, and Chartley.
26. Butler 1974, 99.
27. St John O'Neil 1945, 41–2.

Chapter 3

1. *CLR* 1240–5, 69–70, 129, 140, 180; Alcock 1967, 192–4.
2. Cox 1895, facing p. 376.
3. Clark 1884, 2: 303; Mackenzie 1896, 401; Hunter Blair and Honeyman 1953–5, 206; Pevsner and Richmond 1957, 213; Pevsner and Richmond *et al.* 1992, 391.
4. *CLR* 1245–51, 267.
5. Harvey 1984, 115–16.
6. *CCR* 1247–51, 324.
7. *CLR* 1240–5, 255.
8. *CLR* 1245–51, 300; *CLR* 1251–60, 16.
9. Ludlow 2014, 189–90.

10. Ludlow 2014, 99–113 and 184–8, for a detailed description of the South-East Tower of Carmarthen and comparison with the North Tower of Cardigan.
11. Ludlow 1991, 28–9; 2015, 27.
12. For the chronology of Caerphilly see Johns 1978, 11–17 and 26–35; Renn 1997, 9–11; RCAHMW 2000, 59–66; Turner 2016, 13–19; and Renn 2017–18, 225–9.
13. Renn 2017–18.
14. Ludlow 1991, 28–9; 2015, 10.
15. Ludlow 1998–9, 22; 2015, 34.
16. Renn 1981.
17. RCHME 1973, 75–7, plate 3.
18. King 1782, 272 (early part of Henry III's reign); Wadmore 1886, 26 (1220–40); Toy 1963, 243 (*c.* 1300); Renn 1981, 93–102 (by 1265); Platt 1982, 98; Oliphant 1992, 32 (by 1258); Goodall 2011, 191 (1250s); Newman 2012, 596 (*c.* 1260) Martin and Martin (2013, 271–5) review the evidence but do not come to a firm conclusion other than ruling out the earliest and latest dates.
19. *CPR* 1258–66, 108.
20. Simmons 1998, 45.
21. Simmons 1998.
22. RCAHMW 1991, 258–63.
23. Clark 1850; McLees 2005, 22–4.
24. For differing opinions see Mclees 1998, 7 (early); RCAHMW 2000, 107 (late); Newman 2001, 315 (early); Mclees 2005, 9 (early).

Chapter 4
1. Browne 2010, 59–62.
2. Lloyd 1912, 2: 727; Taylor 1986, 1–5.
3. Taylor 1986, 4.
4. Brownbill 1914, 196.
5. Taylor, 1986, 4 and n. 9.
6. Taylor 1986, 4; Spurgeon 1978–9, 50–1.
7. Spurgeon 1978–9, 55.
8. Taylor 1986, 4.
9. Taylor 1986, 15.
10. Taylor 1986, 8.
11. See Taylor 1977, 285–6 for a discussion of this relationship.
12. Taylor 1986, 13.
13. Hughes 1903 and 1904.
14. Browne 2010.
15. Browne 2010, 66–8.
16. Taylor 1986, 17–18.
17. Owen and Morgan 2008.
18. Miles 1998, 117–20.
19. Taylor 1986, 19.
20. Taylor 1986, 19–20.
21. Taylor 1986, 23.
22. Taylor 1986, 23–4.
23. Taylor 1986, 24.

24. Miles 1998, 104.
25. The older view that the keep contained a central chamber has been propounded by Hemp, 1929; Simpson 1940a; King 1958; and Toy 1963, 167. Taylor's reinterpretation of the central space as a courtyard (Taylor 1957b, 1989) has been followed by Brown 1976. Renn was more circumspect: Renn and Avent 2001, 24–7.
26. As suggested by Taylor 1989, 302.
27. Taylor 1986, 26–9.
28. Manley 1987.
29. Quinnell *et al.* 1994, especially 219–21; Taylor 1984.
30. Of the two sections cut through the Rhuddlan defences, Section DO was at an angle of roughly 90 degrees whilst DP took an oblique line; in comparing the two different sites (Flint and Rhuddlan) it is considered here that DO makes for the better comparison; consequently, the dimensions given are from DO. See Quinnell *et al.* 1994.
31. A number of radio carbon dates were obtained from a series of hearths sealed beneath the banks of the defences. Although these were generally supportive of an early tenth-century date, there were also unexplained anomalies, which introduced a degree of doubt. See Manley *et al.* 1985, and Quinnell *et al.* 1994, 210–13 for the arguments.
32. Quinnell *et al.* 1994, 11–26.
33. Taylor 1954–5.
34. Taylor 1989, 296–9.
35. Taylor 1985, 85–6 and 97.
36. Taylor 1989, especially 296–300.
37. Taylor 1986, 27.
38. Lilley 2010, 110.
39. Hislop 2016, 129–30. See Mayes and Butler 1983, 77 and fig. 40.

Chapter 5

1. Brown *et al.* 1963, 327; Taylor 1986, 35–6.
2. *CPR* 1272–81, 231–2.
3. Taylor 1986, 36.
4. Neaverson 1947, 25.
5. Kenyon *et al.* 2015–16, 108. The outer gatehouse of Chester dates from 1292–3; the date of the inner gatehouse is not recorded, so it is not possible to say which of the three came first.
6. Taylor 1986, 34.
7. The positioning of the West Gate at the end of the ditch dividing the two wards, in also unusual, but has no parallels in the royal works in north Wales. It is, however, reminiscent of the late thirteenth-/early fourteenth-century postern at Barnard Castle (County Durham), which was contrived in the curtain at the end of the great ditch between the middle and inner baileys. Although lords of Barnard (Alexander (d. 1278 and John, later King John of Scotland) did not take part in the Welsh wars, their cousin, Alexander Balliol of Cavers, did serve there; so too did John's father-in-law, John de Warenne, who was to build his own castle in the Welsh Marches at Holt some 20 miles from Ruthin. It has been implied that Warenne was the influence behind the design of inner gatehouse of Barnard, probably erected around the same time as the postern (Hislop 2019, 14).

    8. Taylor 1965–6, 76.
    9. Manley 1994.
   10. Manley 1992.
   11. Manley 1994, 108–9.
   12. King 1974, 135; Kenyon *et al.* 2015–16, 9.
   13. King 1974, 134.
   14. Manley 1994, 95; King 1974, 138.
   15. King 1974, 139.
   16. Taylor 1986, 37; *CPR* 1272–81, 380 and 422.
   17. Robinson 2011, 32.
   18. Turner 2006, 117.
   19. Turner 2006, 117.

Chapter 6

    1. *CWR* 1277–94, 212.
    2. Taylor 1986, 38–40.
    3. Taylor 1986, 44.
    4. Taylor 1992, 25.
    5. Taylor 1992, 31–2.
    6. Taylor 1992, 23–5.
    7. Manley and Cole 1994, 129–30.
    8. Taylor 1986, 53.
    9. Taylor 1986, 56.
   10. Williams 1835, 79–80.
   11. Taylor 1977, 288–9 and plates XLIa and b.
   12. Hart 2010, 50.
   13. The theory that Lausanne was a source for Master James at Conwy has a particular resonance in light of the tentative identification of the principal mason of Lausanne, Master John, with James' father, also Master John, from whom James took over at Yverdon. See Taylor 1985, 22–3 and 23, n. 1.
   14. Shortly after the completion of Conwy, in 1292, the Hospitallers founded St Giles' hospital, in Hereford, the chapel of which had a circular nave.
   15. The course of the Gyffin has since been diverted away from the town walls.
   16. Taylor 1986, 52, n. 1.
   17. Taylor 1985, 152.
   18. Neaverson 1947, 45.
   19. Taylor 1986, 54; Taylor 1985, 152–3.
   20. Taylor locates Master James's *camera* immediately west of the castle to the east end of the current Vicarage Gardens car park and close to the King's Hall: Taylor 1986, p. 53, n. 4 and 50–2.
   21. Taylor 1986, 52. The dividing wall between the two wards ranges between 15.8m (52ft) and 17.7m (58ft) in length, which would amount to more than 3 standard perches of 16½ft (5.03m), but the wall is a little over 3m (10ft) thick, which is approximately twice the thickness of the other main internal walls, so it is probable that the perch was being used here in the sense of a cubic rather than linear measurement.
   22. Ashbee 2017b.
   23. Taylor 1986, 65–6. For an alternative view see Remfry 2013.

24. Clark 1884, 2: 79–80; Hughes 1913, especially 286–8, 296–7 and 299–304; Peers 1921–2, 69; Taylor 1986, 68–9.
25. Taylor 1986, 69–71.
26. Taylor 1963.
27. Taylor 1986, 69.

Chapter 7
1. RCAHMW 1960, 129.
2. RCAHMW 1960, 127–30.
3. RCAHMW 1964, 116–20.
4. Brown *et al.* 1963, 369–71; Taylor 1986, 77–9.
5. Wheatley 2010; Swallow 2019.
6. Taylor 1986, 78–9, n. 4.
7. The Golden Gate of Constantinople wasn't alone in its appellation. Another consideration, for example, is the Golden Gate of Jerusalem.
8. Wheatley 2010, 130–1.
9. RCAHMW 1964, 116–21.
10. A measure of Walter of Hereford's status is that Vale Royal was Edward's most ambitious church building project, in which he set out to create the largest Cistercian Abbey in England. See Brown *et al.* 1963, 248–57.
11. Taylor 1986, 86.
12. Harvey 1984, 136.
13. Taylor 1986, 47 and n. 7.
14. Taylor 1986, 71–2.
15. The argument is set out cogently in Taylor 1986, 99–103.
16. Hislop 2016, 4–5.
17. Taylor 1985, 35.
18. It has to be said that there remains some doubt as to the character of the towers at Saint-Georges-d'Espéranche. The eighteenth-century sketch of the castle that is the main source of its former appearance, shows four towers of uniform size and shape, but their orientation is depicted inaccurately when compared with the surviving one. See Taylor 1986 and compare plate 22c with plate 24b.
19. Wilson 1990, 192–6.
20. Taylor 1949.
21. Thompson 1962, 206, fig. 8: 7, 8.
22. See RCAHMW 1960, fig. 103 K and M.
23. Taylor 1986, 127–38.
24. Guy 2015–16, 174. I am indebted to Neil Guy for first pointing out to me this disparity in form.
25. For a drawing (by Chris Jones-Jenkins) of Beaumaris as it might have been intended see Ashbee 2017a, 10.
26. Taylor 1985, 106–10, which includes a translation of the document.

Chapter 8
1. It is a fashion mostly associated with late fourteenth-century France the most famous example being the Bastille.
2. Goodall 2011, 222 and 223.

3. In the Butler's Pantry and the Conservation Workshop respectively.

4. Hughes 1894, 266; Radford 1953, 18–19; Hubbard 1986, 294–5.

5. The ground-floor fireplace has been converted into an oven, but its segmental relieving arch survives and shows it to have been similar to the surviving one.

6. The passage to the uppermost storey has been extended northwards to link with a mural chamber known as the Magistrate's Court. Originally this latter was entered from the north.

7. *CWR* 1277–94, 240.

8. *CPR* 1307–13, 405.

9. Rather like the fourteenth-century arrangement at Warkworth (Northumberland).

10. For a reconstruction of the castle based on the documentary sources and the existing remains, see Turner and Jones-Jenkins 2016.

11. E.g., Queenborough (Kent), Bolton (Yorkshire), Bodiam (Sussex), Lumley (County Durham), Wressle (Yorkshire), and Old Wardour (Wiltshire).

12. Faulkner 1963, 221–5.

13. Hemp 1926, 64–5.

14. *CWR* 1277–94, 241.

15. Taylor 1986, 41.

16. Hemp 1926, 88–90 and plan facing p. 120; Butler 1976, 15, 26 and plan 6; Butler 2007, 8–10 and 37.

17. I am indebted to Will Davies of Cadw for letting me read his draft report on the work at Denbigh.

18. The timber for the roof was felled in 1288. The vaulting would have been installed after the building had been roofed. See Brown (2003), 51–5 for the dating of the York chapter house.

19. Smith 1988.

20. Arnold 1993, 98.

21. Arnold 1986.

22. Turner *et al.* 2006b, 135–6.

23. Clark 1881–2, 67.

24. Coldstream and Morris 2006. The windows at this level appear to be based on the early thirteenth-century fenestration of the first floor, but their architectural quality is far inferior, suggesting perhaps that there was a hiatus between the first-floor alterations and the construction of the second-floor chamber.

25. Newman 2000, 160.

26. Turner *et al.* 2006a, 151; Turner 2010b, 16, 47.

27. Turner *et al.* 2006a, 163–6.

28. Turner *et al.* 2006a, 162.

29. Clark 1881–2, 63.

30. Turner *et al.* 2006b, 135.

31. Kenyon 2002, 9.

32. Kenyon 2002, 12.

33. Johns 1978, 32–5; Renn 1997, 12–14; RCAHMW 2000, 57–66; Turner 2016, 11–19.

34. Notably the Constable Tower at Dover (*c.* 1220–7), the great gate at Scarborough (1243–5), and the Black Gate at Newcastle (1247–50).

35. *CPR* 1292–1301, 307. *CFR* 1272–1307, 384–5.

Chapter 9

1. Bain 1884, No. 1288; Brown *et al.* 1963, 411.
2. Bain 1884, 352–3.
3. The King was at Roxburgh on 24 May and at Lauder the next day, a distance of some 20 miles.
4. Bain 1884, 457–9.
5. Stevenson 1870, 2: 393.
6. Stevenson 1870, 2: 361.
7. Bain 1888, No. 1112.
8. Bain 1888, No. 1101.
9. Macdonald and Laing 1974–5.
10. Macdonald and Laing 1974–5, 139–45.
11. Macdonald and Laing 1974–5, 124–6.
12. Brown *et al.* 1963, 411.
13. Brown *et al.* 1963, 411.
14. See RCAHMS 1920 for a description of the site.
15. Taylor 1985, 79–80, which includes a transcription of the document.
16. Brown *et al.* 1963, 414.
17. Taylor 1985, 190–4.
18. Brown *et al.* 1963, 217.
19. Taylor 1985, 149, 152; Taylor 1986, 71.
20. Brown *et al.* 1963, 415; RCAHMS 1929, 47–9.
21. Most likely John Comyn (d. 1277), Lord of Badenoch from 1258, or his son, John (d. 1302), who succeeded him.
22. Amours 1907, 239.
23. Dixon and Anderson 2011, 9.
24. Simpson 1927–8, 71–6; Simpson 1928, 37–40; Cruden 1981, 74–5.
25. See the comparative measurements in Simpson 1927–8, 74.
26. Simpson (1923, 78) refers to the insertion of the embrasure arches.
27. Simpson 1927–8, 75–6.
28. Brown *et al.* 1963, 418–19.
29. Bain 1884, Nos 1005 and 1307.
30. Bain 1884, Nos 582 and 589.
31. Bain 1884, No. 1067.
32. Bain 1884, Nos 1112 and 1334.
33. Bain 1884, Nos 1646 and 1305.
34. Although the south tower may have been slightly larger than the others: Dixon *et al.* (2015), 18.
35. However, it should be remembered that the lost masonry details might have told a different story.
36. Although Morton has been dated to the fifteenth century in the past, an Edwardian date is now widely accepted: Simpson 1958–9; Cruden 1981, 95–6; Gifford 1996, 450–3, Rutherford 1998, 224–7.
37. Bain 1884, No. 1807.
38. Bain 1887, No. 76.
39. The licence to crenellate for Dudley dates from 1264. See Hislop 2010a for a consideration of the date of the keep.

40. Bain 1884, Nos 579, 642, 793 and 893.
41. Simpson 1936–7, 105–6, and fig. 8.
42. Bain 1888, 375.
43. Cruden 1981, 125–6.
44. A contrivance that John Goodall has dubbed a 'swallowed forebuilding'.
45. Cruden 1981, 98.
46. Bain 1884, No. 1514.
47. Bain 1884, Nos 1564 and 1705.
48. Fairclough 1984, 43–51.
49. Morris 1901, 287,
50. Hodgson 1904, 103–6.
51. E.g., Simpson 1924–5, 167–8 and 1947, 106; Johnson 1978, 187; Cruden 1981, 78; Goodall 2011, 184; Hislop 2016, 123.
52. Simpson 1947, 102–6.
53. See Tabraham 1994, 18 for a reconstruction drawing of the interior.
54. Ludlow 2018.
55. The general form of these windows has also been noted at Aydon Castle (Northumberland) *c.* 1296, and it is worth adding that it occurs too in the windows of the late thirteenth-century second-floor extension of the great tower of Chepstow, albeit with lancets (Aydon) and shouldered lintels (Chepstow) instead of the trefoil-cusped lights of Bothwell.
56. Wright 1864, 3.
57. Baillie 1999, 184.
58. Cruden 1981, 65; Morris 1998, 74, n. 54.

Chapter 10

1. Taylor 1986, 86.
2. Taylor 1986, 91.
3. Harvey 1984, 92: In 1304 Ellerton petitioned for the payment of arrears of wages (£30 15*s.* 5*d.*) amounting to nearly three years' work at his undermaster rate of 4*s.* per week.
4. Taylor 1986, 95.
5. RCAHMW 1960, 123–4.
6. Peers 1915–16, 15–16.
7. Taylor 1986, 96.
8. Taylor 1986, 96.
9. Taylor 1986, 96.
10. Taylor 1986, 97.
11. *CPR* 1321–4, 353.
12. Taylor 1986, 111–12.
13. *CPR* 1313–17, 457.
14. Harvey 1984, 82–3.
15. Taylor 1985, 205–7.
16. Baynes 1927, 60.
17. *CPR* 1343–5, 56.
18. E163/4/42. The castles were Conwy, Beaumaris, Caernarfon, Criccieth, Harlech, Aberystwyth, Emlyn, Cardigan, Haverfordwest, Carmarthen, Dinefwr, Builth, and Montgomery.

19. Dawes 1930, 46, 61.
20. However, see Morris 1997 on the dating of the east arm of St Augustine's.

Chapter 11

1. Guy 2018b.
2. *CPR* 1282–92, 450.
3. Hislop 2016, 132.
4. *CPR* 1281–92, 110.
5. Radford 1961, 94.
6. Newman and Pevsner 2006, 88.
7. Maddison 1978.
8. Owen 1903, 40–1.
9. Maddison 1993, 65–8.
10. *CPR* 1292–1301, 408, 409.
11. Tringham 1993, 85.
12. Maddison 1993, 67–8.
13. Greenslade 1990; Hislop 2010a.
14. Maddison 1993, 66–8 and plates XIVa and XIVb.
15. Greenslade 1990; Harvey 1984, 105.
16. Reproduced in Kenyon *et al.* 2015–16, 104.
17. Marshall and Samuels 1997, 32–6.
18. Marshall and Samuels 1997, 35.
19. Rodwell 1976; Fasham 1983; Hewitson and Rátkai forthcoming.
20. *CCR* 1288–96, 412.
21. On the other (east) side of the doorway, instead of a capital there is an angular block and a single cusp extending from the corbel to the outer order. Immediately above, a giant chamfered vaulting rib adds to the madness.
22. *CCR* 1279–88, 165, 275.
23. Morris 1901, 288; Wright 1864, 3.
24. Dixon 1990.
25. Dixon 1990, 128.
26. Dixon 1990, 128–9.
27. *CPR* 1301–7, 290.
28. *CIPM* 9, 24–5.
29. Dryden 1891–2.
30. Bateson 1895, 197.
31. Simpson 1949, 2–3; Summerson 1993, 10–11. See also Hartshorne 1854, 9–10, Knoop and Jones 1932, 37, n. 2; and Taylor 1986, 61–2.
32. Summerson 1993, 10.
33. That is to say, the inner gate arch, which is authentic, the outer arch having been destroyed in the fourteenth century when the gateway was blocked and converted into a great tower.
34. *CPR* 1313–17, 278. See Guy 2018–19 for a copiously illustrated discussion of this building.
35. Reproduced with a interpretative scaled drawing in Blair 1988, fig. 5, and in Guy (2018–19), 177, figs 1 and 2.
36. Guy 2018–19, figs 17 and 18.

37. Ludlow 2018, 258–9. There is also a strong parallel at Dudley Castle (Staffordshire) in the main gateway and in entrance to the great tower, which were raised under a licence to crenellate of 1264.
38. Guy 2018–19, fig. 49.
39. Guy 2018–19, fig. 39: 1.
40. Harvey 1984, 136–7.
41. Turner and Parker 1853, 250.
42. Turner and Parker 1853, opposite 249.
43. J. H. Parker records that the foundations of the south-west tower were removed some years previous to his writing: Turner and Parker 1853, 250.
44. The west range was still only two storeys high when Dryden wrote his account of Woodcroft (see Dryden 1903, 207–8) but the additional storey had been added by 1906 (see drawing in Serjeantson *et al.* 1906, 488).
45. A licence had been issued to Bishop Burnell in 1286 'to enclose the churchyard of the cathedral church of Wells and the precinct of the canons' houses in the city with a stone wall, and to crenellate the same for their better security' (*CPR* 1289–92, 229). The 1340 licence granted to Bishop Ralph was 'to build a wall round the churchyard and the precinct of the houses of him and his canons' (*CPR* 1338–40, 466); the episcopal palace had been added to the defended area.
46. Goodall 2011, 276–7.
47. Pickford and Pevsner 2016, 451.
48. Hislop 1991–2.
49. *CPR* 1343–5, 30.
50. Bates 1891, 287–91; Hunter Blair 1910, 102, 178.
51. *CPR* 1340–43, 179.
52. This particular form, with England placed first and third, and France placed second and fourth, is an early form. The order was later reversed by Edward. See Longstaffe 1868, 119, and Michael 1994.
53. Goodall 2011, 267.
54. E.g., the loss of Edinburgh (1341), Roxburgh (1342), and Stirling (1342).
55. Wilson 2002, 55–67; Emery 2006, 203 for a reconstruction drawing of the south elevation.
56. RCHME 1972, 172, plate 58.

Chapter 12

1. Coldstream 2003, 24.
2. Taylor 1963, 312.
3. Taylor 1985, 37.
4. The former Lanthorn Tower, at the Tower of London, which dated from the 1220s has also been cited as possible source, but the evidence for its medieval form (which is based on a sixteenth-century plan) is not so reliable. See Goodall 2011, 218 and n. 43.
5. Henry II's Orford (Suffolk) had a circular plan, but was faceted externally to give a polygonal appearance.
6. Coldstream 2003, 33.
7. Harvey 1984, 137.
8. For a summary of Richard the Engineer's career see Turner 2010a.
9. Taylor 1957b, 6; Turner 2010a, 50.

Bibliography

Abbreviations

CCR	*Calendar of Close Rolls*
CFR	*Calendar of Fine Rolls*
CIPM	*Calendar of Inquisitions Post Mortem*
CLR	*Calendar of Liberate Rolls*
CPR	*Calendar of Patent Rolls*
CWR	*Calendar of Welsh Rolls*
ODNB	*Oxford Dictionary of National Biography*
RCAHMS	Royal Commission on the Ancient and Historical Monuments of Scotland
RCAHMW	Royal Commission on the Ancient and Historical Monuments of Wales
RCHME	Royal Commission on the Historical Monuments of England

Publications

Alcock, L. (1967) 'Excavations at Degannwy Castle, Caernarvonshire, 1961–6', *Archaeological Journal*, 124: 190–201

Amours, F. J. (ed.) (1907) *The Original Chronicle of Andrew of Wyntoun*, Volume 5, Scottish Text Society

Apted, M. R. (1962–3) 'Excavations at Kildrummy Castle, Aberdeenshire, 1952–62', *Proceedings of the Society of Antiquaries of Scotland*, 96: 208–36

Arnold, C. J. (1986) 'Powis Castle: the outer bailey', *The Montgomeryshire Collections*, 74: 70–2

Arnold, C. J. (1990) 'Powis Castle: the outer bailey', *The Montgomeryshire Collections*, 78: 65–71

Arnold, C. J. (1993) 'Powis Castle: the development of the structure', *The Montgomeryshire Collections*, 81: 97–109

Ashbee, J. (2005) *Goodrich Castle*, London: English Heritage

Ashbee, J. (2006) 'Thomas, earl of Lancaster, and the great gatehouse of Dunstanburgh Castle', *English Heritage Historical Review*, 1: 28–35

Ashbee, J. (2007) *Conwy Castle and Town Walls*, Cardiff: Cadw

Ashbee, J. (2010) 'The King's accommodation at his castles', in Williams and Kenyon, 72–84.

Ashbee, J. (2017a) *Beaumaris Castle*, Cardiff: Cadw

Ashbee, J. (2017b) *Harlech Castle*, Cardiff: Cadw

Avent, R. (1983) *Castles of the Princes of Gwynedd*, Cardiff: HMSO

Avent, R. (1995) *Laugharne Castle*, Cardiff: Cadw

Avent, R. (2004) *Dolwyddelan Castle, Dolbadarn Castle, Castell y Bere*, Cardiff: Cadw

Avent, R. (2006) 'William Marshal's castle at Chepstow and its place in military architecture', in Turner and Johnson, 81–90

Avent, R. and Miles, D. (2006) 'The main gatehouse', in Turner and Johnson, 51–62

Avent, R., Suggett, R., and Longley, D. (2011) *Criccieth Castle, Penarth Fawr Medieval Hall-House, St Cybi's Well*, Cardiff: Cadw

Avent, R. and Turner, R. (2006) 'The middle bailey', in Turner and Johnson, 63–70

Baillie, M. G. (1999) 'Dendrochronological dating', in MacIvor and Gallagher, 184–6

Bain, G. (1893) *History of Nairnshire*, Nairn

Bain, J. (1884) *Calendar of Documents Relating to Scotland. Volume 2 A.D. 1272–1307*, Edinburgh: HMSO

Bain, J. (1887) *Calendar of Documents Relating to Scotland. Volume 3 A. D. 1307–1357*, Edinburgh: HMSO

Bain, J. (1888) *Calendar of Documents relating to Scotland. Volume 4 A.D. 1357–1509, Addenda 1221–1435*, Edinburgh: HMSO

Bates, C. J. (1891) *Border Holds*, Society of Antiquaries of Newcastle upon Tyne

Bateson, E. (ed.) (1895) *A History of Northumberland*, Volume 2, Newcastle: Northumberland County History Committee

Baynes, E. N. (1927) 'The early history of Beaumaris Castle', *Transactions of the Anglesey Antiquarian Society and Field Club*, 48–61

Biddle, M. (2000) *King Arthur's Round Table*, Woodbridge: Boydell Press

Blair, J. (1988) *Bampton Castle*, Bampton Research Paper 1

Blondel, L. (1935) 'L'architecture militaire au temps de Pierre II de Savoie: les donjons circulaires', *Genava*, 13: 271–321

Blondel, L. (1949) 'Le château de Brignon', *Vallesia*, 4, 29–34

Blondel, L. (1954) 'Le château de Saxon', *Vallesia*, 9, 165–74

Brodie, H. (2015) 'Apsidal and D-shaped towers of the princes of Gwynedd', *Archaeologia Cambrensis*, 164: 245

Brooks, A. and Pevsner, N. (2012) *Herefordshire*, The Buildings of England, New Haven and London: Yale University Press

Brooks, I. P., Jones, S. and Gwyn, D. (2017) *Chirk Castle: interpretative historic building survey*, Engineering Archaeological Services report for the National Trust

Brown, P. (2003) *Whittington Castle Guidebook*, Whittington Castle Preservation Trust

Brown, S. (2003) *'Our Magnificent Fabrick.' York Minster: An Architectural History c 1220–1500*, Swindon: English Heritage

Brown, R. A. (1976) *English Castles*, 2nd edn, London: Batsford

Brown, R. A., Colvin, H. M. and Taylor, A. J. (1963) *The History of the King's Works. Volumes 1 and 2: The Middle Ages*, London: HMSO

Brownbill, J. (ed.) (1914) *The Ledger Book of Vale Royal Abbey*, Record Society of Lancashire and Cheshire

Browne, D. M. (2010) 'Builth Castle and Aberystwyth Castle 1277–1307', in Williams and Kenyon, 59–71.

Butler, L. A. S. (1974) 'Medieval finds from Castell-y-Bere, Merioneth', *Archaeologia Cambrensis*, 123: 78–112

Butler, L. A. S. (1976) *Denbigh Castle, Town Walls and Friary*. London: HMSO

Butler, L. A. S. (1987) 'Holt Castle: John de Warenne and Chastellion', in Kenyon and Avent, 105–24

Butler, L. A. S. (1989) 'Dolforwyn Castle, Montgomery, Powys. First report: the excavations 1981–1986', *Archaeologia Cambrensis*, 138: 78–98

Butler, L. A. S. (1992) 'Dolforwyn Castle, Powys, Wales: excavations 1985–1990', *Château Gaillard*, 15: 73–82

Butler, L. A. S. (1995) 'Dolforwyn Castle, Montgomery, Powys. Second report: The excavations 1987–1994', *Archaeologia Cambrensis*, 144: 133–203

Butler, L. A. S. (2007) *Denbigh Castle*, Cardiff: Cadw

Butler, L. A. S. (2010) 'The castles of the princes of Gwynedd', in Williams and Kenyon, 27–36

Butler, L. A. S. and Knight, J. (2004) *Dolforwyn Castle, Montgomery Castle*, Cardiff: Cadw

Cannell, J. and Tabraham, C. (1994) 'Excavations at Duffus Castle, Moray', *Proceedings of the Society of Antiquaries of Scotland*, 124: 379–90

Clark, G. T. (1850) 'Castell Coch, Glamorgan: topographical notes', *Archaeologia Cambrensis*, 4: 21–250

Clark, G. T. (1852) *A Description and History of the Castles of Kidwelly and Caerphilly and of Castle Coch*, London: W. Pickering

Clark, G. T. (1881–2) 'Chepstow Castle', *Transactions of the Bristol and Gloucestershire Archaeological Society*, 6: 51–74

Clark, G. T. (1884) *Mediaeval Military Architecture in England*, 2 vols, London: Wyman and Sons

Coad, J. (1995) *Dover Castle*, London: Batsford

Coldstream, N. (2003) 'Architects, advisors and design at Edward I's castles in Wales', *Architectural History*, 46: 19–36

Coldstream, N. (2010) 'James of St George', in Williams and Kenyon, 37–45

Coldstream, N. and Morris, R. (2006) 'The architecture and decoration of the Marshals' great tower', in Turner and Johnson, 101–12

Cox, E. W. (1895) 'Diserth Castle', *Journal of the Chester Archaeological and Historical Society*, new series, 5: 361–79

Cruden, S. (1981) *The Scottish Castle* 3rd edn, Edinburgh: Spurbooks

Curnow, P. E. (1977) 'The Wakefield Tower, Tower of London', in M. R. Apted, R. Gilyard-Beer and A. D. Saunders (eds), *Ancient Monuments and their Interpretation*, London and Chichester: Phillimore

Dawes, M. C. B. (ed.) (1930) *Register of Edward the Black Prince*. Part 1: 1346–1348, London: HMSO

Dixon, P. and Anderson, I. (2011) *Lochindorb Castle*, RCAHMS report

Dixon, P., Anderson, I. and O'Grady, O. (2015) *The Evolution of a Castle. Tibbers, Dumfriesshire: measured and geophysical survey 2013–14*, RCAHMS

Dixon, P. W. (1990) 'The donjon of Knaresborough: the castle as theatre', *Château Gaillard*, 14: 121–39

Dixon, P. W. (2018) 'Patron and Builder', in Guy 2018a, 376–92

Dixon, P. W. and Marshall, P. (1993) 'The great tower at Hedingham Castle: a reassessment', *Fortress*, 18: 16–23

Dryden, H. (1891–2) *Associated Architectural Societies' Reports and Papers*, 21: 247–8

Dryden, H. (1903) *Memorials of Old Northamptonshire*, London: Bemrose and Sons

Dunning, G. C., Hodges, H. W. M. and Jope, E. M. L. (1957–8) 'Kirkcudbright Castle, its pottery and ironwork', *Proceedings of the Society of Antiquaries of Scotland*, 91: 117–38

Edwards, J. G. (1946) 'Edward I's castle building in Wales', *Proceedings of the British Academy*, 32: 15–81

Edwards, J. G. (1951) *The Building of Flint*, Flintshire History Society Publications, 12

Edwards, T. (1912) 'Dyserth Castle', *Archaeologia Cambrensis*, 6th series, 12: 263–94

Ellis, P. (1993) *Beeston Castle, Cheshire: excavations by Laurence Keen and Peter Hough, 1968–85*, London: Historic Buildings and Monuments Commission for England

Emery, A. (1996–2006) *Greater Medieval Houses of England and Wales*, 3 vols: Vol. 1: *Northern England* (1996), Vol. 2: *East Anglia, Central England and Wales* (2000), Vol. 3: *Southern England* (2006), Cambridge: Cambridge University Press

Evans, D. H. (2008) *Valle Crucis Abbey*, 3rd edn, Cardiff: Cadw

Ewart, G. and Fox, P. (2015) 'Bothwell Castle excavation', *Discovery and Excavation in Scotland*, 16: 163–4

Fairclough, G. (1984) 'Edlingham Castle, Northumberland: An interim account of excavations, 1978–82', *Transactions of the Ancient Monuments Society*, new series, 28: 40–59

Fasham, P. J. (1983) 'Excavations in Banbury, 1972: second and final report', *Oxoniensia*, 48: 71–118

Faulkner, P. (1963) 'Castle planning in the fourteenth century', *Archaeological Journal*, 120: 215–35

Fielding. S. (2004) *Phase I. South-west Tower, Wilton Castle, Bridstow, Herefordshire: a report on archaeological building recording and watching brief*, Marches Archaeology Series, 383

Fraser, W. (ed.) (1847) *Liber S. Marie de Dryburgh*, Bannatyne Club, 157: 110

Gifford, J. (1996) *Dumfries and Galloway*, The Buildings of Scotland, New Haven and London: Yale University Press

Giggins, B. (2018–19) 'Barnwell Castle – Part One', *Castle Studies Group Journal*, 32: 293–314

Godfrey, W. H. (1966) *Lewes Castle*, 8th edn, Lewes: Sussex Archaeological Society

Goodall, J. (2010) 'The baronial castles of the Welsh conquest', in Williams and Kenyon, 155–65

Goodall, J. (2011) *The English Castle*, London: Yale University Press

Goodall, J. (2013) 'The early development of Alnwick Castle *c.* 1100–1400', *Newcastle and Northumberland: Roman and Medieval Architecture and Art*, British Archaeological Association Transactions, 36, 232–47

Grandjean, M. (1963) 'A propos de la construction de la cathédrale de Lausanne (XII–XIIIe siècle): notes sur la chronologie et les maîtres d'oeuvre', *Genava*, 11: 261–87

Greenslade, M. W. (ed.) (1990) *A History of the County of Stafford*, Vol. 14, Victoria History of the Counties of England, Oxford: Oxford University Press

Gresham, C. A. (1973) 'The development of Criccieth Castle', *Transactions of the Caernarvonshire Historical Society*, 34: 14–22

Guy, N. (2015–16) 'The portcullis – design and development – 1080–1260', *Castle Studies Group Journal*, 29: 132–201

Guy, N. (2017–18) 'The Harlech Castle garden and privileged spaces of elite accommodation', *Castle Studies Group Journal*, 31: 235–57

Guy, N. (ed.) (2018a) *Castles: History, Archaeology, Landscape, Architecture, and Symbolism: Essays in honour of Derek Renn*, Castle Studies Group

Guy, N. (2018b) 'Broad Gate, Ludlow: James of St George beyond North Wales?', in Guy 2018a, 206–35

Guy, N. (2018–19) 'A few notes on Bampton Castle, Oxfordshire', *Castle Studies Group Journal*, 32: 176–208

Harrison, S. (1994) 'Medieval stonework', in Manley 1994, 118–25

Hart, S. (2010) *Medieval Church Window Tracery in England*, Woodbridge: Boydell

Hartshorne, C. H. (1850) 'Caernarvon Castle', *Archaeological Journal* 7: 237–65

Hartshorne, C. H. (1854) 'Conway Castle', *Archaeologia Cambrensis*, 17: 1–12

Harvey, J. H. (1948) 'The western entrance of the Tower', *Transactions of the London and Middlesex Archaeological Society*, 9: 20–35

Harvey, J. H. (1972) *The Mediaeval Architect*, London: Wayland

Harvey, J. H. (1984) *English Mediaeval Architects*, 2nd edn, Gloucester: Alan Sutton

Haslam, R., Orbach, J., and Voelcker, A. (2009) *Gwynedd*, The Buildings of Wales, New Haven and London: Yale University Press

Hemp, W. J. (1926) 'Denbigh Castle', *Y Cymmrodor*, 36: 64–120

Hemp, W. J. (1929) *Flint Castle*, London: HMSO

Hemp, W. J. (1941) 'Conway Castle', *Archaeologia Cambrensis*, 96: 163–74

Hemp, W. J. (1942–3) 'Castell y Bere', *Archaeologia Cambrensis*, 97: 120–2

Hewitson, C. and Rátkai, S. (forthcoming) *Banbury – The Castle and the Town: archaeological excavations in Banbury town centre, Oxfordshire, 1997–9*

Higham, R. and Barker, P. (1992) *Timber Castles*, London: Batsford

Hislop, M. (1991–2) 'Master John of Burcestre and the castles of Stafford and Maxstoke', *Transactions of the South Staffordshire Archaeological and Historical Society*, 33: 14–20

Hislop, M. (2000) *Medieval Masons*, Princes Risborough: Shire

Hislop, M. (2010a) 'A missing link: a reappraisal of the date, architectural context and significance of the great tower of Dudley Castle', *Antiquaries Journal*, 90: 211–33

Hislop, M. (2010b) 'An early fourteenth-century residential building adjacent to the south gateway of Lichfield Cathedral close', *Staffordshire Archaeological and Historical Society Transactions*, 44: 8–27

Hislop, M. (2016) *Castle Builders: Approaches to Castle Design and Construction in the Middle Ages*, Barnsley: Pen & Sword

Hislop, M. (2019) *Barnard Castle, Egglestone Abbey, Bowes Castle*, London: English Heritage

Hodgson, J. C. (1904) *A History of Northumberland*, Vol. 7, Newcastle-upon-Tyne: The Northumberland County History Committee

Holliday, J. R. (1874) 'Maxstoke Priory', *Birmingham and Midland Institute*, 5: 56–105

Hopewell, D. (2014) *High Status Medieval Sites, Castell Carndochan: conservation and assessment excavation*, Gwynedd Archaeological Trust report 1213

Hopewell, D. (2016) *High Status Medieval Sites, Castell Carndochan: excavation report 2015–16*, Gwynedd Archaeological Trust Report 1305

Hopewell, D. (2017) *High Status Medieval Sites, Castell Carndochan: excavation report 2016–17*, Gwynedd Archaeological Trust report 1381

Hopewell, D. (2018) *High Status Medieval Sites, Castell Carndochan: excavation report 2017–18*, Gwynedd Archaeological Trust report 1420

Hubbard, E. (1986) *Clwyd*, The Buildings of Wales, Harmondsworth: Penguin

Hughes, H. (1894) 'Valle Crucis Abbey', *Archaeologia Cambrensis*, 5th series, 11: 257–75

Hughes, H. (1903) 'Excavations proposed to be carried out at Aberystwyth Castle', *Archaeologia Cambrensis*, 6th series, 3: 272–8

Hughes, H. (1904) Aberystwyth Castle, excavations carried out in the year 1903, *Archaeologia Cambrensis*, 6th series, 4: 317–23

Hughes, H. (1913) 'Harlech Castle', *Archaeologia Cambrensis*, 6th series, 13: 169–85, 275–316

Hughes, H. (1938) 'The Edwardian castle and town defences at Conway', *Archaeologia Cambrensis*, 93: 75–82, 212–25

Huguenin, C. (2016) *A Walk Around the Castle of Chillon*, Chillon: Fondation du Château de Chillon

Humphries, P. H. (2006) *Llansteffan Castle*, 3rd edn, Cardiff: Cadw

Hunter Blair, C. H. (1910) 'The armorials of Northumberland', *Archaeological Aeliana*, 3rd series, 6: 89–190

Hunter Blair, C. H. and Honeyman, H. L. (1953–5) 'Notes on Mitford Castle', *History of the Berwickshire Naturalist Club*, 33, 202–6

Johns, C. N. (1970) *Criccieth Castle*, London: HMSO

Johns, C. N. (1978) *Caerphilly Castle*, Cardiff: HMSO

Johnson, P. (1978) *The National Trust Book of British Castles*, London: Weidenfeld & Nicolson for the National Trust

Jones, W. B. (1998) 'Medieval earthworks at Dinas Brân, Llangollen', *Archaeologia Cambrensis*, 147, 234–9

Kenyon, J. R. (2002) *Kidwelly Castle*, 3rd edn, Cardiff: Cadw

Kenyon, J. R. (2010) *The Medieval Castles of Wales*, Cardiff: University of Wales Press

Kenyon, J. and Avent, R. (eds) (1987) *Castles in Wales and the Marches: essays in honour of D. J. Cathcart King*, Cardiff: University of Wales Press

Kenyon, J. R., Jones-Jenkins, C. and Guy, N. (2015–16) 'The 29th annual CSG conference Wrexham: Castles of North-East Wales conference report', *Castle Studies Group Journal*, 29: 4–120

Kenyon, J. R. and O'Conor, K. (eds) (2003) *The Medieval Castle in Ireland and Wales*, Dublin: Four Courts Press

Kightley, C. J. (2003) *Dinas Brân, Llangollen*, Ruthin: Denbighshire County Council

King, D. J. Cathcart (1958) 'The donjon of Flint', *Journal of the Chester Archaeological Society*, 45: 61–9

King, D. J. Cathcart (1974) 'Two castles in northern Powys: Dinas Brân and Caergwrle', *Archaeologia Cambrensis*, 123: 113–39

King, D. J. Cathcart (1978) 'Pembroke Castle', *Archaeologia Cambrensis*, 127: 75–121

King, D. J. Cathcart (1984–5) 'The castles of Camlais and Sennybridge', *Brycheiniog*, 20: 9–11

King, D. J. Cathcart and Perks, J. C. (1964) 'Carew Castle, Pembrokeshire', *Archaeological Journal*, 119: 270–307

King, E. (1782) 'Sequel to the observations on ancient castles', *Archaeologia*, 6: 269–90

Knight, J. K. (1986) *Chepstow Castle*, Cardiff: Cadw

Knight, J. K. (2000) *The Three Castles*, rev. edn, Cardiff: Cadw

Knoop, D. and Jones, G. P. (1931) 'The first three years of the building of Vale Royal Abbey, 1278–1280', *Ars Quatuor Coronatorum*, 44 (1): 5–47

Knoop, D. and Jones, G. P. (1932) 'Castle building at Beaumaris and Caernarvon in the early fourteenth century', *Ars Quatuor Coronatorum*, 45 (1): 4–47

Knoop, D. and Jones, G. P. (1937) 'The impressment of masons in the Middle Ages', *Economic History Review*, series 1, 8: 57–67

Knoop, D. and Jones, G. P. (1949) *The Mediæval Mason*, Manchester: Manchester University Press

Knowles, W. H. (1909) 'The gatehouse and barbican of Alnwick Castle, with an account of recent discoveries', *Archaeologia Aeliana*, 3rd series, 5: 286–303

Laing, L. R. (1966–7) 'Excavations at Linlithgow Palace, West Lothian, 1966–7', *Proceedings of the Society of Antiquaries of Scotland*, 99: 111–47

Lewis, J. and Smith, H. (1998) 'Excavations at Inverlochy Castle, Inverness-shire, 1983–95', *Proceedings of the Society of Antiquaries of Scotland*, 128: 619–44

Lilley, K. D. (2010) 'The landscapes of Edward's new towns: their planning and design', in Williams and Kenyon, 99–113

Lloyd, J. E. (1912) *A History of Wales from the Earliest Times to the Edwardian Conquest*, 2 vols, 2nd edn, London: Longman, Green and Co.

Longstaffe, W. H. D. (1868) 'Bothal', *Transactions of the Architectural and Archaeological Society of Durham and Northumberland*, 1: 118–21

Ludlow, N. (1991) 'Pembroke Castle and Town Walls', *Fortress*, 8: 25–30

Ludlow, N. (1998–9) 'Pembroke', *Castle Studies Group Newsletter*, 12: 19–23

Ludlow, N. (2014) *Carmarthen Castle: The Archaeology of Government*, Cardiff: University of Wales Press

Ludlow, N. (2015) *Pembroke Castle*, Pembroke: Pembroke Castle Trust

Ludlow, N. (2018) 'Bothwell: a Welsh marches castle in Scotland?', in Guy 2018a, 281–94

Ludlow, N. (2018–19) 'William Marshal, Pembroke Castle and Angevin design', *Castle Studies Group Journal*, 32: 209–92

Macdonald, A. D. S. and Laing, L. R. (1974–5) 'Excavations at Lochmaben Castle, Dumfriesshire', *Proceedings of the Society of Antiquaries of Scotland*, 106: 124–57

MacGibbon, D. and Ross, T. (1887–90) *The Castellated and Domestic Architecture of Scotland from the Twelfth to the Eighteenth Century*, 5 vols, Edinburgh: David Douglas

MacIvor, I. (1995) *Balvenie Castle*, Edinburgh: Historic Scotland

MacIvor, I. and Gallagher, D. (1999) 'Excavations at Caerlaverock Castle, 1955–66', *Archaeological Journal*, 156: 143–245

Mackenzie, J. D. (1896) *The Castles of England*, 2 vols, New York: Macmillan

MacLees, D. (1998) *Castell Coch*, Cardiff: Cadw

MacLees, D. (2005) *Castell Coch*, rev. edn, Cardiff: Cadw

McNeil, R. and Turner, R. C. (1988) 'An architectural and topographical survey of Vale Royal Abbey', *Journal of the Chester Archaeological Society*, 70: 51–79

Maddison, J. (1978) 'Decorated Architecture in the North-West Midlands: An investigation of provincial masons and their sources', University of Manchester PhD thesis

Maddison, J. (1993) 'Building at Lichfield Cathedral during the episcopate of Walter Langton (1296–1321)', in J. Maddison (ed.), *Medieval Archaeology and Architecture at Lichfield*, British Archaeological Association Conference Transactions 13 for 1987, 65–84

Mahler, M. (1912) *A History of Chirk Castle and Chirkland*, London: George Bell and Sons

Manley, J. (1985) 'Salvage excavations at Lôn Hylas, Rhuddlan, Clwyd', *Archaeologia Cambrensis*, 134: 230–5

Manley, J. (1987) '? *Cledemutha*: a late Saxon burh in north Wales', *Medieval Archaeology*, 31: 13–46

Manley, J. (1992) 'The outer enclosure on Caergwrle Hill, Clywd', *Flintshire Historical Society Journal*, 33: 13–20

Manley, J. (1994) 'Excavations at Caergwrle Castle, north Wales: 1988–1990', *Medieval Archaeology*, 38: 83–133

Manley, J. and Cole, J. (1994) 'General interpretation', in Manley 1994, 126–31

Manley, J., Otlet, R. L., Walker, A. J. and Williams, D. (1985) 'Early medieval radiocarbon dates and plant remains from Rhuddlan, Clwyd', *Archaeologia Cambrensis*, 134: 106–19

Marshall, P. and Samuels, J. (1997) *Guardian of the Trent: the story of Newark Castle*, Newark: Newark Castle Trust

Martin, D. and Martin, B. (2013) 'A reinterpretation of the gatehouse at Tonbridge Castle', *Archaeologia Cantiana*, 133: 235–76

Mayes, P. and Butler, L. (1983) *Sandal Castle Excavations 1964–1973*, Wakefield: Wakefield Historical Publications

Meirion-Jones, G., Impey, E. and Jones, M. (2002) *The Seigneurial Residence in Western Europe AD c 800–1600*, BAR International Series 1088, Oxford: Archaeopress

Michael, M. (1994) 'The little land of England is preferred before the great kingdom of France: the quartering of the royal arms by Edward III', in D. Buckton and T. A. Heslop (eds), *Studies in Medieval Art and Architecture presented to Peter Lasko*, Stroud: Alan Sutton, 113–26

Miles, H. (1971–2) 'Excavations at Rhuddlan, 1969–71: Interim report', *Flintshire Historical Society Publications*, 25: 1–8

Miles, T. J. (1998) 'Flint: excavations at the castle and on the town defences 1971–1974', *Archaeologia Cambrensis*, 145: 67–151

Mitchel, A. (ed.) (1906) *Geographical Collections relating to Scotland made by Walter Macfarlane*, Edinburgh: Scottish History Society, Vol. 1

Morris, J. E. (1901) *The Welsh Wars of Edward I*, Oxford: Oxford University Press

Morris, M. (2010) 'Edward I's Building Works in Gascony', in Williams and Kenyon, 166–74

Morris, R. K. (1978) 'The development of later Gothic mouldings in England *c.* 1250–1400 – Part I', *Architectural History*, 21: 18–57

Morris, R. K. (1979) 'The development of later Gothic mouldings in England *c.* 1250–1400 – Part II', *Architectural History*, 22: 1–48

Morris, R. K. (1997) 'European prodigy or regional eccentric? The rebuilding of St Augustine's Abbey Church, Bristol', in L. Keen (ed.), *Almost the Richest City: Bristol in the Middle Ages*, British Archaeological Association Conference Transactions 19

Morris, R. K. (1998) 'The architecture of Arthurian enthusiasm: castle symbolism in the reigns of Edward I and his successors', in M. Strickland (ed.), *Armies, Chivalry and Warfare in Medieval Britain and France*, Harlaxton Medieval Studies 7, Stamford: Paul Watkins

Morris, R. K. (2006) *Kenilworth Castle*, London: English Heritage

Munby, J. (1993) *Stokesay Castle*. London: English Heritage

Neaverson, E. (1947) *Mediaeval Castles in North Wales*, London: Hodder & Stoughton

Naef, A. (1908) *Chillon. Tome 1: La Camera Domini*, Geneva: Boissonnas

Naef, A. (1929) *Château de Chillon. La Chapelle, Le Donjon, Le Bâtiment du Trésor. Tome 1*, Lausanne: Association pour la restauration du château de Chillon

Naef, A. and Schmid, O. (1939) *Château de Chillon. Le Grand Sou-Sol, La Salle de Justice, La Grosse Tour de l'Entrée, Une Inspection au Chateau de Chillon en 1498, La Tour du Duc. Tome 2*, Lausanne: Association pour la restauration du château de Chillon

Newman, J. (2000) *Gwent / Monmouthshire*, The Buildings of Wales, Newhaven and London: Yale University Press

Newman, J. (2001) *Glamorgan*, The Buildings of Wales, Newhaven and London: Yale University Press

Newman, J. (2012) *Kent: West and the Weald*, The Buildings of England, New Haven and London: Yale University Press

Newman, J. and Pevsner, N. (2006) *Shropshire*, The Buildings of England, New Haven and London: Yale University Press

Oliphant, J. (1992) *Tonbridge Castle*, Tonbridge and Malling Borough Council

Oram, R. (1999) 'Dervorgilla, the Balliols and Buittle', *Transactions of the Dumfriesshire and Galloway Natural History and Antiquarian Society*, 73: 165–81

Oswald, A. and Ashbee, J. (2007) *Dunstanburgh Castle*, London: English Heritage

Owen, H. (1903) 'A survey of the lordship of Haverford in 1577', *Archaeologia Cambrensis*, 6th series, 3: 39–41

Owen, H. W. and Morgan, R. (2008) *Dictionary of the Place-Names of Wales*, Ceredigion: Gomer

Palmer, A. N. (1907) 'The town of Holt in County Denbigh: its castle, church, franchise, and demesne', *Archaeologia Cambrensis*, 6th series, 7: 311–34, 389–434

Peers, C. R. (1915–16) 'Caernarvon Castle', *Cymmrodorion Society Transactions*, 28–74

Peers, C. R. (1921–2) 'Harlech Castle', *Cymmrodorion Society Transactions*, 63–82

Pevsner, N. and Richmond, I. A. (1957) *Northumberland*, The Buildings of England, Harmondsworth: Penguin

Pevsner, N. and Richmond, I. A. (1992) *Northumberland*, The Buildings of England, London: Penguin, rev. by J. Grundy, G. McCombie, P. Ryder and H. Welfare

Pickford, C. and Pevsner, N. (2016) *Warwickshire*, The Buildings of England, New Haven and London: Yale University Press

Platt, C. (1982) *The Castle in Medieval England and Wales* London: Secker and Warburg

Quinnel, H., Blockley, R. and Berridge, P. (1994) *Excavations at Rhuddlan, Clwyd 1969–73 Mesolithic to Medieval*, CBA Research Report 95

Radford, C. A. R. (1953) *Valle Crucis Abbey*, London: HMSO

Radford, C. A. R. (1961) 'Acton Burnell Castle', in E. M. Jope (ed.), *Studies in Building History*, London: Odhams, 94–103

Raemy, D. de, Feihl, O., Golay, L., Pedrucci, A., Dresco, J-P. and Nicollier, J. (1999) *Chillon: la chapelle*, Cahiers d'Archaeologie Romande No. 79, Lausanne: Association du Château de Chillon

Reid, R. C. (1925–6) 'The excavation of Auchencas', *Transactions of the Dumfriesshire and Galloway Natural History and Antiquarian Society*, 13: 104–24

Reid, R. C. (1952–3) 'Edward I's peel at Lochmaben', *Transactions of the Dumfriesshire and Galloway Natural History and Antiquarian Society*, 3rd series, 31: 58–73

Remfry, P. (1998) *Wilton Castle 1066 to 1644*, n.p.: SCS Publishing

Remfry, P. (2013) *Harlech Castle and its True Origins*, n.p.: SCS Castle Studies Research and Publishing

Renn, D. F. (1974) *Norman Castles in Britain*, 2nd edn, London: John Baker

Renn, D. F. (1981) 'Tonbridge and some other gatehouses', in A. Detsicas (ed.), *Collectanea Historica*, Kent Archaeological Society, 93–103

Renn, D. F. (1997) *Caerphilly Castle*, 2nd edn, Cardiff: Cadw

Renn, D. F. (2003) 'Two views from the roof: design and defence at Conwy and Stokesay', in Kenyon and O'Conor, 163–75

Renn, D. F. (2017–18) 'Western approaches: the original entrance front of Caerphilly Castle?', *Castles Studies Group Journal*, 31: 211–32

Renn, D. F. and Avent, R. (2001), *Flint Castle, Ewloe Castle*, Cardiff: Cadw

Roberts, E. R. (*c.* 2014) 'Forgotten ruins? The Castles of the Welsh Princes', *Y Cylchgrawn Hanes*, 8

Robinson, D. M. (2011) *Tintern Abbey*. Cardiff: Cadw

Robison, J. and Curle, A. O. (1913–14) 'Account of the excavation of the Edwardian castle at Castledykes, Kirkcudbright', *Proceedings of the Society of Antiquaries of Scotland*, 48: 381–94

Rodwell, K. (1976) 'Excavations on the Site of Banbury Castle, 1973–4', *Oxoniensia*, 41: 90–147

RCAHMS (1920) *Seventh Report with Inventory of Monuments and Constructions in the County of Dumfries*, Edinburgh: HMSO

RCAHMS (1929) *Tenth Report with Inventory of Monuments and Constructions in the Counties of Midlothian and West Lothian*, Edinburgh: HMSO

RCAHMS (1933) *Eleventh report with Inventory of Monuments and Constructions of Fife, Kinross, and Clackmannan*, Edinburgh: HMSO

RCAHMS (1957) *An Inventory of the Ancient and Historical Monuments of Selkirkshire with the Fifteenth Report of the Commission*, Edinburgh: HMSO

RCAHMW (1914) *An Inventory of the Ancient Monuments in Wales and Monmouthshire. IV – County of Denbigh*, London: HMSO

RCAHMW (1917) *An Inventory of the Ancient Monuments in Wales and Monmouthshire. V – County of Carmarthen*, London: HMSO

RCAHMW (1921) *An Inventory of the Ancient Monuments in Wales and Monmouthshire. VI – County of Merioneth*, London: HMSO

RCAHMW (1937) *An Inventory of the Ancient Monuments in Anglesey*, London: HMSO

RCAHMW (1956, 1960, 1964) *An Inventory of the Ancient Monuments in Caernarvonshire*, 3 vols, London: HMSO

RCAHMW (1991) *An Inventory of the Ancient Monuments in Glamorgan. Volume 3, Part 1a: The Early Castles*, London: HMSO

RCAHMW (2000) *An Inventory of the Ancient Monuments in Glamorgan. Volume 3, Part 1b: The Later Castles*, London: HMSO

RCHME (1931) *An Inventory of the Historical Monuments in Herefordshire. Volume 1: South West*, London: HMSO

RCHME (1970) *An Inventory of the Historical Monuments in Dorset. Volume 2: South East*, London: HMSO

RCHME (1972) *An Inventory of the Historical Monuments in the City of York. Volume 2: The Defences*, London: HMSO

Rowlands, M. J. L. (1994) *Monnow Bridge and Gate*, Stroud: Alan Sutton

Rutherford, A. G. (1998) 'A Social Interpretation of the Castle in Scotland', University of Glasgow doctoral thesis

St John Hope, W. H. (1913) *Windsor Castle: An Architectural History*, 2 vols, London: Country Life

St John O'Neil, B. H. (1944–5) 'Criccieth Castle, Caernarvonshire', *Archaeologia Cambrensis*, 98: 1–51

Salzman, L. F. (1952) *Building in England Down to 1540*, Oxford: Oxford University Press

Scourfield, R. and Haslam, R. (2013) *Powys. The Buildings of Wales*, London: Yale University Press

Serjeantson, R. M., Ryland, W. and Adkins, D. (eds) (1906) *The Victoria History of the County of Northampton*, Vol. 2, London

Sharples, J., Walker, D. W. and Woodworth, M. (2015) *Aberdeenshire: South and Aberdeen*, The Buildings of Scotland, New Haven and London: Yale University Press

Shelby, L. (1972) 'The geometrical knowledge of medieval master masons', *Speculum* 47: 395–421

Shoesmith, R. (ed.) (2014) *Goodrich Castle: Its History and its Buildings*, Logaston: Logaston Press

Shoesmith, R. and A. Johnson (eds) (2000) *Ludlow Castle: Its History and its Buildings*, Logaston: Logaston Press

Simmons, S. (1998) 'The lords and ladies of Tonbridge Castle', *Archaeologia Cantiana*, 118: 45–62

Simon, M. E. (1999) 'The Lovells of Titchmarsh: An English baronial family, 1297–148?', University of York D. Phil. thesis

Simpson, W. D. (1923) *The Castle of Kildrummy: Its Place in Scottish History and Architecture*, Aberdeen: D. Wylie

Simpson, W. D. (1924–5) 'The architectural history of Bothwell Castle', *Proceedings of the Society of Antiquaries of Scotland*, 59: 165–93

Simpson, W. D. (1925–6) 'The development of Balvenie Castle', *Proceedings of the Society of Antiquaries of Scotland*, 60: 132–48

Simpson, W. D. (1927–8) 'A new survey of Kildrummy Castle', *Proceedings of the Society of Antiquaries of Scotland*, 62: 36–80

Simpson, W. D. (1928) 'James de Sancto Georgio, Master of Works to King Edward I in Wales and Scotland', *Transactions of the Anglesey Antiquarian Society and Field Club*, 31–41, repr. in *Scottish Archaeological Studies*, 2nd series (1936), 159–69

Simpson, W. D. (1936–7) 'Rait Castle and Barevan church', *Proceedings of the Society of Antiquaries of Scotland*, 71: 98–115

Simpson, W. D. (1938–9) 'Morton Castle', *Transactions of the Dumfriesshire and Galloway Natural History and Antiquarian Society*, 3rd series, 22: 26–35

Simpson, W. D. (1940a) 'Flint Castle', *Archaeologia Cambrensis*, 95: 20–6

Simpson, W. D. (1940b) 'Belsay Castle and the Scottish Tower-Houses', *Archaeologia Aeliana*, 4th series, 17: 75–84

Simpson, W. D. (1947) 'Bothwell Castle reconsidered', *Transactions of the Glasgow Archaeological Society*, 11: 97–116

Simpson, W. D. (1949) 'Further notes on Dunstanburgh Castle', *Archaeologia Aeliana*, 4th series, 27: 1–28

Simpson, W. D. (1958–9) 'The castles of Duffus, Rait and Morton reconsidered', *Proceedings of the Society of Antiquaries of Scotland*, 92: 10–14

Simpson, W. D. (1978) *Kildrummy and Glenbuchat Castles*, 4th edn, Edinburgh: HMSO

Smith, C. (1988) 'The excavation of the Exchequer Gate, Denbigh 1982–3', *Archaeologia Cambrensis*, 137: 108–12

Spurgeon, C. J. (1975) *The Castle and Borough of Aberystwyth*, repr. of 1973 edn with addition of a bibliography, Ceredigion District Council

Spurgeon, C. J. (1978–9) 'Builth Castle', *Brycheiniog*, 18: 47–59

Stephenson, D. (2007) 'Powis Castle; a reappraisal of its medieval development', *Montgomeryshire Collections*, 95: 9–21

Stephenson, D. (2015) 'A reconsideration of the siting, function and dating of Ewloe Castle', *Archaeologia Cambrensis*, 164: 245–53

Stevenson, J. (1870) *Documents Illustrative of the History of Scotland*, 2 vols, Edinburgh

Summerson, H. (1993) *Dunstanburgh Castle*, London: English Heritage

Summerson, H., Trueman, M. and Harrison, S. (1998) *Brougham Castle, Cumbria*, Cumberland and Westmorland Antiquarian and Archaeological Society Research Series No. 8

Swallow, R. (2014) 'Gateways to power: the castles of Ranulf III of Chester and Llywelyn the Great of Gwynedd', *Archaeological Journal* 171: 1, 289–311

Swallow, R. (2019) 'Living the dream: the legend, lady and landscape of Caernarfon Castle, Gwynedd, North Wales', *Archaeologia Cambrensis*, 168: 153–95

Tabraham, C. (1986) *Kildrummy Castle*, Edinburgh: HMSO

Tabraham, C. (1994) *Bothwell Castle*, Edinburgh: Historic Scotland

Tabraham, C. (2010) 'Scottorum Malleus: Edward I and Scotland', in Williams and Kenyon, 181–92

Tatton-Brown, T. (2009) *Salisbury Cathedral: the making of a medieval masterpiece*, London: Scala

Taylor, A. J. (1948a) 'English builders in Scotland during the wars of independence: a record of 1304', *Scottish Historical Review*, 34: 44–6

Taylor, A. J. (1948b) 'A note on Walter of Hereford builder of Carnarvon Castle', *Transactions of the Carnarvonshire Historical Society*, 9: 16–19

Taylor, A. J. (1949) *Rhuddlan Castle, Flintshire*, London: HMSO

Taylor, A. J. (1949) 'The cloister of Vale Royal Abbey', *Journal of the Chester Archaeological and Historical Society*, 37: 295–7

Taylor, A. J. (1950) 'Master James of St George', *English Historical Review*, 65: 433–57

Taylor, A. J. (1950–1) 'Builth Castle', *Archaeologia Cambrensis*, 101: 174–5

Taylor, A. J. (1952) 'The date of Caernarvon Castle', *Antiquity*, 26: 25–34

Taylor, A. J. (1954–5) 'Rhuddlan Cathedral: a "might have been" of Flintshire history', *Flintshire Historical Publications*, 15: 43–51

Taylor, A. J. (1957a) *Conway Castle and Town Walls*, London: HMSO

Taylor, A. J. (1957b) 'The building of Flint: a postscript', *Flintshire Historical Society Journal*, 17, 34–41

Taylor, A. J. (1958) 'The castle of St. Georges-d'Espéranche', *Antiquaries Journal*, 33: 33–47

Taylor, A. J. (1961) 'Castle building in Wales in the later thirteenth century: the prelude to construction', in E. M. Jope (ed.), *Studies in Building History* London: Odhams, 104–33

Taylor, A. J. (1963) 'Some notes on the Savoyards in north Wales, 1277–1300. With special reference to the Savoyard element in the construction of Harlech Castle', *Genava*, 11: 289–315

Taylor, A. J. (1965–6) 'The earliest reference to works at Hope Castle', *Flintshire Historical Society Publications*, 22: 76–7

Taylor, A. J. (1972) *Caernarvon Castle and Town Walls*, London: HMSO

Taylor, A. J. (1977) 'Castle-building in thirteenth-century Wales and Savoy', *Proceedings of the British Academy*, 63: 265–92

Taylor, A. J. (1984) 'A shipwreck near Rhuddlan in 1310', *Flintshire Historical Society Journal*, 31: 57–70

Taylor, A. J. (1985) *Studies in Castles and Castle Building*, London: Hambledon Press

Taylor, A. J. (1986) *The Welsh Castles of Edward I*, London: Hambledon Press

Taylor, A. J. (1987) 'The Beaumaris Castle building account of 1295–1298', in Kenyon and Avent, 125–42

Taylor, A. J. (1989) 'Master Bertram, *ingeniator regis*', in C. Harper-Bill, C. J. Holdsworth, J. L. Nelson, *Studies in Medieval History*, Woodbridge: Boydell, 289–316

Taylor, A. J. (1992) 'The Hope Castle account of 1282', *Flintshire Historical Society Journal*, 33: 21–53

Taylor, A. J. (1999) *Beaumaris Castle*, 4th edn, Cardiff: Cadw

Taylor, A. J. (2002) *Harlech Castle*, 4th edn, Cardiff: Cadw

Taylor, A. J. (2004) *Caernarfon Castle and Town Walls*, 6th edn, Cardiff: Cadw

Taylor, A. J. (2018) 'St George, James [*known as* Master James of St George]', in *ODNB* online version, accessed 8.8.19

Taylor, H. (1922) 'Ewloe Castle', *Flintshire Historical Society Publications*, 9: 51–4

Thompson, F. H. (1962) 'Excavations at the Cistercian abbey of Vale Royal, Cheshire, 1958', *Antiquaries Journal*, 42 (2): 183–207

Thompson, M. W. (1977) *Kenilworth Castle*, London: English Heritage

Thompson, M. W. (2000) 'The great hall and great chamber block', in Shoesmith and Johnson, 167–74

Toulmin Smith, L. (1906–10) *The Itinerary of John Leland in or About the Years 1535–1543*, 5 vols, London: G. Bell and Sons

Toy, S. (1936) 'The town and castle of Conway', *Archaeologia*, 86: 163–71, 176–93

Toy, S. (1963) *The Castles of Great Britain*, 3rd edn, London: Heinemann

Tringham, N. (1993) 'The palace of Bishop Walter Langton in Lichfield Cathedral close', in J. Maddison (ed.), *Medieval Archaeology and Architecture at Lichfield*, British Archaeological Association Conference Transactions 13 for 1987, 85–100

Turnbull, D. (1979) 'Some problems about the origin of Criccieth Castle', *Fort*, 7: 52–68

Turner, R. (2006) 'The Upper Barbican', in Turner and Johnson, 113–18

Turner, R. (2010a) 'The life and career of Richard the engineer', in Williams and Kenyon, 46–58

Turner, R. (2010b) *Chepstow Castle,* 3rd edn, Cardiff: Cadw

Turner, R. (2016) *Caerphilly Castle*, Cardiff: Cadw

Turner, R. and Johnson, A. (eds) (2006) *Chepstow Castle: its history and buildings*, Logaston: Logaston Press

Turner, R., Priestley, S., Coldstream, N. and Sale, B. (2006a) 'The New or Marten's Tower', in Turner and Johnson, 151–166.

Turner, R., Priestley, S., Coldstream, N. and Sale, B. (2006b) 'The "Gloriette" in the lower bailey', in Turner and Johnson, 135–50

Turner, R., Priestley, S. and Jones-Jenkins, C. (2006) 'The Marshals' use of the Great Tower', in Turner and Johnson, 91–100

Turner, T. H. and Parker, J. H. (1851–9) *Some Account of Domestic Architecture in England*, 3 vols, Vol. 1: *From the Conquest to the end of the Thirteenth Century* (1851); Vol. 2: *From Edward I to Richard II* (1853); Vol. 3: *From Richard II to Henry VIII* (1859), London: J. H. Parker

Wadmore, J. F. (1886) 'Tonbridge Castle and its lords', *Archaeologia Cantiana*, 16: 12–57

West, J. (1981) 'Acton Burnell Castle, Shropshire', in A. Detsicas (ed.), *Collectanea Historica: essays in memory of Stuart Rigold*, Kent Archaeological Society, 86–92

Wheatley, A. (2010) 'Caernarfon Castle and its mythology', in Williams and Kenyon, 129–39

Williams, D. M., and Kenyon, J. R. (eds) (2010) *The Impact of the Edwardian Castle in Wales*, the proceedings of a conference held at Bangor University, 7–9 September 2007, Oxford: Oxbow Books

Williams, R. (1835) *The History and Antiquities of the Town of Aberconwy and its Neighbourhood*, Denbigh for the author

Willis, R. and Clarke, J. W. (1886) *The Architectural History of the University of Cambridge* Vol. 1, Cambridge: Cambridge University Press

Wilson, C. (1990) *The Gothic Cathedral* London: Thames & Hudson

Wilson, C. (2002) 'The royal lodgings of Edward III at Windsor Castle', in S. Brown (ed.), *Winsdor: medieval archaeology, art and architecture of the Thames valley*, British Archaeological Association Conference Transactions 15

Wilson, P. R. (1989) 'Excavations at Helmsley Castle', *Yorkshire Archaeological Journal*, 61: 29–33

Wright, T. (ed.) (1864) *The Roll of Caerlaverock*, London: John Camden Hotten

Wynne, W. W. E. (1861) 'Castell y Bere – county of Merioneth', *Archaeologia Cambrensis*, 16: 105–10

Index